LINCOLN CHRISTIAN COLLEGE
P9-CFV-747

THE CHRISTIAN VISION

MAN AND CREATION

Perspectives on Science and Theology

THE CHRISTIAN VISION

MAN AND CREATION

Perspectives on Science and Theology

Michael Bauman, Executive Editor
Lissa Roche, General Editor
Jon Corombos, Editorial Assistant

Hillsdale College Press
Hillsdale, Michigan 49242

Hillsdale College Press

Books by the Hillsdale College Press include *The Christian Vision* series; the *Champions of Freedom* series; and other works.

The views expressed in this volume are not necessarily the views of Hillsdale College.

The Christian Vision Series
MAN AND CREATION:
PERSPECTIVES ON SCIENCE AND THEOLOGY
© 1993 by the Hillsdale College Press
Hillsdale, Michigan 49242

Printed in the United States of America

Photo: Andromeda Galaxy, Photri, Inc.

All rights reserved. No part of this publication may be reproduced without the prior written permission of the publisher.

First printing 1993
Library of Congress Catalog Card Number 93-078627
ISBN 0-916308-74-X

Contents

90351

Introduction

In their own very different ways, science and theology attempt to raise and answer ultimate questions: Where did we come from? Why is there anything at all? Why is the universe intelligible? How will it all end? What does it mean to be human? But these common concerns do not result in commonly agreed upon answers. Neither do they imply that both sorts of answers are correct. Both sorts of answers exist and thinking people everywhere must wrestle with them in hope of discovering precisely what the truth is and how best to apply it.

Such considerations, of course, are not new. As the opening chapter of this volume by Mark Kalthoff suggests, the relationship between science and religion dates from ancient times and is surprisingly variegated. But although science and theology have contributed significantly to our common heritage, considerable disagreement continues over what relationship has existed and should exist between them. John Draper's *History of the Conflict Between Religion and Science* (1874) and Andrew White's *A History of the Warfare of Science with Theology in Christendom* (1896), for example, presuppose an irreconcilable "war" between science and religion, a common notion that persists even today. A second view, advanced by Reijer Hooykaas' *Religion and the Rise of Science* (1972), Stanley Jaki's *The Road of Science and the Ways to God* (1978), and Colin Russell's *Cross-Currents: Interactions Between Science and Faith* (1985), argues that modern science was born in a religious context and that theological considerations undergird the entire scientific enterprise, though scientists today seldom acknowledge the debt. A third and increasingly common position says that science and theology are complementary disciplines that do well at answering questions in their own respective domains but that have little to say directly to one another. Complementarians can be, as some of the contributors to this volume are, atheists or agnostics, as well as practicing Christians.

This volume also reveals that some of the most ardent debate is not between militant atheists and Christians but among Christians themselves, who disagree about how high the "wall of separation" between science and theology ought to be and indeed whether there is or ought to be a wall at all. As in the lay community, great controversy still centers on the theory of evolution and the origins of life. Many complementarians, like Howard Van Till, Owen Gingerich and Donald Heckenlively, suggest that not only is it possible to be a devout Christian and support evolution, but that the doctrine of divine Creation is simply irrelevant to scientific considerations regarding the physical world and its operations. Other Christian scholars, however, like J. P. Moreland, Phillip Johnson and myself, contend that theology is relevant to all scientific inquiry. Specifically, we argue that, for a plethora of reasons, what is often presented as empirical proof of scientific theories like evolution is both theory-laden and inconclusive. As a result, we call for theologians to play a more active role in the debate and for scientists to recognize the theological and philosophical underpinnings of their methods and conclusions.

In one of the initial chapters, Richard Bube surveys various competing views on the relationship between science and theology and identifies the fundamental ideas that distinguish them. Other chapters deal with a variety of specific science/theology issues. One, an historical overview by Ronald Numbers, seeks to confirm the antiscientific nature and relative newness of the "Young Earth" movement. Richard Alexander argues for the superiority of biology as the supreme method of discovering the truth about the mystery of human nature. And Craig Chester brings both scientific and theological considerations to bear in exploring another compelling mystery: the Star of Bethlehem.

No matter where one stands on these issues, science and theology continue to influence the way we think about and act on life's most fundamental questions. We hope, therefore, that you will enjoy *Man and Creation: Perspectives on Science and Theology,* which is the sixth volume in our Christian Vision series, and which is based on lectures delivered during a recent seminar sponsored by Hillsdale College's Center for Constructive Alternatives and Christian Studies program.

July, 1993
Hillsdale College

Michael Bauman

God and Creation: An Historical Look at Encounters Between Christianity and Science

Mark A. Kalthoff

Mark Kalthoff is an assistant professor of history at his alma mater, Hillsdale College, where he earned a B.S. in history, biology and mathematics. He is a Ph.D. candidate in the history and philosophy of science at Indiana University-Bloomington and has published nearly a half dozen reviews as well an article entitled, "The Harmonious Dissonance of Evangelical Scientists," in *Perspectives on Science and Christian Faith* (December 1991).

Preface

If you seek here a presentation of pioneering new research, then you will be disappointed. For instead the task before me is to survey terrain that has been plowed again and again by historians more learned than I. Indeed, much of this essay relies upon the ground-breaking work of others. My premise, however, is that most people are not stricken with my bizarre yearning—a yearning to learn about the ways "dead white male" scientists have regarded the Creator and accounted for God's relationship to the created world. I believe, accordingly, that the way to begin a volume like this one is to offer an introductory overview of some pertinent themes. Experts may consider the following discussion a lullaby, for they will learn nothing new. My goal, however, is to offer those who are newcomers to the history of science a brief overview of the way some historians (and some non-historians) have tried to understand the encounters between Christianity and science.

Introduction

The intellectual fabric of Western civilization is woven from three principal strands—one from Greece and Rome, another commonly referred to as the Judeo-Christian tradition, and the third, which was born in the sixteenth and seventeenth centuries from a complicated union of the first two, we have named modern science.[1] One of my professors in graduate school used to remind us that prior to the rise of the third strand (modern science), the most fitting adjective to characterize European civilization was the word "Christian." By the close of the seventeenth century, however, "Christian" would no longer serve as the best descriptive word. Instead my professor suggested that by the beginning of the eighteenth century the adjective of choice for describing European civilization was the word "scientific."[2]

If he was correct—and I think he was—then the seventeenth century challenges us to learn how this change occurred. Indeed, if we hold any hope of understanding our Western intellectual heritage, then I suggest that we must go one step further and answer this question: "What has been the relation between science and Christianity?" Notice that the question calls for a descriptive, historical answer. I did not ask, "What *ought* to be the relationship between science and Christianity?" This question, too, is of great importance. Perhaps it is of greater ultimate importance than the historical question. First, however, we should inquire regarding how it *has been* between science and Christianity.[3] For in learning about the history of encounters between science and Christianity, we equip ourselves to speak responsibly about the nature of their contemporary interactions.

I. On Defining "Science" and "Religion"

Were I to stand before you today as a scientist, philosopher or theologian purporting to defend a model of the way science and religion *ought* to be related, then presumably it would be my duty to begin by *defining my terms.* What exactly do we mean when we say "science"? What exactly do we mean when we say "religion" (or "Christianity" or "theology")? Get the categories straight first. Define "authentic" science. Define "authentic" religion. Then the task will be simplified and the intellectual conundrums will dissolve. Yet while there may be some truth in these claims, the rewards of simplicity and brevity can be gained only by paying the exorbitant price of disregarding the way the world really is. For the historian, in other words, there are very good reasons to reject the temptation to construct rigid definitions at the outset, for such an approach cannot avoid twisting and ignoring historical realities.[4] Consider a few brief examples.

When in 1687 Isaac Newton (1642–1727) published his monumental account of universal gravitation, he entitled his work *The Mathematical Principles of Natural Philosophy,* not *The Mathematical Principles of Natural Science.* As a natural philosopher, Newton saw no problem with taking up questions of God's associations with this world. In the "General Scholium," with which he concluded Book Three of the *Principia,* Newton wrote, "This most beautiful system of the sun, planets and comets, could only proceed from the counsel and dominion of an intelligent and powerful being.... Blind metaphysical necessity, which is certainly the same always and everywhere, could produce no variety of things. All that diversity of natural things which we find suited to different times and places could arise from nothing but the ideas and will of a Being necessarily existing.... And thus much concerning God; to discourse of whom from the appearances of things, does certainly belong to Natural Philosophy."[5] Clearly, when discussing natural philosophers like Newton, rigidly separating science and religion can become an exercise in spurious contrivance. Here was a man whose theological writings—in excess of three million words—were of greater significance in his own mind than the scientific works for which he became so famous. Indeed, to his thinking, his scientific pursuits were made possible and legitimated by his theological convictions. His biographer, Richard Westfall, has noted in plain language, "The fact is that Newton was convinced from the beginning that the universe is an ordered cosmos because he knew as a Christian that God had created it."[6] For Newton, then, the two enterprises (science and Christian belief) were woven together into the now largely obsolete fabric called natural philosophy.

Newton's contemporary, John Ray (1627–1705), the leading naturalist of the day, published in 1691 his scientific celebration of divine craftsmanship. His book was entitled *The Wisdom of God Manifested in the Works of Creation.* Science became a religious tool in the hands of those men who studied the Creator's handiwork in order to magnify the glory of the Creator. In Ray, and like-minded contemporaries like Robert Boyle, we have examples of men who, as John Hedley Brooke affirms, "envisaged scientific inquiry itself as a form of worship."[7] This being the case, we can only offer hearty agreement with Charles Webster's assessment of seventeenth century science that it would be "perverse to deny religious motivation in the numerous cases where this was made explicit by the scientists themselves, often with painful emphasis."[8]

When the seventeenth-century geologist Thomas Burnet published his theological cosmogony, *The Sacred Theory of the Earth* (1684), his ostensibly "scientific" account of the earth relied heavily upon biblical history and assigned a prominent role to Noah's flood. Yet it was the same Burnet who had concurred with St. Augustine's warning that science and religion not be intermingled and who had taken Augustine to task for using the Bible to settle a question of human population distribution. Had Burnet ignored Augustine's advice and committed the same error of blending science and religion? He did not think so. But in giving his account of the earth's history, he gives us evidence that over the centuries the boundaries between "science" and "religion" have been redrawn again and again. What counted as the interference of religion with science for Burnet seems to have been different than what might count for us or what counted for Augustine.[9]

Furthermore, "science" and "Christianity" have not always stood as autonomous entities which submit to neat extraction from the social, political and cultural contexts within which scientists—who have often been Christians—act. As a result, to pretend that science and Christianity could somehow be excised from their contexts would be to construct a fictional scenario of little help to those exploring the way the world really works.[10]

Still, one may protest, is there not a sense in which we all know how to define science and religion? Science deals with indifferent forces and the natural physical world. Religion involves the supernatural, the spiritual, the realm of personalized divine beings like angels. Science entails objective methods for testing. Religion is typified by strident dogmatism. While such behavior as ceremony and worship may be fine for religion, science knows nothing of them. These distinctions may be appealing, but, as I have briefly tried to demonstrate, the history of science shows that each is overly simplistic.[11] In fact, if there is to be any *simple* message from this discussion, it is this: If while investigating the history of science and religion one reaches a simple conclusion, it is probably a wrong conclusion. The real story is almost always complex.

Speaking as an historian, then, I flinch at the insistence that "authentic" science and "authentic" Christianity must be defined at the outset. To do so would be to impose upon the past categories that belong to the late twentieth century. Such an artificial method might offer an appealing tidiness; and while wholly appropriate for the philosopher of science or the theologian, it can undermine the historian's goal of viewing the past on its own terms.[12] As a result, I prefer to move on and look at the history of science without presupposing any unyielding categories.

II. The Origin and Persistence of Military Metaphors

Consider the recent "Bloom County" comic strip in which boy genius Oliver announces to his penguin friend Opus, "Let me tell you about 'The Grand Unification Theory.' When finally discovered by me, it will unify all the disparate elements of existential physics. We'll know how and why the universe, galaxies, stars, earth... even time... began. We'll even know the origins of man himself." To this momentous proclamation Opus replies, "Where does Noah's Ark fit into all this?" We laugh. Why? Because living in the shadow of Darwinism in the late twentieth century, we somehow know that Noah's Ark *does not* "fit into all this." In fact, we all know that at some fundamental level, science and religion are opposing forces (even if we don't give airtight definitions of each). Have not historians, scientists and philosophers taught us that the forward progression of science has occurred only gradually, as free-thinking experimentalists managed to discard the oppressive religious shackles of ignorance, superstition and narrow-minded biblical literalism? The answer is, yes; many historians (as well as scientists and philosophers) have taught us to believe just that. Who are these historians (scientists and philosophers)? What exactly did they say? What follows is a brief attempt to answer these questions.

On Friday evening, December 17, 1869, before an audience gathered at the hall of the Cooper Union in New York City, the first president of Cornell University, Andrew Dickson White (1832–1918), gave a lecture entitled "The Warfare of Science." White began his talk with the statement that "the great sacred struggle for the liberty of Science ... has been going on for centuries ... with battles fiercer, with sieges more persistent, with strategy more vigorous than in any of the comparatively petty warfares of Alexander, or Caesar, or Napoleon." Indeed, continued White, "In all modern history, interference with Science in the supposed interest of religion—no matter how conscientious such interference may have been—has resulted in the direst evils both to Religion and Science, and *invariably*. And on the other hand all untrammeled scientific investigation, no matter how dangerous to religion some of its stages may have seemed, temporarily to be, has invariably resulted in the highest good of Religion and Science."[13]

Over the following decades, White expanded his research and refined his position.[14] When his two-volume magnum opus *A History of the Warfare of Science with Theology in Christendom* finally appeared in 1896, White had shifted his polemic somewhat. The real villain was not "Religion" but

"Dogmatic Theology."[15] This did not, however, mitigate his disdain for Christianity; nor did it weaken his conviction that organized religion stood as the bitter enemy of science. "The establishment of Christianity," proclaimed White, "arrested the normal development of the physical sciences for over fifteen hundred years."[16] White's enormously influential work remained in print through the majority of the twentieth century, cementing in the minds of many the validity of the "Warfare Thesis."[17]

Meanwhile, while White was undertaking his review of the battlefields of science, John William Draper (1811–1882), the son of a Methodist minister and sometime science teacher and historian, put the final touches on his 1874 volume. *History of the Conflict between Religion and Science.*[18] Despite similarities between the titles of his and White's books, Draper's thesis was different. "Draper's book," notes historian Ronald L. Numbers, "would more accurately have been titled 'History of the Conflict Between Roman Catholicism and Science.'"[19] Draper was much more inclined to look with favor upon Protestantism than was White, who denounced all stripes of dogmatic theology as impotent fossils of a fruitless medievalism. All the same, Draper's anti-Catholic rhetoric could easily be read as a denunciation of all religious belief. "Religion must relinquish that imperious, that domineering position which she has so long maintained against Science," wrote Draper. "There must be absolute freedom for thought. The ecclesiastic must learn to keep himself within the domain he has chosen, and cease to tyrannize over the philosopher. . . ."[20] Draper's book had appeared as a volume in the popular International Scientific Series. His text outsold every other title in the series, was translated into ten languages, and went through some fifty printings.[21] By the turn of the century, then, Draper's "Conflict Thesis" was widely known.

As the twentieth century began, the legacy of the Draper-White theses remained strong. Many who spoke of the relations between science and religion did so with military metaphors. As the century wore on, nearly all discourse regarding the relationship between science and Christianity was cast in a militaristic framework. Consider a few examples.

In 1923 biologist and Stanford President David Starr Jordan praised White's book in a letter to a friend, "Have you ever read President White's *Warfare of Science with Theology*? You will find it very valuable in showing science from my point of view."[22] In 1927 Maynard Shipley, president of the Science League of America, brought out his volume, *The War on Modern Science,* in which he proclaimed "the superiority of the scientific method ... against the 'revelation' of those afflicted with the disease of traditionalism."[23] The back cover of the 1960 Dover reprint of *The Warfare of Science with Theology* praises White's book as "the most thorough account ever written of the great religious-scientific battles, and remains an eloquent testament to the scientific spirit." As the decades have worn on, one still encounters pronouncements of the fundamental incompatibility of science and religion. Historian of biology William Provine insists that "religion is compatible with modern evolutionary biology (and indeed all of modern science) if the religion is effectively indistinguishable from atheism." Richard Dawkins, in his best-selling sermon on evolution, *The Blind Watchmaker,* testifies that "Darwin made it possible to be an intellectually fulfilled atheist." And philosopher Tad Clements, in his book *Science vs. Religion,* wishes to demonstrate that "none of the reasons offered to deny incompatibility between science and religion is successful."[24] I offer these examples, aware that not all are cases of historical opinion, as evidence of how widespread the conflict thesis has become. The litany of choruses proclaiming the warfare between or fundamental incompatibility of science and religion reveals the widespread legacy of Draper and White. Perhaps historian of science James R. Moore captures this reality best in his study, *The Post-Darwinian Controversies:* "Through constant repetition in historical and philosophical exposition of every kind, from pulpit, platform and printed page, the idea of science and religion at 'war' has become an integral part of Western intellectual culture."[25] A conflict metaphor is perhaps appealing because it is simple. But recall the warning issued above: If while investigating the history of science and religion one reaches a simple conclusion, it is probably a wrong conclusion. I suggest that this is undeniably the case with the opinions of Draper and White.[26]

I have now approached the midway point of my discussion describing a view that I announce to be illegitimate. It is incumbent upon me, therefore, to turn to the tasks of explaining why this is so and then conclude by offering some suggestions to help evade the blunders of militaristic language.

III. Why Military Metaphors Make Bad History

Scholarship of recent decades has increasingly shown that the Draper-White military metaphors are deeply flawed and virtually useless for any honest attempt to elucidate the relations between science and religion.[27] The history of science and its encounters with Christianity is complex. It resists being tailored to fit preconceived apologetic agendas. Draper and White had axes to grind. They "read the past through battle-scarred glasses."[28] Consequently their histories emerged as warped pictures bearing only vague resemblance to historical realities. To support this claim I offer three brief reviews of significant themes from the history of science—one from the early church, one from the middle ages, and one from the scientific revolution of the sixteenth and seventeenth centuries.[29] The topics I have chosen are important for at least three reasons. First, none are merely anecdotal historical tidbits. Each is truly important in the history of science. Second, each could be interpreted upon cursory inspection as an example of conflict between science and religion. Third, honest investigation of each case points, instead to the conclusion that militaristic language does not offer a helpful tool for interpreting the past. Ultimately "complexity" rather than "simplicity" is the appropriate term for characterizing encounters between Christianity and science.

1. The Early Church—Science as Handmaiden

It is common knowledge that the decline of Western civilization—popularly, although perhaps inappropriately, referred to as "the dark ages"—coincided substantially with the ascendancy of the Christian religion. This has led some to lay the blame for alleged medieval scientific stagnation at the door of the Church. Andrew Dickson White summed up the first millennium of the Christian era by portraying the shapers of Christian thought as archenemies of scientific learning. "The greatest thinkers in the Church," insisted White, "generally poured contempt upon all investigators into a science of Nature and insisted that everything except the saving of souls was folly."[30] The shred of truth in this statement is that the chief concerns of the Church fathers were theological and ultimately other-worldly.

Yet historian of medieval science David C. Lindberg observes that "during the Middle Ages, science was in decline quite apart from the Church. The fathers of the church saw no need to rescue it. After all, during the crumbling of a civilization why worry about spheres of the heavens, the form of the rainbows and the paths of projectiles?"[31] Indeed, the Church fathers had other priorities. But when considered in comparison to pagan culture and ideologies that offered virtually no incentives to study nature, the Church emerges as "*the* major patron" of scientific learning. Lindberg argues, "If we compare the early church with a modern research university or the National Science Foundation, the church will prove to have failed abysmally as a supporter of science and natural philosophy. But such a comparison is obviously unfair. If instead we compare the support given to the study of nature by the early church with the support available from any other contemporary social institution, it will become apparent that the church was one of the major patrons."[32]

The question to ask, then, is "What form did this patronage take?" The answer comes through an understanding of the Church's view of "science as handmaiden to theology"—a position originally expressed in the first century A.D. by Philo Judaeus and later embraced by Clement of Alexandria (ca. 150–ca. 215), St. Augustine (354–430), Hugh of Saint-Victor (d. 1141), and St. Bonaventure (1221–1274). The handmaiden position discounted the value of scientific learning as an end in itself. Rather, science (or, for that matter, any other division of knowledge) was to be pursued insofar as it could glorify God, assist in the interpretation of Scripture, and offer defense against heresy.[33] One implication of this was that Christianity encouraged the study of the physical world because such investigation caused one to marvel at God's creation. This would inspire worship at the same time that it would empower man with the knowledge to exercise dominion over the earth as recommended in Psalm 8: 6–9.[34] At the very least, however, the Christian should know enough science to avoid talking nonsense to unbelievers. This was Augustine's position:

> Usually, even a non-Christian knows something about the earth, the heavens and the other elements of this world, about the motion and orbit of the stars and even their size and relative positions, about the predictable eclipses of the sun and moon, the cycles of the years and the seasons, about the kinds of animals, shrubs stones, and so forth, and this knowledge he holds to as being certain from reason and experience. Now, it is a disgraceful and dangerous thing for an infidel to hear a Christian, presumably giving the meaning of Holy Scripture, talking nonsense on these topics; and we should take all means to prevent such an embarrassing situation, in which people show up vast ignorance in a Christian and laugh it to scorn.[35]

The point is that although science was "a far cry from its modern status, characterized by autonomy and intellectual hegemony," it was also "far from the victim of Christian intolerance that White portrayed."[36] To suggest that because Church fathers placed the highest emphasis upon theology—as one would expect of theologians—they were anti-intellectuals who preferred blind faith and ignorance to reason and learning is absurd. Instead the handmaiden philosophy suggests that Christianity assisted science insofar as it provided sanction for investigation of God's creation.

2. Science and the Church in the Middle Ages— The Condemnation of 1277

Although the Church sanctioned the investigation of nature and scientists were beneficiaries of ecclesiastical patronage, the handmaiden philosophy also provided the Church with a supervisory role. In this controlling mode, the Church could function as a "coercive agent" and actually supervise the activity and content of scientific work.[37] Suppose, then, that science were to become an unruly servant. If man's investigation of God's handiwork ever failed to square neatly with traditional doctrines, then what? The likelihood of this sort of "conflict" seemed rather high given the nature of Aristotelian natural philosophy, which by the mid-thirteenth century had emerged as a staple item in the university curriculum. Certain features of Aristotle's worldview seemed to contradict crucial Christian teachings. For example, while Christianity comprehended the world as the contingent creation of an omnipotent God, Aristotle's universe was an uncreated, eternal and rigidly deterministic cosmos with no place for free will, the miraculous or divine omnipotence.

The classic example of the medieval Church "meddling" with science occurred in the late thirteenth century when the bishop of Paris, Etienne Tempier, issued a sweeping condemnation of 219 propositions, many of which stemmed from Aristotelian thought. The arts master found guilty of holding or teaching even one of the condemned propositions faced excommunication. The ensuing strife, which carried over into the fourteenth century, powerfully symbolizes the complexity of the encounter between science and Christianity.[38] For although it is true that the condemnation of 1277 placed real limitations upon the speculation of Aristotelian natural philosophers, it is not at all clear that this episode can be interpreted as a battle between science and religion. First, because all the participants involved were Christians, if there was any conflict it was "among Christians holding different views of the proper relationship between Christianity and science."[39] Second, although the Church may have played a supervisory role, its Christian theology was imposed upon scientists by persuasion rather than by coercion.[40] Because all the participants were Christians, they respected the Church's pronouncements as being true. It seems, therefore, that the effect of banning certain Aristotelian teachings was to open fresh avenues for non-Aristotelian natural philosophy. These included speculation about the nature of empty space and the possibility of the motion of the earth—concepts certainly more in tune with modern science than with Aristotelianism. In fact, rather than interpreting the Condemnation of 1277 as a case of the Church thwarting scientific growth, some historians, crediting the Bishop of Paris with calling for a new physics, have ventured to name 1277 as the birth date of modern science.[41] While it is not my intent to defend that bold thesis, it is important to acknowledge that science and Christianity did penetrate one another so deeply during the middle ages that it really makes no sense at all to speak of conflict between two opposing camps.

3. The Scientific Revolution—Copernicus, Galileo and the Church

If we adjust our focus chronologically forward from the thirteenth century to the sixteenth and seventeenth centuries, then we come face to face with one of the most provocative periods in the history of the Western intellectual tradition—the so-called scientific revolution. Were I to attempt anything resembling a comprehensive survey of the place of religion in the scientific revolution, this essay would carry on for several volumes. I will instead focus upon one related set of episodes, with my remarks framed to demonstrate that military language is wholly deficient as a tool for coming to terms with the relationship between Christianity and science during this period of intellectual ferment.

One of the central themes of the scientific revolution was the emergence of a sun-centered (heliocentric) cosmology to replace the dominant earth-centered (geocentric) world picture. The Polish astronomer and church administrator Nicolaus Copernicus (1473–1543) presented to the world his heliocentric astronomy in the year of his death with the publication of his *De Revolutionibus Orbium Coelestium [On the Revolutions of the Heavenly Spheres]*. A few generations later, the Italian Catholic mathematician and astronomer Galileo Galilei (1564–1642) turned his homemade telescope heavenward and viewed what he believed to be compelling evidence for the truth of Copernicanism. In 1616 the Theological Consultors of the Holy Office of the Catholic Church declared the theory of the immobility of the sun to be both heretical and foolish, and Copernicus' book was officially placed on the Index of prohibited books until "corrected." In 1633 Galileo knelt before the Inquisitors-General and upon order recanted his Copernican convictions; after which he was sentenced as vehemently suspected of heresy to house arrest. These facts, while themselves beyond dispute, have spawned much scholarly debate regarding their meaning.[42]

If ever we could find a case of science at war with religion, is this not it? Was not Galileo a martyr for science and freedom of thought who suffered at the hands of the Church's anti-intellectual authoritarian traditionalism? If we believe White, this would be our conclusion.[43] Yet his polemical oversimplification plays fast and loose with the facts and, in the words of one Galileo expert, "shows a total lack of understanding regarding the theological doctrines he tries so hard to destroy."[44] It is not necessary to rehearse all the nuanced complexities of Copernicanism and the churches in order to demonstrate that the popular conception of Galileo as martyr misses the mark. Consider a few points of information.

Although White would have us believe that Copernicus delayed publication of his 1543 book from fear of clerical opposition, the fact of the matter was that it was mathematically inclined churchmen who encouraged its publication and ultimately saw *De Revolutionibus* through the press. The second half of the sixteenth century saw slow acceptance of the Copernican sun-centered model, not because the Church stood in the way, but rather because the authoritarian scientific establishment was deeply biased against Copernicanism via its prior commitments to Aristotelian physics and Ptolemaic (earth-centered) cosmology. In fact, we only know of ten Copernicans dating from between 1543 and 1600. Of these, all were professing Christians—seven Protestants and three Catholics.[45]

As for Galileo, he was never the point-man for a scientific community which was united in affirming the truth of

Copernicanism. To the contrary, Galileo's true opponents were the university scientists who had become entrenched in an unyielding commitment to Aristotelian cosmology. These university scientists prodded the Church into joining the affair only when they had failed to beat Galileo's arguments on scientific terms. When Galileo did finally run into difficulties with Church officials, he erred in two ways. First, he overstated the degree of proof he could offer for the sun-centered system—indeed, he had not himself become a Copernican by examining the "evidence." Second, he brazenly trod into the sensitive territory of biblical interpretation. In the wake of the Council of Trent "modern liberal values were far from commanding the assent that we have come to take for granted."[46] His overconfidence in the truth of Copernicanism led Galileo to make some bold statements about how the Scriptures ought to be read. He was especially fond of the statement, "That the intention of the Holy Ghost is to teach us how one goes to heaven, not how heaven goes."[47] Thus he placed himself upon very tenuous ground by defending principles of interpretation that ran contrary to the Council of Trent. And he did so possessing no unassailable fortress of scientific truth into which to retreat.

How are we to assess this complex affair? Galileo's greatest opposition came originally not from the Church, but from scientific establishment elites whom he had upstaged with rhetorical acumen. By branching into the realm of hermeneutics, i.e., biblical interpretation, however, without sufficient supporting proof for his position, Galileo exposed his Achilles' heel. We may conclude by agreeing with other historians who have denounced as simplistic and wrongheaded the warfare model which attempts to cast Galileo as the proponent of scientific fact being derailed by biblical literalists:

> It was not a matter of Christianity waging war on science. All of the participants called themselves Christians, and all acknowledged biblical authority. This was a struggle between opposing theories of biblical interpretation: a conservative theory issuing from the Council of Trent versus Galileo's more liberal alternative. Both were precedented in the history of the church. Personal and political factors also played

> a role, as Galileo demonstrated his flair for cultivating enemies in high places.[48]

We are presented once again, in the story of Galileo, with an illustration of the fact that the history of the encounter between science and Christianity is one of complexity rather than of simple warfare.

IV. A Farewell to Arms: Science and Christianity, Neither Armed nor Arm-in-Arm

Although my discussion has of necessity been incomplete, it should be clear that casting the history of science and Christianity as a struggle between two opposing forces does gross injustice to the historical realities. I agree with John Hedley Brooke who suggests that science and religion should "be seen as complex social activities involving different expressions of human concern, the same individuals often participating in both."[49] As I have shown, many of the players in our drama have been scientists of deep religious convictions. Knowing this, some opponents of the conflict thesis have transformed their critiques into forms of Christian apologetics. Their denial of warfare evolves into an argument for the converse position—namely, that science and religion have been thoroughgoing partners allied in a brotherly quest for knowledge.[50] There are components of this position that strike me as fundamentally sound. For example, no one can easily deny that religious beliefs have offered scientists philosophical *presuppositions* that have helped get their science off the ground (viz. the world and the human mind are ordered, the world is intelligible, etc.). Furthermore, religious beliefs have supplied *motivation* for doing science and have provided *sanction* for the investigation of the created world.[51] Yet to affirm these truths one does not have to travel the whole route of the apologist and argue that the historical relationship between science and Christianity is understood correctly only in terms of harmony. Some historians have done this though. For example, in his search for an explanation of the fact that Copernicus,

Descartes, Kepler, Galileo, and others easily accepted the idea of a moving earth, Stanley Jaki concludes with the bold assertion: "The explanation is that all those in question believed in a saving Birth that once took place in a manger."[52] If this is true, might one question the orthodoxy and commitment of those Christians from the first millennium who believed the earth was stationary?

It seems to me that, like the Draper-White theses, the positions that take the opposite extreme also founder upon the dictum that ultimately the history of science and its encounters with Christianity is a very complex affair. In the end, history resists being tailored to fit preconceived apologetic agendas. That, too, is fine. As a Christian, I am not sure that I would be comfortable claiming responsibility for the rise of modern science. To be sure, it has offered many blessings to be thankful for—thankful to God, for all that is good comes ultimately from His hand. Yet human scientific knowledge of the world has not resulted in universal blessing.

Perhaps a more fruitful although much more arduous way of understanding the historical relationships between science and Christianity will come from a willingness to turn away from our tendency to be cheerleaders for a cause, be it science or the Church. Instead we should approach the encounters between science and Christianity in ways that transcend the practice of "assigning credit and blame." If we do not, we can never achieve true understanding of these principal strands in the fabric of our Western intellectual heritage.[53]

A Concluding Non-Historical Postscript

My unwillingness to define science and religion at the outset of this essay was not, as I indicated, indicative of a principled opposition to such an enterprise. It simply is not a fruitful way to begin an historical investigation. I would, however, like now to remove my historian's cap and offer a few tentative suggestions that might serve to inspire further reflection.

We live in one world, not separate scientific and religious worlds—one world. As human beings created in the image of God we have an insatiable desire to interpret our world. I think this (at least in part) is because we and our world are the creations of a God who wants to be known. He has made Himself known too—in His works (the physical world) and in His words (the Scriptures).[54] Human beings possess a variety of tools to use in the tasks of interpreting God's works and words. The theologian's tools are best suited for interpreting God's word and acquiring knowledge of God. The scientist's tools are most appropriate for reading the book of God's works and acquiring knowledge of His creation.[55] It is not the case that scientists and theologians can never share tools. There must be certain methods and modes of thought which scientists and theologians hold in common. After all, both are thinking human beings trying to understand parts of the same world. But just as I would not use a toothbrush to clean the streets or a jackhammer to pound a finishing nail, I would not want to use the wrong tools to interpret God's works and words. To assemble lists of tools and to undertake a reasoned comparison of those lists is, however, the task of another essay. My point here is merely to suggest that God's works and word never present themselves to us without need of interpretation. First and foremost, the scientist and the theologian are interpreters. The scientist can never employ an uninterpreted Bible as a tool for interpreting nature, nor can an uninterpreted physical world serve the theologian as a tool for interpreting the Bible. What could happen, to be sure, is that the scientist in doing his science may be inspired or informed by the theologian's "interpretation" of written revelation.[56] Likewise, the theologian may be inspired or informed by the scientist's "interpretation" of the physical world.[57]

Two points, then, need emphasis in conclusion. First, if both the physical world and the written Scriptures are expressions of God, then correct interpretations of these two books (the book of God's words and the book of God's works) will not make contradicting claims. Second, even if the theologian or the scientist succeeds individually in offering a complete and accurate interpretation of the portion of the world that he interprets, he cannot claim that his individual interpretation is *the* exhaustive story. Any complete interpretation of God's revelation (His words and works taken together) will demonstrate the inability of any one level of interpretation (the theological or the scientific) to stand alone as the whole picture.

Thus a complete interpretation of God's works and words can emerge only from a considered reflection that takes seriously the works of both scientists and theologians and that presents these works as a consonant pair of interacting interpretations. We know that the history of the relationship between science and Christianity does not echo with a simple harmony, but instead sounds a complex cacophony of dissonant chords. This, I suggest, is not because science and religion are fundamentally at odds. Rather it is a signal that the job of using our tools correctly remains unfinished.

Notes

1. John C. Greene and James R. Moore, "Introductory Conversation," in *History, Humanity and Evolution: Essays for John C. Greene,* ed. James R. Moore (Cambridge University Press, 1989), 1–2.
2. Richard S. Westfall, "The Rise of Science and the Decline of Orthodox Christianity: A Study of Kepler, Descartes and Newton," in *God and Nature: Historical Essays on the Encounter Between Christianity and Science,* ed. David C. Lindberg and Ronald L. Numbers (University of California Press, 1986), 218–219.
3. Of course, this question rapidly splinters into a host of subsidiary queries about science and Christianity that cry to be tended to individually. For example, John Hedley Brooke asks, "Were they complementary in their effects, or were they antagonistic? Did religious movements assist the emergence of the scientific movement, or was there a power struggle from the start? Were scientific and religious beliefs constantly at variance, or were they perhaps more commonly integrated, both by clergy and by practicing men of science? How has the relationship changed over time?" See John Hedley Brooke, *Science and Reli-*

gion: Some Historical Perspectives (Cambridge University Press, 1991), 1.

4. This position is also argued by J. H. Brooke, 6–11; 16–19. My discussion of this question follows his line of thinking and employs some of the examples from his account.
5. Isaac Newton, *Mathematical Principles of Natural Philosophy,* 2 vols., trans. Andrew Motte, translations rev. Florian Cajori, (University of California Press, 1962), 544, 546.
6. Richard S. Westfall, *Science and Religion in Seventeenth-Century England* (Yale University Press, 1958; reprint, University of Michigan Press, 1973), 197.
7. Brooke, 18. For a good overview of Ray and Boyle, see Westfall, passim. On Ray, see, Charles E. Raven, *John Ray Naturalist: His Life and Works* (Cambridge University Press, 1942), especially 452–480.
8. Charles Webster, "Puritanism, Separatism and Science," in *God and Nature,* 213.
9. This case of Burnet is taken from Brooke, *Science and Religion,* 7–10.
10. The infamous case of Galileo and the Church has been misunderstood and misinterpreted by those who fail to acknowledge the complex social and political contexts within which this intramural Catholic dispute regarding biblical hermeneutics occurred. See discussion in the third section of Part 3.
11. Brooke, *Science and Religion,* 17–18. Here Brooke provides good counter-examples to demonstrate how each of these generalizations breaks down under historical scrutiny.
12. I do not mean to suggest that by refusing to define science and religion I can now claim complete objectivity. Everyone argues from a point of view. Yet the historian should not saddle himself with more presuppositions when less will do. Furthermore, I do not wish to imply that all attempts to define science and religion are inappropriate or ill-advised. To the contrary, such exercises can be very fruitful; and for some pursuits they are absolutely necessary. But for the historian to offer historical definitions is a complex job, well beyond the scope of this brief treatment. And to offer theological or philosophical discussion of these terms, while of tremendous value, would lead us astray from the immediate historical task.

13. "First of the Course of Scientific Lectures—Prof. White on 'The Battlefields of Science,'" *New York Daily Tribune,* December 18, 1869, 4.
14. In 1876 he published a brief study, *The Warfare of Science,* in which he pointed to "ecclesiasticism" in particular, as opposed to religion in general, as the culprit guilty of thwarting scientific progress.
15. White wrote in his introduction, "My conviction is that Science, though it has evidently conquered Dogmatic Theology based on biblical texts and ancient modes of thought, will go hand in hand with Religion; and that, although theological control will continue to diminish, Religion, as seen in the recognition of 'a Power in the universe, not ourselves which makes for righteousness,' and in the love of God and of our neighbor, will steadily grow stronger and stronger, not only in the American institutions of learning but in the world at large." Andrew Dickson White, *A History of the Warfare of Science with Theology in Christendom,* 1 (D. Appleton and Company, 1896), xii.
16. Ibid., 375.
17. Historians of science and religion Lindberg and Numbers affirm the significance of White's book. "No work... has done more than White's to instill in the public mind a sense of the adversarial relationship between science and religion." See David C. Lindberg and Ronald L. Numbers, "Beyond War and Peace: A Reappraisal of the Encounter between Christianity and Science," *Church History* 55 (September 1986): 340.
18. John William Draper, *History of the Conflict Between Religion and Science* (D. Appleton & Co., 1874). On Draper, see Donald Fleming, *John William Draper and the Religion of Science* (University of Pennsylvania Press, 1950).
19. Ronald L. Numbers, "Science and Religion," *Osiris,* 2nd series, 1 (1985): 61.
20. Draper, 367.
21. "Introduction," David C. Lindberg and Ronald L. Numbers, in *God and Nature,* 2.
22. David Starr Jordan to Scudder Klyce, December 26, 1923, quoted in Edward A. White, *Science and Religion in American Thought: The Impact of Naturalism* (Stanford University Press, 1950), 2.

23. Maynard Shipley, *The War on Modern Science: A Short History of the Fundamentalist Attacks on Evolution and Modernism* (Alfred A. Knopf, 1927), 18.
24. William B. Provine, review of *Trial and Error: The American Controversy over Creation and Evolution* by Edward J. Larson in *Academe* (January-February, 1987), 52; Richard Dawkins, *The Blind Watchmaker* (W. W. Norton & Co., 1986), 6; Tad S. Clements, *Science vs. Religion* (Prometheus Books, 1990), 3.
25. James R. Moore, *The Post-Darwinian Controversies: A Study of the Protestant Struggle to Come to Terms with Darwin in Great Britain and America, 1870–1900* (Cambridge University Press, 1979), 20.
26. This suggestion, of course, is not original with me. Many have affirmed Moore's conclusion that "the military metaphor has taken a dreadful toll in historical interpretation." Ibid., 99.
27. Serious questioning of the validity of warfare theses has been around for some time. Perhaps the most significant early challenge was issued in 1938 by sociologist Robert K. Merton. See Robert K. Merton, *Science, Technology and Society in Seventeenth-Century England* (*Osiris,* 4, part 2, 1938; reprint, Harper & Row, 1970). James R. Moore, *The Post-Darwinian Controversies,* 19–122, offers the best detailed critique of the Draper-White thesis. Also indispensable are the works by Lindberg and Numbers cited above. See as well, Colin A. Russell, R. Hooykaas and David C. Goodman, "The 'Conflict Thesis' and Cosmology," Block 1, Units 1–3 of *Science and Belief: From Copernicus to Darwin* (The Open University Press, 1974).
28. Lindberg and Numbers, "Beyond War and Peace," 340.
29. I have resisted the strong temptation to add discussion of a fourth theme—Darwin, Evolution and Creation—only because other papers in this volume (most notably that of Ronald L. Numbers) treat this issue, not because it is not eminently worthy of attention.
30. White, *Warfare,* 375.
31. David C. Lindberg, "Science and the Early Church," Presentation to a conference of the Institute for Advanced Christian Studies, Madison, WI, August 11, 1986.
32. David C. Lindberg, *The Beginnings of Western Science: The European Scientific Tradition in Philosophical, Religious and Institu-*

tional Context, 600 B.C. *to* A.D. *1450* (University of Chicago Press, 1992), 151.

33. Edward Grant, "Science and Theology in the Middle Ages," in *God and Nature: Historical Essays on the Encounter Between Christianity and Science* (University of California Press, 1986), 50.
34. Ibid.
35. St. Augustine, *The Literal Meaning of Genesis,* trans. John Hammond Taylor, S.J., 2 vols., *Ancient Christian Writers: The Works of the Fathers in Translation,* Nos. 41–42 (Newman Press, 1982), 41: 42–43.
36. Lindberg and Numbers, "Beyond War and Peace," 342.
37. See David C. Lindberg, "Critical Problems in the History of Medieval Science: The Case of Science and Religion," in proceedings of the "Conference on Critical Problems and Research Frontiers in the History of Science and Technology," Madison, WI, 1991, 191–198.
38. The most helpful sources in my study of the Condemnation of 1277 have been Edward Grant, "The Condemnation of 1277, God's Absolute Power and Physical Thought in the Late Middle Ages," *Viator,* 10 (1979): 211–244; Edward Grant, "Late Medieval Thought, Copernicus and the Scientific Revolution," *Journal of the History of Ideas,* 23 (1962): 197–220; Gordon Leff, *Paris and Oxford Universities in the Thirteenth and Fourteenth Centuries: An Institutional and Intellectual History* (John Wiley and Sons, 1968); and Edward Grant, "Science and Theology in the Middle Ages," in *God and Nature,* 49–75.
39. Lindberg and Numbers, "Beyond War and Peace," 343.
40. David C. Lindberg, "Early Encounters Between Christianity and Science: The Case of the Middle Ages," lecture presented to the 50th Anniversary Meeting of the American Scientific Affiliation, Wheaton, IL, July 25, 1991.
41. Pierre Duhem in his *Etudes sur Leonard de Vinci* (1906–1913) wrote: "[I]f we must assign a date for the birth of modern science, we would, without doubt, choose the year 1277." Quoted in Grant, "Late Medieval Thought," 200. And in his monumental *Le System du monde* Duhem remarked that modern science "was born, one may say, on March 7, 1277, from a decree issued by Monsignor Etienne, bishop of Paris." *Le*

Systeme du monde: Histoire des doctrines cosmologiques de Platon E Copernic, 6 (1914; reprint, Hermann, 1965), 66. This reference is from a sympathetic citation by Stanley L. Jaki, *The Origin of Science and the Science of Its Origin* (Regnery Gateway, 1979), 139.

42. The literature on Copernicanism, Galileo and the Church is vast. Helpful and important places to start include Robert S. Westman, "The Copernicans and the Churches," in *God and Nature,* 76–113; William R. Shea, "Galileo and the Church," in *God and Nature,* 114–135; Maurice A. Finocchiaro, *The Galileo Affair: A Documentary History* (University of California Press, 1989); Giorgio De Santillana, *The Crime of Galileo* (University of Chicago Press, 1955); Jerome J. Langford, *Galileo, Science and the Church* (University of Michigan Press, 1971); Stillman Drake, *Discoveries and Opinions of Galileo* (Doubleday and Company, 1957); and Richard J. Blackwell, *Galileo, Bellarmine and the Bible* (University of Notre Dame Press, 1991).
43. See White, *A History of the Warfare,* vol. 1, chap. 3, 114–170.
44. Langford, *Galileo, Science and the Church,* 99.
45. Westman, "The Copernicans and the Churches," 85.
46. Shea, "Galileo and the Church," 114.
47. Galileo attributes this saying to Cardinal Baronius whom Galileo probably met in Padua in 1598. See Galileo's "Letter to the Grand Duchess Christina," in Drake, *Discoveries and Opinions of Galileo,* 186.
48. Lindberg and Numbers, "Beyond War and Peace," 347.
49. Brooke, *Science and Religion,* 42.
50. See, for example, Stanley Jaki, *The Road of Science and the Ways to God* (University of Chicago Press, 1978); Colin A. Russell, *Cross-Currents: Interactions Between Science and Faith* (William B. Eerdmans Publishing Company, 1985); and R. Hooykaas, *Religion and the Rise of Modern Science* (William B. Eerdmans Publishing Company, 1972).
51. John Hedley Brook, "Religious Belief and the Natural Sciences: Mapping the Historical Landscape," paper presented to the Pascal Centre International Conference on Science and Belief, Ancaster, Ontario, August 12, 1992. To be published

in forthcoming proceedings of the conference. See also Brooke, *Science and Religion,* 19–33.

52. Stanley L. Jaki, *The Savior of Science* (Regnery Gateway, 1988), 50.
53. Lindberg and Numbers, "Beyond War and Peace," 354.
54. I am echoing here the ancient doctrine of the "two books" that can be traced back at least to Tertullian and that found expression in Augustine, Bonaventure, Francis of Assisi, and numerous thinkers since the reformation and rise of modern science.
55. I would suggest that Theology (with a capital "T") involves the task of interpreting *all* of God's *revelation.* To the degree that God has *revealed* Himself in the created physical world, the scientist's job of interpreting that physical world may be understood as doing a sort of natural "Theology." Indeed, it has been suggested that science is, in the end, "thinking God's thoughts after Him."
56. There is no reason why theologians may not suggest fruitful lines of scientific inquiry. And it seems to be the case that many of the philosophical presuppositions of modern science emerge from a view of the universe consonant with Christian doctrines.
57. Scientific knowledge of all sorts—from philology to astronomy—has proven helpful in biblical interpretation.

The Evolution of Scientific Creationism

Ronald L. Numbers

Ronald L. Numbers is the William Coleman Professor of the History of Science and Medicine at the University of Wisconsin-Madison where he has taught since 1974. The editor of the journal, *Isis,* he has written, co-written or edited 14 books. Among them are *Almost Persuaded: American Physicians and Compulsory Health Insurance, 1912–1920* (1978), *The Education of American Physicians: Historical Essays* (1980), *God and Nature: A History of the Encounter Between Christianity and Science* (1986), and *The Creationists* (1992), which won the Albert C. Outler Prize from the American Society of Church History. He is currently at work on *Science and the Americans: A History* for Cambridge University Press.

Scarcely twenty years after the publication of Charles Darwin's *Origin of Species* in 1859, special creationists could name only two working naturalists in North America, John William Dawson (1820–1899) of Montreal and Arnold Guyot (1806–1884) of Princeton, who had not succumbed to some theory of organic evolution. The situation in Great Britain looked equally bleak for creationists, and on both sides of the Atlantic liberal churchmen were beginning to follow their scientific colleagues into the evolutionist camp. By the closing years of the nineteenth century evolution was infiltrating even the ranks of the evangelicals and, in the opinion of many observers, belief in special creation seemed destined to go the way of the dinosaur. Contrary to the hopes of liberals and the fears of conservatives, however, creationism did not become extinct. The majority of late nineteenth-century Americans remained true to a traditional reading of

From *The Creationists* (New York: Alfred A. Knopf, 1992). Reprinted by permission.

Genesis and, as late as 1982, a public-opinion poll revealed that 44 percent of Americans, nearly a fourth of whom were college graduates, continued to believe that "God created man pretty much in his present form at one time within the last 10,000 years."[1]

Such surveys failed, however, to disclose the great diversity of opinion among those professing to be creationists. Risking oversimplification, we can divide creationists into two main camps: "strict creationists," who interpret the days of Genesis literally, and "progressive creationists," who construe the Mosaic days to be immense periods of time. But even within these camps substantial differences exist. Some strict creationists, for example, believe that God created all terrestrial life—past and present—less than ten thousand years ago, while others postulate one or more creations prior to the seven days of Genesis. Similarly, some progressive creationists believe in numerous creative acts, while others limit God's intervention to the creation of life and perhaps the human soul. Since this last species of creationism is practically indistinguishable from theistic evolutionism, this essay focuses on the strict creationists and the more conservative of the progressive creationists, particularly on the small number who claimed scientific expertise. Drawing on their writings, it traces the ideological development of creationism from the crusade to outlaw the teaching of evolution in the 1920s to the current battle for equal time. During this period the leading apologists for special creation shifted from an openly biblical defense of their views to one based largely on science. At the same time they grew less tolerant of notions of an old earth and symbolic days of creation, which had been common among creationists early in the century, and became more doctrinaire in their insistence on both a recent creation in six literal days and a universal flood.

The Loyal Majority

The general acceptance of organic evolution by the intellectual elite of the late Victorian era has often obscured the fact that the majority of Americans remained loyal to the doctrine of special creation. In addition to the masses who said nothing, there were many people who vocally rejected kinship with the apes and other, more reflective, persons who concurred with the Princeton theologian Charles Hodge (1797–1878) that Darwinism was atheism. Among the most intransigent foes of organic evolution were the premillennialists, whose predictions of Christ's imminent return depended on a literal reading of the Scriptures. Because of their conviction that one error in the Bible invalidated the entire book, they had little patience with scientists who, as described by the evangelist Dwight L. Moody (1837–1899), "dug up old carcasses . . . to make them testify against God."[2]

Such an attitude did not, however, prevent many biblical literalists from agreeing with geologists that the earth was far older than six thousand years. They did so by identifying two separate creations in the first chapter of Genesis: the first, "in the beginning," perhaps millions of years ago, and the second, in six actual days, approximately four thousand years before the birth of Christ. According to this so-called gap theory, most fossils were relics of the first creation, destroyed by God prior to the Adamic restoration. In 1909 the *Scofield Reference Bible,* the most authoritative biblical guide in fundamentalist circles, sanctioned this view.[3]

Scientists like Guyot and Dawson, the last of the reputable nineteenth-century creationists, went still further to accommodate science by interpreting the days of Genesis as ages and correlating them with successive epochs in the natural history of the world. Although they believed in special creative acts, especially of the first human beings, they tended to minimize the number of supernatural interventions and to maximize the operation of natural law. During the late nineteenth century their theory of progressive creation circulated widely in the colleges and seminaries of America.[4]

The early Darwinian debate focused largely on the implications of evolution for natural theology; so long as these discussions remained confined to scholarly circles, those who objected to evolution on biblical grounds saw little reason to participate. When the debate spilled over into the public arena during the 1880s and 1890s, however, creationists grew alarmed. "When these vague speculations, scattered to the four winds by the million-tongued press, are caught up by ignorant and untrained men," declared one premillennialist in 1889, "it is time for earnest Christian men to call a halt."[5]

The questionable scientific status of Darwinism undoubtedly encouraged such critics to speak up. Although the overwhelming majority of scientists after 1880 accepted a long earth history and some form of organic evolution, many in the late nineteenth century were expressing serious reservations about the ability of Darwin's particular theory of natural selection to account for the origin of species. Their published criticisms of Darwinism led creationists mistakenly to conclude that scientists were in the midst of discarding evolution. The appearance of books with such titles as *The Collapse of Evolution* and *At the Death Bed of Darwinism* bolstered this belief and convinced antievolutionists that liberal Christians had capitulated to evolution too quickly. In view of this turn of events it seemed likely that those who had "abandoned the stronghold of faith out of sheer fright will soon be found scurrying back to the old and impregnable citadel, when they learn that 'the enemy is in full retreat.'"[6]

For the time being, however, those conservative Christians who would soon call themselves fundamentalists perceived a greater threat to orthodox faith than evolution: higher criticism, which treated the Bible more as an historical document than as God's inspired word. Their relative apathy toward evolution is evident in *The Fundamentals,* a mass-produced series of twelve booklets published between 1910 and 1915 to revitalize and reform Christianity around the world. Although one contributor identified evolution as the principal cause of disbelief in the Scriptures and another traced the roots of higher criticism to Darwin, the collection as a whole lacked the strident antievolutionism that would characterize the fundamentalist movement of the 1920s.[7]

This is particularly true of the writings of George Frederick Wright (1838–1921), a Congregational minister and amateur geologist of international repute. At first glance he seems an anomalous representative of the fundamentalist point of view. As a prominent Christian Darwinist in the 1870s he had argued that the intended purpose of Genesis was to protest polytheism, not teach science. By the 1890s, however, he had come to espouse the progressive creationism of Guyot and Dawson, partly, it seems, in reaction to the claims of higher critics regarding the accuracy of the Pentateuch. Because of his standing as a scientific authority and his conservative view of the Scriptures, the editors of *The Fundamentals* selected him to address the question of the relationship between evolution and the Christian faith.[8]

In an essay misleadingly titled "The Passing of Evolution," Wright attempted to steer a middle course between the theistic evolution of his early days and the traditional views of some special creationists. On the one hand, he argued that the Bible itself taught evolution, "an orderly progress from lower to higher forms of matter and life." On the other hand, he limited evolution to the origin of species, pointing out that even Darwin had postulated the supernatural creation of several forms of plants and animals, endowed by the Creator with a "marvelous capacity for variation." Furthermore, he argued that, despite the physical similarity between human beings and the higher animals, the former "came into existence as the Bible represents, by the special creation of a single pair, from whom all the varieties of the race have sprung."[9]

Although Wright represented the left wing of fundamentalism, his moderate views on evolution contributed to the conciliatory tone that prevailed during the years leading up to World War I. Fundamentalists may not have liked evolution, but few, if any, at this time saw the necessity or desirability of launching a crusade to eradicate it from the schools and churches of America.

The Antievolution Crusade

Early in 1922 William Jennings Bryan (1860–1925), Presbyterian layman and thrice-defeated Democratic candidate for the presidency of the United States, heard of an effort in

Kentucky to prohibit evolution from being taught in public schools. "The movement will sweep the country," he predicted hopefully, "and we will drive Darwinism from our schools."[10] His prophecy proved overly optimistic, but before the end of the decade more than twenty state legislatures did debate antievolution laws, and four—Oklahoma, Tennessee, Mississippi, and Arkansas—banned the teaching of evolution in public schools. At times the controversy became so tumultuous that it looked to some as though "America might go mad." Many persons shared responsibility for these events, but none more than Bryan. His entry into the fray had a catalytic effect and gave antievolutionists what they needed most: "a spokesman with a national reputation, immense prestige and a loyal following."[11]

The development of Bryan's own attitude toward evolution closely paralleled that of the fundamentalist movement. Since early in the century he had occasionally alluded to the silliness of believing in monkey ancestors and to the ethical dangers of thinking that might makes right, but until the outbreak of World War I he saw little reason to quarrel with those who disagreed. The war, however, exposed the darkest side of human nature and shattered his illusions about the future of Christian society. Obviously something had gone awry, and Bryan soon traced the source of the trouble to the paralyzing influence of Darwinism on the human conscience. By substituting the law of the jungle for the teaching of Christ, it threatened both democracy and Christianity, the principles he valued most deeply. Two books in particular confirmed his suspicion. The first, Vernon Kellogg's *Headquarters Nights* (1917), recounted firsthand conversations with German officers that revealed the role Darwin's biology had played in persuading the Germans to declare war. The second, Benjamin Kidd's *Science of Power* (1918), purported to demonstrate the historical and philosophical links between Darwinism and German militarism.[12]

About the time that Bryan discovered the Darwinian origins of the war, he also became aware, to his great distress, of unsettling effects the theory of evolution was having on America's own young people. From frequent visits to college campuses and from talks with parents, pastors and Sunday-school teachers, he heard about an epidemic of unbelief that was sweeping the country. Upon investigating the cause, his wife reported, "he became convinced that the teaching of evolution as a fact instead of a theory caused the students to lose faith in the Bible, first, in the story of creation, and later in other doctrines, which underlie the Christian religion." Again Bryan found confirming evidence in a recently published book. In *Belief in God and Immortality* (1916) the Bryn Mawr psychologist James H. Leuba demonstrated statistically that college attendance endangered traditional religious beliefs.[13]

Armed with this information about the cause of moral decay in the world and the nation, Bryan launched a nationwide crusade against the offending doctrine. In one of his most popular and influential lectures, "The Menace of Darwinism," he summed up his case against evolution, arguing that it was both un-Christian and unscientific. Darwinism, he declared, was nothing but "guesses strung together," and poor guesses at that. Borrowing from a turn-of-the-century tract, he illustrated how the evolutionist explained the origin of the eye:

> The evolutionist guesses that there was a time when eyes were unknown—that is a necessary part of the hypothesis. . . . [A] piece of pigment, or, as some say, a freckle appeared upon the skin of an animal that had no eyes. This piece of pigment or freckle converged the rays of the sun upon that spot and when the little animal felt the heat on that spot it turned the spot to the sun to get more heat. The increased heat irritated the skin—so the evolutionists guess, and a nerve came there and out of the nerve came the eye!

"Can you beat it?" he asked incredulously—and that it happened not once but twice? As for himself, he would take one verse in Genesis over all that Darwin wrote.[14]

Throughout his political career Bryan had placed his faith in the common people, and he resented the attempt of a few thousand scientists "to establish an oligarchy over the forty million American Christians," to dictate what should be taught in the schools.[15] To a democrat like Bryan it seemed preposterous that this "scientific soviet" would not only demand to teach its insidious philosophy but impudently insist that society pay its salaries. Confident that nine-tenths of the Christian citizens agreed with him, he decided to appeal directly to them, as he had done so successfully in fighting the liquor interests. "Commit your case to the people," he advised creationists. "Forget, if need be, the high-brows both in the political and college world, and carry this cause to the people. They are the final and efficiently corrective power."[16]

And who were the people who joined Bryan's crusade? As recent studies have shown, they came from all walks of life and from every region of the country. They lived in New York, Chicago and Los Angeles as well as in small towns and rural areas. Few possessed advanced degrees, but many were not without education. Nevertheless, Bryan undeniably found his staunchest supporters and won his greatest victories in the conservative and still largely rural South, described hyperbolically by one fundamentalist journal as "the last stronghold of orthodoxy on the North American continent," a region where the "masses of the people in all denominations 'believe the Bible from lid to lid.'"[17]

It is more difficult to determine the strength of Bryan's following within the churches, because not all fundamentalists were creationists, and many creationists refused to participate in the crusade against evolution. A 1929 survey of the theological beliefs of seven hundred Protestant ministers does provide some valuable clues. The question "Do you believe that the creation of the world occurred in the manner and time recorded in Genesis?" elicited the following positive responses:

Lutheran	89%
Baptist	63%
Evangelical	62%
Presbyterian	35%
Methodist	24%
Congregational	12%

Episcopalian	11%
Other	60%

Unfortunately, these statistics tell us nothing about the various ways respondents may have interpreted the phrase "in the manner and time recorded in Genesis," nor do they reveal anything about the level of political involvement in the campaign against evolution. For example, Lutherans overwhelming rejected evolution but generally preferred education to legislation and tended to view legal action against evolution as "a dangerous mingling of church and state." Similarly, premillennialists, who saw the spread of evolution as one more sign of the world's impending end, sometimes lacked incentive to correct the evils around them.[18]

Baptists and Presbyterians, who dominated the fundamentalist movement, participated actively in the campaign against evolution. The Southern Baptist Convention, spiritual home of some of the most outspoken foes of evolution, lent encouragement to the creationist crusaders by voting unanimously in 1926 that "this Convention accepts Genesis as teaching that man was the special creation of God, and rejects every theory, evolution or other, which teaches that man originated in, or came by way of, a lower animal ancestry." The Presbyterian Church contributed Bryan and other leaders to the creationist cause but, as the above survey indicates, also harbored many evolutionists. In 1923 the General Assembly turned back an attempt by Bryan and his fundamentalist cohorts to cut off funds to any church school found teaching human evolution, approving instead a compromise measure that condemned only materialistic evolution. The other major Protestant bodies paid relatively little attention to the debate over evolution, and Catholics, though divided on the question of evolution, seldom favored restrictive legislation.[19]

Leadership of the antievolution movement came not from the organized churches of America but from individuals like Bryan and interdenominational organizations such as the World's Christian Fundamentals Association, a predominantly premillennialist body founded in 1919 by William Bell Riley (1861–1947), pastor of the First Baptist Church in Minneapolis. Riley became active as an antievolutionist after discovering, to his apparent surprise, that evolutionists were teaching their views at the University of Minnesota. As part of an unprecedented expansion of public education in the early twentieth century, enrollment in public high schools nearly doubled between 1920 and 1930. Fundamentalists like Riley and Bryan wanted to make sure that students attending these institutions would not lose their faith. Thus they resolved to drive every evolutionist from public school payrolls. Those who lost their jobs as a result deserved little sympathy, for, as one rabble-rousing creationist put it, the German soldiers who killed Belgian and French children with poisoned candy were angels compared with the teachers and textbook writers who corrupted the souls of children and thereby sentenced them to eternal death.[20]

The creationists, we should remember, did not always act without provocation. In many instances their opponents displayed equal intolerance and insensitivity. In fact, one contemporary observer blamed the creation-evolution controversy in part on the "intellectual flapperism" of irresponsible and poorly informed teachers who delighted in shocking naive students with unsupportable statements about evolution. It was understandable, wrote an Englishman, that American parents would resent sending their sons and daughters to public institutions that exposed them to "a multiple assault upon traditional faiths."[21]

Creationist Science and Scientists

In 1922 William Bell Riley outlined the reasons why fundamentalists opposed the teaching of evolution. "The first and most important reason for its elimination," he explained, "is the unquestioned fact that evolution is not a science; it is a hypothesis only, a speculation." Bryan often made the same point, defining true science as "classified knowledge . . . the explanation of facts."[22] Although creationists had far more compelling reasons for rejecting evolution than its alleged unscientific status, their insistence on this point was not merely an obscurantist ploy. It stemmed from their commitment to a once-respected tradition, associated with the English philosopher Sir Francis Bacon (1561–1626), that emphasized the factual, non-theoretical nature of science. By identifying with the Baconian tradition, creationists could label evolution as false science, claim equality with scientific authorities in comprehending facts, and deny the charge of being opposed to science. "It is not 'science' that orthodox Christians oppose," a fundamentalist editor insisted defensively. "No! no! a thousand times, No! They are opposed only to the theory of evolution, which has not yet been proved, and therefore is not to be called by the sacred name of science."[23]

Their conviction that evolution was unscientific led creationists to assure themselves that the world's best scientists agreed with them. At the beginning of their campaign in 1921, they received an important boost from an address by the distinguished British biologist William Bateson (1861–1926), in which he declared that scientists had *not* discovered "the actual mode and process of evolution." Although he warned creationists against misinterpreting his statement as a rejection of evolution, they paid no more attention to that caveat than they did to the numerous pro-evolution resolutions passed by scientific societies.[24]

Unfortunately for the creationists, they could claim few legitimate scientists of their own: a couple of self-made men of science, one or two physicians, and a handful of teachers who, as one evolutionist described them, were "trying to hold down, not a chair, but a whole settee, of 'Natural Science' in some little institution."[25] Of this group the most influential were Harry Rimmer (1890–1952) and George McCready Price (1870–1963).

Rimmer, Presbyterian minister and self-styled "research scientist," obtained his limited exposure to science during a term or two at San Francisco's Hahnemann Medical College, a small homeopathic institution that required no more than a high-school diploma for admission. As a medical student he picked up a vocabulary of "double-jointed, twelve cylinder, knee-action words" that later served to impress the uninitiated. After his brief stint in medical school he attended Whittier College and the Bible Institute of Los Angeles for a year each before entering full-time evangelistic work. About 1919 he settled in Los Angeles and set up a small laboratory at the rear of his house to conduct experiments in embryology and related sciences. Within a year or two he established the Research Science Bureau "to prove through findings in biology, paleontology and anthropology that science and the literal Bible were not contradictory." The bureau staff—that is, Rimmer—apparently used income from the sale of memberships to finance anthropological field trips in the western United States, but Rimmer's dream of visiting Africa to prove the dissimilarity of gorillas and humans failed to materialize. By the late 1920s the bureau lay dormant, and Rimmer signed on with Riley's World's Christian Fundamentals Association as a field secretary.[26]

Besides engaging in research, Rimmer delivered thousands of lectures, primarily to student groups, on the scientific accuracy of the Bible. Posing as a scientist, he attacked Darwinism and poked fun at the credulity of evolutionists. To attract attention, he repeatedly offered one hundred dollars to anyone who could discover a scientific error in the Scriptures; not surprisingly, the offer never cost him a dollar. By his own reckoning, he never lost a public debate. Following one encounter with an evolutionist in Philadelphia, he wrote home gleefully that "the debate was a simple walkover, a massacre—murder pure and simple. The eminent professor was simply scared stiff to advance any of the common arguments of the evolutionists, and he fizzled like a wet firecracker."[27]

George McCready Price, a Seventh-day Adventist geologist, was less skilled at debating than was Rimmer, but he wielded more scientific influence. As a young man, Price attended an Adventist college in Michigan for two years and later completed a teacher-training course at the provincial normal school in his native New Brunswick. The turn of the century found him serving as principal of a small high school in an isolated part of eastern Canada, where one of his few companions was a local physician. During their many conversations the doctor almost converted his fundamentalist friend to evolution. On each occasion that Price wavered, however, he was saved by prayer and by reading the works of the Seventh-day Adventist prophetess Ellen G. White (1827–1915), who claimed divine inspiration for her view that Noah's flood accounted for the fossil record on which evolutionists based their theory. As a result of these experiences, Price vowed to devote his life to promoting creationism of the strictest kind.[28]

By 1906 he was working as a handyman at an Adventist sanitarium in southern California. That year he published a slim volume entitled *Illogical Geology: The Weakest Point in the Evolution Theory,* in which he brashly offered one thousand dollars "to any one who will, in the face of the facts here presented, show me how to prove that one kind of fossil is older than another." (Like Rimmer, he never had to pay.) According to Price's argument, Darwinism rested "logically and historically on the succession of life idea as taught by geology" and, "if this succession of life is not an actual scientific fact, then Darwinism ... is a most gigantic hoax."[29] Although a few fundamentalists praised Price's polemic, David Starr Jordan (1851–1931), president of Stanford University and an authority on fossil fishes, warned him that he should not expect "any geologist to take [his work] seriously." Jordan conceded that the unknown author had written "a very clever book" but described it as:

> a sort of lawyer's plea, based on scattering mistakes, omissions and exceptions against general truths that anybody familiar with the facts in a general way cannot possibly dispute. It would be just as easy and just as plausible and just as convincing if one should take the facts of European history and attempt to show that all the various events were simultaneous.[30]

As Jordan recognized, Price lacked any formal training or field experience in geology. He was, however, a voracious reader of geological literature, an armchair scientist who self-consciously minimized the importance of field experience.

During the next fifteen years Price occupied scientific "settees" in several Seventh-day Adventist schools and authored six more books attacking the geological foundation of evolution. Although not unknown outside his own church before the early 1920s, he did not attract national attention until that time. Shortly after Bryan declared war on evolution, Price published *The New Geology* (1923), the most systematic and comprehensive of his many books. Uninhibited by false modesty, he presented his "great *law of conformable stratigraphic sequences* ... by all odds the most important law ever formulated with reference to the order in which the strata occur." This law stated that "*any kind of fossiliferous beds whatever, 'young' or 'old,' may* be *found occurring conformably on any other fossiliferous beds, 'older' or 'younger.'*"[31] To Price, so-called deceptive conformities (where strata seem to be missing) and thrust faults (where the strata are apparently in the wrong order) proved that there was no natural order to the fossil-bearing rocks, all of which he attributed to the Genesis flood.

A Yale geologist reviewing the book for *Science* accused Price of "harboring a geological nightmare." Despite such criticism from the scientific establishment—and the fact that his theory contradicted both the day-age and gap interpretations of Genesis—Price's reputation among fundamentalists rose dramatically. Rimmer, for example, hailed *The New Geology* as "a masterpiece of REAL science [that] explodes in a convincing manner some of the ancient fallacies of science 'falsely so called.'"[32] By the mid-1920s, Price's byline was appearing with increasing frequency in a broad spectrum of conservative religious periodicals, and the editor of *Science* could accurately describe him as "the principal scientific authority of the Fundamentalists."[33]

The Scopes Trial and Beyond

In the spring of 1925, John Thomas Scopes, a high school teacher in the small town of Dayton, Tennessee, confessed to having violated the state's recently passed law banning the teaching of human evolution in public schools. His subsequent trial focused international attention on the antievolution crusade and brought William Jennings Bryan to

Dayton to assist the prosecution. In anticipation of arguing the scientific merits of evolution, Bryan sought out the best scientific minds in the creationist camp to serve as expert witnesses. The response to his inquiries could only have disappointed the aging crusader. Price, then teaching in England, sent his regrets—along with advice for Bryan to stay away from scientific topics. Howard A. Kelly, a prominent Johns Hopkins physician who had contributed to *The Fundamentals* confessed that, except for Adam and Eve, he believed in evolution. Louis T. More, a physicist who had just written a book on *The Dogma of Evolution* (1925), replied that he accepted evolution as a working hypothesis. Alfred W. McCann, author of *God—or Gorilla* (1922), took the opportunity to chide Bryan for supporting Prohibition in the past and for trying now "to bottle-up the tendencies of men to think for themselves."[34]

At the trial itself, things scarcely went better. When Bryan could name only Price and the deceased George Frederick Wright as scientists for whom he had respect, the caustic Clarence Darrow (1857–1938), attorney for the defense, scoffed: "You mentioned Price because he is the only human being in the world so far as you know that signs his name as a geologist that believes like you do . . . every scientist in this country knows [he] is a mountebank and a pretender and not a geologist at all." Eventually Bryan conceded that the world was indeed far more than six thousand years old and that the six days of creation had probably been longer than twenty-four hours each—concessions that may have harmonized with the progressive creationism of Wright but hardly with the strict creationism of Price.[35]

Though one could scarcely have guessed it from some of his public pronouncements, Bryan had long been a progressive creationist. In fact, his beliefs regarding evolution diverged considerably from those of his more conservative supporters. Shortly before his trial he had confided to Dr. Kelly that he, too, had no objection to "evolution before man but for the fact that a concession as to the truth of evolution up to man furnishes our opponents with an argument which they are quick to use, namely, if evolution accounts for all the species up to man, does it not raise a presumption in behalf of evolution to include man?" Until biologists could actually demonstrate the evolution of one species into another, he thought it best to keep them on the defensive.[36]

Bryan's admission at Dayton spotlighted a serious and longstanding problem among antievolutionists: their failure to agree on a theory of creation. Even the most visible leaders could not reach a consensus. Riley, for example, followed Guyot and Dawson (and Bryan) in viewing the days of Genesis as ages, believing that the testimony of geology necessitated this interpretation. Rimmer favored the gap theory, which involved two separate creations, in part because his scientific mind could not fathom how, given Riley's scheme, plants created on the third day could have survived thousands of years without the light of the sun, which appeared on the fourth.

According to the testimony of acquaintances, he also believed that the Bible taught a local, rather than a universal, flood. Price, who cared not a whit about the opinion of geologists, insisted on nothing less than a recent creation in six literal days and a worldwide deluge. He regarded the day-age theory as "the devil's counterfeit" and the gap theory as only slightly more acceptable. Rimmer and Riley, who preferred to minimize the differences among creationists, attempted the logically impossible, if ecumenically desirable, task of incorporating Price's "new geology" into their own schemes.[37]

Although the court in Dayton found Scopes guilty as charged, creationists had little cause for rejoicing. The press had not treated them kindly, and the taxing ordeal no doubt contributed to Bryan's death a few days after the end of the trial. Nevertheless, the antievolutionists continued their crusade, winning victories in Mississippi in 1926 and Arkansas two years later. By the end of the decade, however, their legislative campaign had lost its steam. The presidential election of 1928, pitting a Protestant against a Catholic, offered fundamentalists a new cause, and the onset of the Great Depression in 1929 further diverted their attention.[38]

Contrary to appearances, the creationists were simply

changing tactics, not giving up. Instead of lobbying state legislatures, they shifted their attack to local communities, where they engaged in what one critic described as "the emasculation of textbooks, the 'purging' of libraries and, above all, the continued hounding of teachers." Their new approach attracted less attention but paid off handsomely, as school boards, textbook publishers, and teachers in both urban and rural areas, North and South, bowed to their pressure. Darwinism virtually disappeared from high school texts, and for years many American teachers feared being identified as evolutionists.[39]

Creationism Underground

During the heady days of the 1920s, when their activities made front-page headlines, creationists dreamed of converting the world; a decade later, forgotten and rejected by the establishment, they turned their energies inward and began creating an institutional base of their own. Deprived of the popular press and frustrated by their inability to publish their views in organs controlled by orthodox scientists, they determined to organize their own societies and edit their own journals.[40] Their early efforts, however, encountered two problems: the absence of a critical mass of scientifically trained creationists and lack of internal agreement.

Hoping to create "a united front against the theory of evolution," Price joined forces in 1935 with Dudley Joseph Whitney, a farm journalist, and L. Allen Higley, a Wheaton College science professor, to form the Religion and Science Association. Among those invited to participate in the association's first—and only—convention were representatives of the three major creationist parties, including Price himself, Rimmer, and one of Dawson's sons, who, like his father, advocated the day-age theory. As soon as the Price faction discovered that its associates had no intention of agreeing on a short earth history, it withdrew from the organization, leaving it a shambles.[41]

Shortly thereafter, in 1938, Price and some Seventh-day Adventist friends in the Los Angeles area, several of whom were physicians associated with the College of Medical Evangelists (now part of Loma Linda University), organized their own Deluge Geology Society. Between 1941 and 1945, they published a *Bulletin of Deluge Geology and Related Science.* As described by Price, the group consisted of "a very eminent set of men.... In no other part of this round globe could anything like the number of scientifically educated believers in Creation and opponents of evolution be assembled, as here in Southern California."[42] Perhaps the society's most notable achievement was its sponsorship in the early 1940s of a secret project to study giant fossil footprints, believed to be human, in rocks far older than the theory of evolution would allow. This find, the society announced excitedly, thus demolished that theory "at a single stroke" and promised to "*astound the scientific world!*" Despite such activity and the group's religious homogeneity, it, too, soon foundered—on "the same rock," as a disappointed member put it, that wrecked the Religion and Science Association, that is "*pre-Genesis time for the earth.*"[43]

By this time creationists were also beginning to face a new problem: the presence within their own ranks of young university-trained scientists who wanted to bring evangelical Christianity into greater agreement with mainstream science. The encounter between the two generations often proved traumatic, as the case of Harold W. Clark illustrates. A former student of Price, Clark had subsequently earned a master's degree in biology from the University of California and taken a position at a small Adventist college in northern California. By 1940 his training and field experience had convinced him that Price's *New Geology* was "entirely out of date and inadequate" as a text, especially in its rejection of the geological column. When Price learned of this, he angrily accused his former disciple of suffering from "the modern mental disease of university-itis" and currying the favor of "tobacco-smoking, Sabbath-breaking, God-defying" evolutionists. Despite Clark's protests that he still believed in a literal six-day creation and universal flood, Price kept up his attack for the better part of a decade, at one point addressing a vitriolic pamphlet, *Theories of Satanic Origin,* to his erstwhile friend and fellow creationist.[44]

The inroads of secular scientific training also became apparent in the American Scientific Affiliation (ASA), created by evangelical scientists in 1941.[45] Although the society took no official stand on creation, strict creationists found the atmosphere congenial during its early years. In the late 1940s, however, some of the more progressive members, led by J. Laurence Kulp, a young geochemist on the faculty of Columbia University, began criticizing Price and his followers for their allegedly unscientific effort to squeeze earth history into less than ten thousand years. Kulp, a Wheaton alumnus and member of the Plymouth Brethren, had acquired a doctorate in physical chemistry from Princeton University and completed all the requirements, except a dissertation, for a Ph.D. in geology. Although initially suspicious of the conclusions of geology regarding the history and antiquity of the earth, he had come to accept them. As one of the first evangelicals professionally trained in geology, he felt a responsibility to warn his colleagues in the ASA about Price's work, which, he believed, had "infiltrated the greater portion of fundamental Christianity in America primarily due to the absence of trained Christian geologists." In what was apparently the first systematic critique of the "new geology," Kulp concluded that the "major propositions of the theory are contraindicated by established physical and chemical laws." Conservatives within the ASA suspected, not unreasonably, that Kulp's exposure to "the orthodox geological viewpoint" had severely undermined his faith in a literal interpretation of the Bible.[46]

Before long it became evident that a growing number of ASA members, like Kulp, were drifting from strict to progressive creationism and, sometimes, to theistic evolutionism. For many, the transition involved immense personal stress, as another Wheaton alumnus, J. Frank Cassel revealed in his autobiographical testimony:

> First to be overcome was the onus of dealing with a "verboten" term and in a "non-existent" area. Then, as each made

> an honest and objective consideration of the data, he was struck with the validity and undeniability of datum after datum. As he strove to incorporate each of these facts into his Biblico-scientific frame of reference, he found that—while the frame became more complete and satisfying—he began to question first the feasibility and then the desirability of an effort to refute the total evolutionary concept, and finally he became impressed by its impossibility on the basis of existing data. This has been a heart-rending, soul-searching experience for the committed Christian as he has seen what he had long considered the *raison d'être* of God's call for his life endeavor fade away and as he has struggled to release strongly held convictions as to the close limitations of Creationism.

Cassel went on to note that the struggle was "made no easier by the lack of approbation (much less acceptance) of some of his less well-informed colleagues, some of whom seem to question motives or even to imply heresy."[47] Strict creationists, who suffered their own agonies, found it difficult not to conclude that their liberal colleagues were simply taking the easy way out. To both parties a split seemed inevitable.

Creationism Abroad

During the decades immediately following the crusade of the 1920s, American antievolutionists were buoyed by reports of a European creationist revival that was strongest in England, where creationism was thought to be all but dead. The Victoria Institute in London, a haven for English creationists in the nineteenth century, had become a stronghold of theistic evolution by the 1920s. When Price visited the institute in 1925 to receive its Langhorne-Orchard Prize for an essay on "Revelation and Evolution," several members protested his attempt to export the fundamentalist controversy to England. Even evangelicals refused to get caught up in the turmoil that engulfed the United States. As historian George Marsden has explained, English evangelicals, always a minority, had developed a tradition of theological toleration stronger than that of revivalist Americans, who had never experienced minority status prior to the twentieth century. Thus while the displaced Americans fought to recover their lost position, English evangelicals adopted a nonmilitant, live-and-let-live philosophy that stressed personal piety.[48]

The sudden appearance of a small but vocal group of British creationists in the early 1930s caught nearly everyone by surprise. The central figure in this movement was Douglas Dewar (1875–1957), a Cambridge graduate and amateur ornithologist, who had served for decades as a lawyer in the Indian Civil Service. Originally an evolutionist, he had gradually become convinced of the necessity of adopting "a provisional hypothesis of special creation ... supplemented by a theory of evolution." This allowed him to accept unlimited development within biological families. His published views, unlike those of most American creationists, betrayed little biblical influence. His greatest intellectual debt was not to Moses but to Louis Vialleton (1859–1929), a French zoologist who had attracted considerable attention in the 1920s for suggesting a theory of discontinuous evolution, which antievolutionists eagerly—but erroneously—equated with special creation.[49]

Soon after announcing his conversion to creationism in 1931, Dewar submitted a short paper on mammalian fossils to the Zoological Society of London, of which he was a member. The secretary of the society subsequently rejected the piece, noting that a competent referee thought Dewar's evidence "led to no valuable conclusion." Such treatment infuriated Dewar and convinced him that evolution had become "a scientific creed." Those who questioned scientific orthodoxy, he complained, "are deemed unfit to hold scientific offices; their articles are rejected by newspapers or journals; their contributions are refused by scientific societies; and publishers decline to publish their books except at the author's expense. Thus the independents are today pretty effectually muzzled." Because of such experiences, Dewar and other British dissidents organized the Evolution Protest Movement, which after two decades claimed a membership of two hundred.[50]

Henry M. Morris and the Revival of Creationism

In 1964 one historian predicted that "a renaissance of the [creationist] movement is most unlikely." And so it seemed. But even as these words were penned, Henry M. Morris (b. 1918), a Texas engineer, was launching just such a revival. Raised a nominal Southern Baptist and, as such, a believer in creation, Morris had drifted unthinkingly into evolutionism and religious indifference during his youth. Following his graduation from college, a thorough study of the Bible convinced Morris of its absolute truth and prompted him to reevaluate his belief in evolution. After an intense period of soul-searching, he concluded that creation had taken place in six literal days, because the Bible clearly said so and "God doesn't lie." Corroborating evidence came from the book of nature. While sitting in his office at Rice Institute, where he was teaching civil engineering, he would study the butterflies and wasps that flew in through the window. Being familiar with structural design, he calculated the improbability of such complex creatures developing by chance. Nature, as well as the Bible, seemed to argue for creation.[51]

Apart from the writings of Rimmer and Price, he found little creationist literature that would assist in answering the claims of evolutionists. Although he rejected Price's peculiar theology, he took an immediate liking to the Adventist's flood geology and incorporated it into *That You Might Believe* (1946) which, to his knowledge was the first book, "published since the Scopes trial in which a scientist from a secular university advocated recent special creation and a worldwide flood." In the late 1940s he joined the American Scientific Affiliation—just in time to protest Kulp's attack on Price's geology. But his words fell largely on deaf ears. In 1953 when he presented some of his own views on the flood to the ASA, one of the few compliments came from a young theologian, John C. Whitcomb, Jr., who belonged to the Grace Brethren. The two subsequently became friends and decided to collaborate on a major defense of the Noachian flood. By the time they finished their project, Morris had earned a

Ph.D. in hydraulic engineering from the University of Minnesota and was chairing the civil engineering department at Virginia Polytechnic Institute; Whitcomb was teaching Old Testament studies at Grace Theological Seminary in Indiana.[52]

In 1961 they brought out *The Genesis Flood,* the most impressive contribution to strict creationism since the publication of Price's *New Geology* in 1923. One reader described the book as "a reissue of G. M. Price's views, brought up to date." Beginning with a statement of their belief in "the verbal inerrancy of Scripture," Whitcomb and Morris went on to argue for a recent creation of the entire universe, a Fall that triggered the second law of thermodynamics and a worldwide flood that in one year laid down most of the geological strata. Given this history, they argued, "the last refuge of the case for evolution immediately vanishes away, and the record of the rocks becomes a tremendous witness . . . to the holiness and justice and power of the living God of Creation!"[53]

Despite the book's lack of conceptual novelty, it provoked an intense debate among evangelicals. Progressive creationists denounced it as a travesty on geology that threatened to set Christian scientific study back a generation, while strict creationists praised it for making belief in biblical catastrophes intellectually respectable. One critic suggested that the book had such appeal because, unlike previous creationist works, it "looked *legitimate* as a scientific contribution," accompanied as it was by footnotes and other scholarly appurtenances. In responding to their detractors, Whitcomb and Morris repeatedly refused to be drawn into a scientific debate, arguing that "the real issue is not the correctness of the interpretation of various details of the geological data, but simply what God has revealed in His Word concerning these matters."[54]

Whatever its merits, *The Genesis Flood* unquestionably "brought about a stunning renaissance of flood geology," symbolized by the establishment in 1963 of the Creation Research Society. Shortly before the publication of his book, Morris had sent the manuscript to Walter E. Lammerts (b.

1904), a Missouri-Synod Lutheran with a doctorate in genetics from the University of California. As an undergraduate at Berkeley, Lammerts had discovered Price's *New Geology* and, while teaching at UCLA during the early 1940s, had worked with Price in the Creation-Deluge Society. After the mid-1940s, however, his interest in creationism had flagged—until it was awakened by reading the Whitcomb and Morris manuscript. Disgusted by the ASA's flirtation with evolution, he organized a correspondence network with Morris and eight other strict creationists, dubbed the "team of ten." In 1963 seven of the ten met with a few other like-minded scientists at the home of a team member in Midland, Michigan, to form the Creation Research Society (CRS).[55]

The society began with a carefully selected, eighteen-man "inner-core steering committee," which included the original team of ten. The composition of this committee reflected, albeit imperfectly, the denominational, regional and professional bases of the creationist revival. There were six Missouri-Synod Lutherans, five Baptists, two Seventh-day Adventists, and one each from the Reformed Presbyterian Church, the Reformed Christian Church, the Church of the Brethren and an independent Bible church. Information about one member is not available. Eleven lived in the Midwest, three in the South, and two in the Far West. The committee included six biologists, but only one geologist, an independent consultant with a master's degree. Seven members taught in church-related colleges, five in state institutions; the others worked for industry or were self-employed.[56]

To ensure that the society remained loyal to the Price-Morris tradition and free of the creeping evolutionism that had infected the ASA, the CRS required members to sign a statement affirming the inerrancy of the Bible, the special creation of "all basic types of living things," and a worldwide deluge. It restricted membership to Christians. (Although creationists liked to stress the scientific evidence for their position, one estimated that "only about five percent of evolutionists-turned-creationists did so on the basis of the overwhelming evidence for creation in the world of nature"; the remaining 95 percent became creationists because they believed in the Bible.) To legitimize its claim to being a scientific society, the CRS published a quarterly journal and limited full membership to persons possessing a graduate degree in a scientific discipline.[57]

At the end of its first decade the society claimed 450 regular members and 1,600 additional sustaining members who failed to meet the scientific qualifications. Eschewing politics, the CRS devoted itself almost exclusively to education and research, funded "at very little expense, and . . . with no expenditure of public money." CRS-related projects included expeditions to search for Noah's ark, studies of fossilized human footprints and pollen grains that occurred out of the predicted evolutionary order, experiments on radiation-induced mutations in plants, and theoretical studies in physics that demonstrated a recent origin of the earth. A number of members collaborated in preparing a biology textbook based on creationist principles. In view of the previous history of creation science, it was an auspicious beginning.[58]

While the CRS catered to the needs of scientists, a second, predominantly lay organization carried creationism to the masses. The interest surrounding *The Genesis Flood* spurred formation of the Bible-Science Association, a group that came to be identified with Walter Lang, an ambitious Missouri-Synod pastor who self-consciously prized spiritual insight above scientific expertise. As editor of the widely circulated *Bible-Science Newsletter,* he vigorously promoted the Price-Morris line—and occasionally provided a platform for individuals on the fringes of the creationist movement, including some who questioned the heliocentric theory and others who believed that Einstein's theory of relativity "was invented in order to circumvent the evidence that the earth is at rest." Needless to say, the pastor's broad-mindedness greatly embarrassed creationists seeking scientific respectability, who feared that such bizarre behavior would tarnish the entire movement.[59]

Scientific Creationism

The creationist revival of the 1960s attracted little public attention until fundamentalists became aroused about the federally-funded Biological Sciences Curriculum Study texts, which featured evolution. The California State Board of Education voted to require public-school textbooks to include creation and evolution. Nell Segraves and Jean Sumrall, two southern California housewives who were associates of both the Bible-Science Association and the CRS, played a pivotal role in the board's decision. In 1961 Segraves learned of the U.S. Supreme Court's ruling in the Madalyn Murray case that protected atheist students from required prayers in public schools. Murray's ability to shield her child from religious exposure suggested to Segraves that creationist parents like herself "were entitled to protect our children from the influence of beliefs that would be offensive to our religious beliefs." It was this line of argument that finally persuaded the Board of Education to grant creationists equal rights.[60]

Flushed with victory, Segraves and her son, Kelly, joined an effort to organize a Creation-Science Research Center (CSRC). Affiliated with Christian Heritage College in San Diego, the group would prepare creationist literature suitable for adoption in public schools. Henry Morris, who resigned his position at Virginia Polytechnic Institute to help establish a center for creation research, was associated with them in this enterprise. Because of differences in personalities and objectives, the Segraveses left the college in 1972, taking the CSRC with them; Morris thereupon set up the Institute for Creation Research (ICR), a new research division of the college. He announced with obvious relief that the ICR would be "controlled and operated by scientists" and would engage in research and education, not political action. During the 1970s Morris added five scientists to his staff and, funded largely by small gifts and royalties from institute publications, turned the ICR into the world's leading center for the propagation of strict creationism.[61] Meanwhile, the CSRC continued campaigning for the legal recognition of special creation, often citing a direct relationship between the acceptance of evolution and the breakdown of law and order. Its own research, the CSRC announced, proved that evolution fostered "the moral decay of spiritual values which contribute to the destruction of mental health and ... [the prevalence of] divorce, abortion and rampant venereal disease."[62]

The 1970s witnessed a major shift in creationist tactics. Instead of trying to outlaw evolution, as they had done in the 1920s, antievolutionists now fought to give creation equal time. And instead of appealing to the authority of the Bible, as Morris and Whitcomb had done as recently as 1961, they consciously downplayed the Genesis story in favor of what they called "scientific creationism." Several factors contributed to this shift. One sociologist has suggested that creationists began stressing the scientific legitimacy of their enterprise because "their theological legitimation of reality was no longer sufficient for maintaining their world and passing on their worldview to their children." But there were also practical considerations. In 1968 the U.S. Supreme Court declared the Arkansas antievolution law unconstitutional, giving creationists reason to suspect that legislation requiring the teaching of biblical creationism would meet a similar fate. They also feared that requiring the biblical account "would open the door to a wide variety of interpretations of Genesis" and produce demands for the inclusion of non-Christian versions of creation.[63]

In view of such potential hazards, Morris recommended that creationists ask public schools to teach "only the scientific aspects of creationism," which in practice meant omitting all reference to the six days of Genesis and Noah's ark, and focusing instead on evidence for a recent worldwide catastrophe and arguments against evolution. Thus the product remained virtually the same; only the packaging changed. The ICR textbook *Scientific Creationism* (1974), for example, came in two editions: one for public schools that contained no references to the Bible, and another for Christian schools that included a chapter on "Creation According to Scripture."[64]

In defending creation as a scientific alternative to evolution, creationists relied less on Francis Bacon and his conception of science and more on two new philosopher-heroes: Karl Popper and Thomas Kuhn. Popper required all scientific theories to be falsifiable; since evolution could not be falsified, reasoned the creationists, it was, by definition, not science. Kuhn described scientific progress in terms of competing models or paradigms rather than the accumulation of objective knowledge. Thus creationists saw no reason why their flood-geology model should not be allowed to compete on an equal scientific basis with the evolution model. In selling this two-model approach to school boards, creationists were advised:

> Sell more SCIENCE.... Who can object to teaching more science? What is controversial about that? ... [D]o not use the word "creationism." Speak only of science. Explain that withholding scientific information contradicting evolution amounts to "censorship" and smacks of getting into the province of religious dogma.... Use the "censorship" label as one who is against censoring science. YOU are for science; anyone else who wants to censor scientific data is an old fogey and too doctrinaire to consider.

This tactic proved extremely effective, at least initially. State legislatures in Arkansas and Louisiana and various school boards adopted the two-model approach, and an informal poll of school-board members in 1980 showed that only 25 percent favored teaching nothing but evolution. In 1982, however, a federal judge struck down the Arkansas law, which had required a "balanced treatment" of creation and evolution.[65] Three years later a similar decision was reached regarding the Louisiana law.

Except for the battle to get scientific creationism into public schools, nothing brought more attention to the creationists than their public debates with prominent evolutionists, which were usually held on college campuses. During the 1970s the ICR staff alone participated in more than a hundred of these contests and, according to their own reckoning, never lost one. Although Morris preferred delivering straight lectures—and likened debates to the bloody confrontations between Christians and lions in ancient Rome—

he recognized their value in carrying the creationist message to "more non-Christians and non-creationists than almost any other method." Fortunately for him, an associate, Duane T. Gish, holder of a doctorate in biochemistry from the University of California, relished such confrontations. If the mild-mannered, professorial Morris was the Darwin of the creationist movement, then the bumptious Gish was its Huxley. He "hits the floor running" just like a bulldog, observed an admiring colleague, and Gish himself added, "I go for the jugular vein." Such enthusiasm helped draw crowds of up to five thousand.[66]

Early in 1981 the ICR announced the fulfillment of a recurring dream among creationists: a program offering graduate degrees in various creation-oriented sciences. Besides hoping to fill an anticipated demand for teachers trained in scientific creationism, the ICR wished to provide an academic setting in which creationist students would be free from discrimination. Over the years a number of creationists had reportedly been kicked out of secular universities because of their heterodox views, prompting leaders to warn graduate students to keep silent, "because if you don't, in almost 99 percent of the cases you will be asked to leave." To avoid anticipated harassment, several graduate students took to using pseudonyms when writing for creationist publications.[67]

Creationists also feared—with good reason—that their students might defect while studying under evolutionists. Since the late 1950s the Seventh-Day Adventist Church had invested hundreds of thousands of dollars to staff its Geoscience Research Institute with well-trained young scientists, only to discover several instances in which exposure to orthodox science had destroyed belief in strict creationism. To reduce the incidence of apostasy, the church established its own graduate programs at Loma Linda University, where George McCready Price had once taught.[68]

To All the World

It is still too early to assess the full impact of the creationist revival sparked by Whitcomb and Morris, but its influence, especially among evangelical Christians, seems to have been immense. Not least, it has elevated the strict creationism of Price and Morris to a position of apparent orthodoxy. It has also endowed creationism with a measure of scientific respectability unknown since the deaths of Guyot and Dawson. Yet it is impossible to determine how much of the creationists' success stemmed from converting evolutionists as opposed to mobilizing the already converted, and how much it owed to widespread disillusionment with established science. A sociological survey of church members in northern California in 1963 revealed that over a fourth of those polled—30 percent of Protestants and 28 percent of Catholics—were already opposed to evolution when the creationist revival began.[69] Broken down by denomination, it showed:

Liberal Protestants (Congregationalists, Methodists, Episcopalians, Disciples)	11%
Moderate Protestants (Presbyterians, American Lutherans, American Baptists)	29%
Church of God	57%
Missouri-Synod Lutheran	64%
Southern Baptists	72%
Church of Christ	78%
Nazarenes	80%
Assemblies of God	91%
Seventh-day Adventists	94%

Thus the creationists had a large reservoir of potential support when they launched their crusade.

But has belief in creationism increased since the early 1960s? The scanty evidence available suggests that it has. A nationwide Gallup poll in 1982, cited earlier, showed that the number of Americans who believed in a recent special creation (44 percent) was nearly as great as the number who accepted theistic (38 percent) or nontheistic (9 percent) evolution. These figures, when compared with the roughly 30 percent of northern California church members who opposed evolution in 1963, suggest, in a grossly imprecise way, a substantial gain in the actual number of American creationists. Bits and pieces of additional evidence lend credence to this conclusion. For example, in 1935 only 36 percent of the students at Brigham Young University, a Mormon school, rejected human evolution; in 1973 the rate had climbed to 81 percent. Also, during the 1970s both the Missouri-Synod Lutheran and Seventh-day Adventist churches, traditional bastions of strict creationism, took strong measures to reverse a trend toward greater tolerance of progressive creationism. In at least these instances, strict creationism did seem to be gaining ground.[70]

Unlike the antievolution crusade of the 1920s, which remained confined mainly to North America, the revival of the 1960s rapidly spread overseas as American creationists and their books circled the globe. Partly as a result of stimulation from America, including the publication of a British edition of *The Genesis Flood* in 1969, the lethargic Evolution Protest Movement in Great Britain was revitalized, and two new creationist organizations, the Newton Scientific Association and the Biblical Creation Society, sprang into existence.[71] On the Continent the Dutch, encouraged by visits from ICR scientists and the translation of books on flood geology, assumed the lead in promoting creationism. Similar developments occurred elsewhere in Europe, as well as in Australia, Asia and South America. By 1980, Morris's books alone had been translated into Chinese, Czech, Dutch, French, German, Japanese, Korean, Portuguese, Russian, and Spanish. Strict creationism had become an international phenomenon.[72]

Notes

1. "Poll Finds Americans Split on Creation Idea," *New York Times*, August 29, 1982, 22. Nine percent of the respondents favored an evolutionary process in which God played no part, 38 per-

cent believed God directed the evolutionary process, and 9 percent had no opinion. Regarding Dawson and Guyot, see Edward J. Pfeifer, "United States," in *The Comparative Reception of Darwinism,* ed. Thomas F. Glick (University of Texas Press, 1974), 203, and Asa Gray, *Darwiniana: Essays and Reviews Pertaining to Darwinism,* ed. A. Hunter Dupree, (Harvard University Press, 1963), 202–203. In *The Darwinian Revolution: Science Red in Tooth and Claw* (University of Chicago Press, 1979), Michael Ruse argues that most British biologists were evolutionists by the mid-1860s, while David L. Hull, Peter D. Tessner and Arthur M. Diamond point out in "Planck's Principle," *Science,* 202 (1978): 721, that more than a quarter of British scientists continued to reject the evolution of species as late as 1869. On the acceptance of evolution among religious leaders, see, e.g., Frank Hugh Foster, *The Modern Movement in American Theology: Sketches in the History of American Protestant Thought from the Civil War to the World War* (Fleming H. Revell Co., 1939), 38–58; and Owen Chadwick, *The Victorian Church,* Part 2, 2nd ed. (Adam & Charles Black, 1972), 23–24.

2. William G. McLoughlin, Jr., *Modern Revivalism: Charles Grandison Finney to Billy Graham* (Ronald Press, 1959), 213. In *Protestant Christianity Interpreted Through Its Development* (Charles Scribner's Sons, 1954), 227, John Dillenberger and Claude Welch discuss the conservatism of the common people. On the attitudes of premillennialists, see Robert D. Whalen, "Millenarianism and Millennialism in America, 1790–1880" (Ph.D. dissertation, State University of New York at Stony Brook, 1972), 219–229; and Ronald L. Numbers, "Science Falsely So-Called: Evolution and Adventists in the Nineteenth Century," *Journal of the American Scientific Affiliation,* 27 (March 1975): 18–23.

3. Ronald L. Numbers, *Creation by Natural Law: Laplace's Nebular Hypothesis in American Thought* (University of Washington Press, 1977), 89–90; Bernard Ramm, *The Christian View of Science and Scripture* (William B. Eerdmans Publishing Co., 1954), 195–198. On the influence of the *Scofield Reference Bible,* see Ernest R. Sandeen, *The Roots of Fundamentalism: British and American Millenarianism, 1800–1930* (University of Chicago Press, 1971), 222.

4. Charles E. O'Brien, *Sir William Dawson: A Life in Science and Religion* (American Philosophical Society, 1971). On Guyot

and his influence, see Numbers, *Creation by Natural Law,* 91–100. On the popularity of the Guyot-Dawson view, also associated with the geologist James Dwight Dana, see William North Rice, *Christian Faith in an Age of Science,* 2nd ed. (A. C. Armstrong & Son, 1904) 101; and Dudley Joseph Whitney, "What Theory of Earth History Shall We Adopt?" *Bible Champion,* 34 (1928): 16.

5. H. L. Hastings, preface to the 1889 edition of *The Errors of Evolution: An Examination of the Nebular Theory, Geological Evolution, the Origin of Life and Darwinism,* by Robert Patterson, 3rd ed. (Scriptural Tract Repository, 1893), iv. On the Darwinian debate, see James R. Moore, *The Post-Darwinian Controversies: A Study of the Protestant Struggle to Come to Terms with Darwin in Great Britain and America, 1870–1900* (Cambridge University Press, 1979).
6. G. L. Young, "Relation of Evolution and Darwinism to the Question of Origins," *Bible Student and Teacher,* 11 (July 1909): 41. On anti-Darwinian books, see "Evolution in the Pulpit," in *The Fundamentals,* 12 vols. (Testimony Publishing Company, 1910–1915), 8:28–30. See also Peter J. Bowler, *The Eclipse of Darwinism: Anti-Darwinian Evolution Theories in the Decades around 1900* (Johns Hopkins University Press, 1983).
7. Philip Mauro, "Modern Philosophy," in *The Fundamentals,* 2:85–105; and J. J. Reeve, "My Personal Experience with the Higher Criticism," ibid., 3: 98–118.
8. G. Frederick Wright, *Story of My Life and Work* (Bibliotheca Sacra Co., 1916); idem, "The First Chapter of Genesis and Modern Science," *Homiletic Review,* 35 (1898): 392–399; idem, introduction to *The Other Side of Evolution,* by Alexander Patterson (Winona Publishing Co., 1902), xvii-xix.
9. George Frederick Wright, "The Passing of Evolution," in *The Fundamentals,* 7:5–20. The Scottish theologian James Orr contributed an equally tolerant essay, "Science and Christian Faith," ibid., 4:91–104.
10. Lawrence W. Levine, *Defender of the Faith—William Jennings Bryan: The Last Decade, 1915–1925* (Oxford University Press, 1965), 277.
11. Ibid., 272. The quotation about America going mad appears in Roland T. Nelson, "Fundamentalism and the Northern

Baptist Convention" (Ph.D. dissertation, University of Chicago, 1964), 319. On antievolution legislation, see Maynard Shipley, *The War on Modern Science: A Short History of the Fundamentalist Attacks on Evolution and Modernism* (Alfred A. Knopf, 1927); and idem, "Growth of the Antievolution Movement," *Current History,* 32 (1930): 330–332. On Bryan's catalytic role, see Ferenc Morton Szasz, *The Divided Mind of Protestant America, 1889–1930* (University of Alabama Press, 1982), 107–116.

12. Levine, *Defender of the Faith,* 261–265.
13. Ibid., 266–267. Mrs. Bryan's statement appears in Wayne C. Williams, *William Jennings Bryan* (G. P. Putnam, 1936), 448.
14. William Jennings Bryan, *In His Image* (Fleming H. Revell Co., 1922), 94, 97–98. "The Menace of Darwinism" appears in this work as Chapter 4, "The Origin of Man." Bryan apparently borrowed his account of the evolution of the eye from Patterson, *The Other Side of Evolution,* 32–33.
15. Paolo E. Coletta, *William Jennings Bryan,* vol. 3, *Political Puritan, 1915–1925* (University of Nebraska Press, 1969), 230.
16. "Progress of Antievolution," *Christian Fundamentalist,* 2 (1929): 13. Bryan's reference to a "scientific soviet" appears in Levine, *Defender of the Faith,* 289. Bryan gives the estimate of nine-tenths in a letter to W. A. McRae, April 5, 1924, box 29, Bryan papers, Library of Congress.
17. "Fighting Evolution at the Fundamentals Convention," *Christian Fundamentals in School and Church,* 7 (July-September, 1925): 5. The best state histories of the antievolution crusade are Kenneth K. Bailey, "The Enactment of Tennessee's Antievolution Law," *Journal of Southern History,* 16 (1950): 472–510; Willard B. Gatewood, Jr., *Preachers, Pedagogues and Politicians: The Evolution Controversy in North Carolina, 1920–1927* (University of North Carolina Press, 1966); and Virginia Gray, "Antievolution Sentiment and Behavior: The Case of Arkansas," *Journal of American History,* 57 (1970): 352–366. Ferenc Morton Szasz stresses the urban dimension of the crusade in "Three Fundamentalist Leaders: The Roles of William Bell Riley, John Roach Straton and William Jennings Bryan in the Fundamentalist-Modernist Controversy" (Ph.D. dissertation, University of Rochester, 1969), 351.

18. George Herbert Betts, *The Beliefs of 700 Ministers and Their Meaning for Religious Education* (Abingdon Press, 1929), 26, 44; Milton L. Rudnick, *Fundamentalism and the Missouri Synod: A Historical Study of Their Interaction and Mutual Influence* (Concordia Publishing House, 1966), 88–90; Sandeen, *Roots of Fundamentalism,* 266–268, which discusses the premillennialists. Lutheran reluctance to join the crusade is also evident in Szasz, "Three Fundamentalist Leaders," 279. For examples of prominent fundamentalists who stayed aloof from the antievolution controversy, see Ned B. Stonehouse, *J. Gresham Machen: A Biographical Memoir* (William B. Eerdmans Publishing Co., 1954), 401–402, and William Bryant Lewis, "The Role of Harold Paul Sloan and His Methodist League for Faith and Life in the Fundamentalist-Modernist Controversy of the Methodist Episcopal Church" (Ph.D. dissertation, Vanderbilt University, 1963), 86–88.
19. Edward Lassiter Clark, "The Southern Baptist Reaction to the Darwinian Theory of Evolution" (Ph.D. dissertation, Southwestern Baptist Theological Seminary, 1952), 154; James J. Thompson, Jr., "Southern Baptists and the Antievolution Controversy of the 1920s," *Mississippi Quarterly,* 29 (1975–1976): 65–81; Lefferts A. Loetscher, *The Broadening Church: A Study of Theological Issues in the Presbyterian Church Since 1869* (University of Pennsylvania Press, 1954), 111; John L. Morrison, "American Catholics and the Crusade Against Evolution," *Records of the American Catholic Historical Society of Philadelphia,* 64 (1953): 59–71. Norman F. Furniss, *The Fundamentalist Controversy 1918–1931* (Yale University Press, 1954), includes chapter-by-chapter surveys of seven denominations.
20. T. T. Martin, *Hell and the High School: Christ or Evolution, Which?* (Western Baptist Publishing Co., 1923), 164–165. On Riley, see Marie Acomb Riley, *The Dynamic of a Dream: The Life Story of Dr. William B. Riley* (William B. Eerdmans Publishing Co., 1938), 101–102; Szasz, *The Divided Mind of Protestant America,* 89–91. George M. Marsden, *Fundamentalism and American Culture: The Shaping of Twentieth-Century Evangelicalism, 1870–1925* (Oxford University Press, 1980), 169–170, stresses the interdenominational character of the antievolution crusade. On the expansion of public education, see Kenneth K. Bailey, *Southern White Protestantism in the Twentieth Century* (Harper & Row, 1964), 72–73.

21. Both quotations come from Howard K. Beale, *Are American Teachers Free? An Analysis of Restraints Upon the Freedom of Teaching in American Schools* (Charles Scribner's Sons, 1936), 249–251.
22. [William B. Riley], "The Evolution Controversy," *Christian Fundamentals in School and Church,* 4 (April-June 1922): 5; Bryan, *In His Image,* 94.
23. L. S. K[eyserl, "No War against Science—Never!" *Bible Champion,* 31 (1925): 413. On the fundamentalist affinity for Baconianism, see Marsden, *Fundamentalism and American Culture,* 214–215.
24. William Bateson, "Evolutionary Faith and Modern Doubts," *Science,* 55 (1922): 55–61. The creationists' use of Bateson provoked the evolutionist Henry Fairfield Osborn into repudiating the British scientist; see Osborn, *Evolution and Religion in Education: Polemics of the Fundamentalist Controversy of 1922 to 1926* (Charles Scribner's Sons, 1926), 29. On pro-evolution resolutions, see Shipley, *War on Modern Science,* 384.
25. Heber D. Curtis to W. J. Bryan, May 22, 1923, box 37, Bryan Papers, Library of Congress. Two physicians, Arthur I. Brown of Vancouver and Howard A. Kelly of Johns Hopkins, achieved prominence in the fundamentalist movement, but Kelly leaned toward theistic evolution.
26. William D. Edmondson, "Fundamentalist Sects of Los Angeles, 1900–1930" (Ph.D. dissertation, Claremont Graduate School, 1969), 276–336; Steward G. Cole, *The History of Fundamentalism* (Richard R. Smith, 1931), 264–265; F. J. B[oyer], "Harry Rimmer, D.D.," *Christian Faith and Life* (1939), 6–7; "Two Great Field Secretaries—Harry Rimmer and Dr. Arthur I. Brown," *Christian Fundamentals in School and Church,* 8 (July-September 1926): 17. Harry Rimmer refers to his medical vocabulary in *The Harmony of Science and Scripture,* 11th ed. (William B. Eerdmans Publishing Co., 1945), 14.
27. Edmondson, "Fundamentalist Sects of Los Angeles," 329–330, 333–334. Regarding the $100 reward, see "World Religious Digest," *Christian Faith and Life,* 45 (1939): 215.
28. This and the following paragraphs on Price closely follow my account in "'Sciences of Satanic Origin': Adventist Attitudes toward Evolutionary Biology and Geology," *Spectrum,* 9 (January 1979): 22–24.

29. George McCready Price, *Illogical Geology: The Weakest Point in the Evolution Theory* (Modern Heretic Co., 1906), 9. Four years earlier Price had published his first antievolution book, *Outlines of Modern Science and Modern Christianity* (Pacific Press, 1902).
30. David Starr Jordan to G. M. Price, May 5, 1911, Price Papers, Andrews University Library.
31. George McCready Price, *The New Geology* (Pacific Press, 1923), 637–638. Price first announced the discovery of his law in *The Fundamentals of Geology and Their Bearings on the Doctrine of a Literal Creation* (Pacific Press, 1913), 119.
32. Charles Schuchert, review of *The New Geology* by George McCready Price, *Science,* 59 (1924): 486–487; Harry Rimmer, *Modern Science, Noah's Ark and the Deluge* (Research Science Bureau, 1925), 28.
33. *Science,* 63 (1926): 259.
34. Howard A. Kelly to W. J. Bryan, June 15, 1925; Louis T. More to W. J. Bryan, July 7, 1925; and Alfred W. McCann to W. J. Bryan, June 30, 1925, box 47, Bryan Papers, Library of Congress. Regarding Price, see Numbers, "'Sciences of Satanic Origin,'" 24.
35. Numbers, "'Sciences of Satanic Origin,'" 24; Levine, *Defender of the Faith,* 349.
36. W. J. Bryan to Howard A. Kelly, June 22, 1925, box 47, Bryan Papers, Library of Congress. In a letter to the editor of the *Forum,* 70 (1923): 1852–1853, Bryan asserted that he had never taught that the world was made in six literal days. I am indebted to Paul M. Waggoner for bringing this document to my attention.
37. W. B. Riley and Harry Rimmer, *A Debate: Resolved, That the Creative Days in Genesis Were Aeons, Not Solar Days,* (undated pamphlet); [W. B. Riley], "The Creative Week," *Christian Fundamentalist,* 4 (1930): 45; Price, *Outlines,* 125–127; idem, *The Story of the Fossils* (Mountain View: Pacific Press, 1954), 39. On Rimmer's acceptance of a local flood, see Robert D. Culver, "An Evaluation of *The Christian View of Science and Scripture* by Bernard Ramm from the Standpoint of Christian Theology," *Journal of the American Scientific Affiliation,* 7 (December 1955): 7.

38. Shipley, "Growth of the Anti-Evolution Movement," 330–332; Szasz, *The Divided Mind of Protestant America,* 117–125.

39. Beale, *Are American Teachers Free?* 228–237; Willard B. Gatewood, Jr., ed., *Controversy in the Twenties: Fundamentalism, Modernism and Evolution* (Vanderbilt University Press, 1969), 39. The quotation comes from Shipley, "Growth of the Antievolution Movement," 330. See also Judith V. Grabiner and Peter D. Miller, "Effects of the Scopes Trial," *Science,* 185 (1974): 832–837; and Estelle R. Laba and Eugene W. Gross, "Evolution Slighted in High-School Biology," *Clearing House,* 24 (1950): 396–399.

40. Joel A. Carpenter, "Fundamentalist Institutions and the Rise of Evangelical Protestantism, 1929–1942," *Church History,* 49 (1980): 62–75, provides an excellent analysis of this trend. For a typical statement of creationist frustration, see George McCready Price, "Guarding the Sacred Cow," *Christian Faith and Life,* 41 (1935): 124–127. The title for this section comes from Henry M. Morris, *The Troubled Waters of Evolution* (Creation-Life Publishers, 1974), 13.

41. "Announcement of the Religion and Science Association," Price Papers, Andrews University; "The Religion and Science Association," *Christian Faith and Life,* 42 (1936): 159–160; "Meeting of the Religion and Science Association," ibid., 209; Harold W. Clark, *The Battle over Genesis* (Review & Herald Publishing Association, 1977), 168. On the attitude of the Price faction, see Harold W. Clark to G. M. Price, September 12, 1937, Price Papers, Andrews University.

42. Numbers, "'Sciences of Satanic Origin,'" 26.

43. Ben F. Allen to the Board of Directors of the Creation-Deluge Society, August 12, 1945 (courtesy of Molleurus Couperus). Regarding the fossil footprints, see the *Newsletters* of the Creation-Deluge Society for August 19, 1944 and February 17, 1945.

44. Numbers, "'Sciences of Satanic Origin,'" 25.

45. On the early years of the ASA, see Alton Everest, "The American Scientific Affiliation—The First Decade," *Journal of the American Scientific Affiliation,* 3 (September, 1951): 33–38.

46. J. Laurence Kulp, "Deluge Geology," ibid., 2, no. 1 (1950): 1–15; "Comment on the 'Deluge Geology' Paper of J. L. Kulp,"

ibid., 2 (June 1950): 2. Kulp mentions his initial skepticism of geology in a discussion of "Some Presuppositions in Evolutionary Thinking," ibid., 1 (June 1949): 20.

47. J. Frank Cassel, "The Evolution of Evangelical Thinking on Evolution," ibid., 11 (December, 1959): 26–27. For a fuller discussion, see Ronald L. Numbers, "The Dilemma of Evangelical Scientists," in *Evangelicalism and Modern America,* ed. George M. Marsden (William B. Eerdmans Publishing Co., 1984), 150–160.

48. Numbers, "'Sciences of Satanic Origin,'" 25; George Marsden, "Fundamentalism as an American Phenomenon: A Comparison with English Evangelicalism,'" *Church History,* 46 (1977): 215–232; idem, *Fundamentalism and American Culture,* 222–226.

49. Douglas Dewar, *The Difficulties of the Evolution Theory* (Edward Arnold & Co., 1931), 158; Arnold Lunn, ed., *Is Evolution Proved? A Debate between Douglas Dewar and H. S. Shelton* (Hollis & Carter, 1947), 1, 154; *Evolution Protest Movement Pamphlet No. 125* (April 1965). On Vialleton, see Harry W. Paul, *The Edge of Contingency: French Catholic Reaction to Scientific Change from Darwin to Duhem* (University Presses of Florida, 1979), 99–100.

50. Douglas Dewar, "The Limitations of Organic Evolution," *Victoria Institute,* 64 (1932): 142; "EPM—40 Years On; Evolution—114 Years Off," supplement to *Creation,* 1 (May 1972): no pagination.

51. R. Halliburton, Jr., "The Adoption of Arkansas' Antievolution Law," *Arkansas Historical Quarterly,* 23 (1964): 283; interviews with Henry M. Morris, October 26, 1980 and January 6, 1981. See also the autobiographical material in Henry M. Morris, *History of Modern Creationism* (Master Book Publishers, 1984).

52. Interviews with Morris; Henry M. Morris, introduction to the revised edition, *That You Might Believe* (Creation-Life Publishers, 1978), 10.

53. John C. Whitcomb, Jr., and Henry M. Morris, *The Genesis Flood: The Biblical Record and Its Scientific Implications* (Presbyterian & Reformed Publishing Co., 1961), xx, 451.

54. Henry M. Morris and John C. Whitcomb, Jr., "Reply to Reviews in the March 1964 Issue," *Journal of the American Scientific Affiliation,* 16 (June 1964): 60. The statement regarding the

appearance of the book comes from Walter Hearn, quoted in Vernon Lee Bates, "Christian Fundamentalism and the Theory of Evolution in Public School Education: A Study of the Creation Science Movement" (Ph.D. dissertation, University of California, Davis, 1976), 52. See also Frank H. Roberts, review of *The Genesis Flood,* by Henry M. Morris and John C. Whitcomb, Jr., *Journal of the American Scientific Affiliation,* 16 (March 1964): 28–29; J. R. Van de Fliert, "Fundamentalism and the Fundamentals of Geology," ibid., 21 (September, 1969): 69–81; and Walter E. Lammerts, "Introduction," Creation Research Society, *Annual,* 1964, no pagination. Among Missouri-Synod Lutherans, John W. Klotz, *Genes, Genesis and Evolution* (Concordia Publishing House, 1955), may have had an even greater influence than Morris and Whitcomb.

55. Walter E. Lammerts, "The Creationist Movement in the United States: A Personal Account," *Journal of Christian Reconstruction,* 1 (Summer 1974): 49–63. The first quotation comes from Davis A. Young, *Creation and the Flood: An Alternative to Flood Geology and Theistic Evolution* (Baker Book House, 1977), 7.

56. Names, academic fields, and institutional affiliations are given in *Creation Research Society Quarterly,* 1 (July 1964): 31; for additional information I am indebted to Duane T. Gish, John N. Moore, Henry M. Morris, Harold Slusher, and William J. Tinkle.

57. *Creation Research Society Quarterly,* 1 (July 1964): [13]; [Walter Lang], "Editorial Comments," *Bible-Science Newsletter,* 16 (June 1978): 2. Other creationists have disputed the five percent estimate.

58. Lammerts, "The Creationist Movement in the United States," 63; Duane T. Gish, "A Decade of Creationist Research," *Creation Research Society Quarterly,* 12 (June 1975): 34–46; John N. Moore and Harold Schultz Slusher, eds., *Biology: A Search for Order in Complexity* (Zondervan Publishing House, 1970).

59. Walter Lang, "Fifteen Years of Creationism," *Bible Science Newsletter,* 16 (October 1978): 1–3; "Editorial Comments," ibid., 15 (March 1977): 2–3; "A Naturalistic Cosmology vs. a Biblical Cosmology," ibid., 15 (January-February 1977): 4–5; Gerald Wheeler, "The Third National Creation Science Conference," *Origins,* 3 (1976): 101–102.

60. Bates, "Christian Fundamentalism," 58; "15 Years of Creationism," *Five Minutes with the Bible and Science,* supplement to *Bible-Science Newsletter,* 17 (May 1979): 2; Nicholas Wade, "Creationists and Evolutionists: Confrontation in California," *Science,* 178 (1972): 724–729. Regarding the BSCS texts, see Gerald Skoog, "Topic of Evolution in Secondary School Biology Textbooks: 1900–1977," *Science Education,* 63 (1979): 621–640; and "A Critique of BSCS Biology Texts," *Bible-Science Newsletter,* 4 (March 15, 1976): 1. See also John A. Moore, "Creationism in California," *Daedalus,* 103 (1974): 173–189; and Dorothy Nelkin, *The Creation Controversy: Science or Scripture in the Schools* (W. W. Norton, 1982).

61. Henry M. Morris, "Director's Column," *Acts & Facts,* 1 (June-July 1972): no pagination; Morris interview, January 6, 1981.

62. Nell J. Segraves, *The Creation Report* (Creation-Science Research Center, 1977), 17; "15 Years of Creationism," 2–3.

63. Bates, "Christian Fundamentalism," 98; Henry M. Morris, "Director's Column," *Acts & Facts,* 3 (September 1974): 2. See also Edward J. Larson, "Public Science vs. Popular Opinion: The Creation-Evolution Legal Controversy" (Ph.D. dissertation, University of Wisconsin, Madison, 1984).

64. Morris, "Director's Column," 2; Henry M. Morris, ed., *Scientific Creationism,* General Edition (Creation-Life Publishers, 1974).

65. The quotation comes from Russel H. Leitch, "Mistakes Creationists Make," *Bible-Science Newsletter,* 18 (March 1980): 2. Regarding school boards, see "Finding: Let Kids Decide How We Got Here," *American School Board Journal,* 167 (March 1980): 52; and Segraves, *Creation Report,* 24. On Popper's influence, see, e.g., Ariel A. Roth, "Does Evolution Qualify as a Scientific Principle?" *Origins,* 4 (1977): 4–10. In a letter to the editor of *New Scientist,* 87 (August 21, 1980): 611, Popper affirmed that the evolution of life on earth was testable and, therefore, scientific. On Kuhn's influence, see, e.g., Ariel A. Roth, "The Pervasiveness of the Paradigm," *Origins,* 2 (1975): 55–57; Leonard R. Brand, "A Philosophic Rationale for a Creation-Flood Model," ibid., 1 (1974): 73–83; and Gerald W. Wheeler, *The Two-Taled Dinosaur: Why Science and Religion Conflict over the Origin of Life* (Southern Publishing Association, 1975), 192–210. For the judge's decision, see "Creationism in

Schools: The Decision in McLean versus the Arkansas Board of Education," *Science,* 215 (1982): 934–943.

66. Henry M. Morris, "Two Decades of Creation: Past and Future," *Impact,* supplement to *Acts & Facts,* 10 (January 1981): iii; idem, "Director's Column," ibid., 3 (March 1974): 2. The reference to Gish comes from an interview with Harold Slusher and Duane T. Gish, January 6, 1981.
67. "ICR Schedules M.S. Programs," *Acts & Facts,* 10 (February 1981): 1–2. Evidence for alleged discrimination and the use of pseudonyms comes from: "Grand Canyon Presents Problems for Long Ages," *Five Minutes with the Bible and Science,* supplement to *Bible-Science Newsletter,* 18 (June 1980): 1–2; interview with Ervil D. Clark, January 9, 1981; interview with Steven A. Austin, January 6, 1981; and interview with Duane T. Gish, October 26, 1980, the source of the quotation.
68. Numbers, "'Sciences of Satanic Origin,'" 27–28; Molleurus Couperus, "Tensions between Religion and Science," *Spectrum,* 10 (March 1980): 74–88.
69. William Sims Bainbridge and Rodney Stark, "Superstitions: Old and New," *Skeptical Inquirer,* 4 (Summer, 1980): 20.
70. "Poll Finds Americans Split on Evolution Idea," 22; Harold T. Christensen and Kenneth L. Cannon, "The Fundamentalist Emphasis at Brigham Young University: 1935–1973," *Journal for the Scientific Study of Religion,* 17 (1978): 53–57; "Return to Conservatism," *Bible-Science Newsletter,* 11 (August 1973): 1; Numbers, "'Sciences of Satanic Origin,'" 27–28.
71. Eileen Barker, "In the Beginning: The Battle of Creationist Science Against Evolutionism," in *On the Margins of Science: The Social Construction of Rejected Knowledge,* ed. Roy Wallis, Sociological Review Monograph 27 (University of Keele, 1979), 179–200, who greatly underestimates the size of the E.P.M. in 1966; [Robert E. D. Clark], "Evolution: Polarization of Views," *Faith and Thought,* 100 (1972–1973): 227–229; [idem], "American and English Creationists," ibid., 104 (1977): 6–8; "British Scientists Form Creationist Organization," *Acts & Facts,* 2 (November-December 1973): 3; "EPM—40 Years On; Evolution—114 Years Off," supplement to *Creation,* 1 (May 1972): no pagination.

72. W. J. Ouweneel, "Creationism in the Netherlands," *Impact,* supplement to *Acts & Facts,* 7 (February 1978): i–iv. Notices regarding the spread of creationism overseas appeared frequently in *Bible-Science Newsletter* and *Acts & Facts.* On translations, see "ICR Books Available in Many Languages," *Acts & Facts,* 9 (February 1980: 2, 7.

Seven Patterns for Relating Science and Theology

Richard H. Bube

Richard H. Bube is Emeritus Professor of Materials Science and Electrical Engineering at Stanford University, where he served as a department chairman for over a decade and as a member of the faculty since 1962. During his career, he has been president of the American Scientific Affiliation and editor of *Solid State Electronics, Annual Reviews of Materials Science* and *Christians in Science.* He is the author of nearly 300 articles and reviews as well as nine books, including *A Textbook of Christian Doctrine: To Every Man an Answer* (1955), *The Human Quest: A New Look at Science and Christian Faith* (1971) and *Science and the Whole Person: A Personal Integration of Scientific and Biblical Perspectives* (1985). In addition, he has just completed a new volume, *Putting It All Together: Seven Patterns for Relating Science and Christian Faith.*

Introduction

Trying to reconcile the demands of modern scientific thinking with the inputs of religious faith is often a formidable task. One of the main reasons is that there is a wide variety of opinion about what "science" and "faith" really mean. I would like to suggest that the meaningful terms to define for our purpose here are "science" and "Christian theology." "Science" is a human endeavor to describe and understand the physical universe; "theology" is a human endeavor to describe and understand the broader relationships involved in human life before God.

This paper was written at the invitation of Prof. Koan-sik Chon, Editor of the *Journal of Integrated Studies* in Korea.

We want to see how people who have made a personal commitment to Jesus Christ can live a consistent life in the midst of a secular, scientifically oriented world. We start our discussion, therefore, with suggested definitions of authentic science and authentic Christian theology, to which we can refer as we look deeper into each of the seven proposed patterns for relating them. [1-4]

Authentic Science

By the term "authentic science" we mean *a particular way of knowing based on human interpretation in natural categories of publicly observable and reproducible data obtained by sense interaction with the world.* This definition in no way rules out creative thinking or uninhibited speculation; it does demand that such efforts at interpretation be testable in the ways specified. To say that something is not included within this definition of science is *not* to say that it is not true, important, or meaningful. It is only to claim that such a concept or event is outside the domain of authentic science, which by itself describes only a part of reality, and that it cannot therefore claim whatever validating support science might give. It is adherence to this definition of science that gives science integrity and value; once we begin to depart appreciably from such a definition, we have an enterprise that no longer shares in the reliability and trust appropriate to authentic science. Each of the terms in the definition is significant.

(1) To say that science is *a* way of knowing is to deny that science is *the* way of knowing. The belief that science is *the* way of knowing is often called "scientism"; it affirms that science is the only source of truth and that the scientific method is truth's only guide. We offer two other non-sophisticated definitions of important terms necessary for our discussion: (a) Reality corresponds to "what is"; and (b) truth is that which corresponds to reality. Clearly the distinction between science and scientism is an essential one. Science can tell us how things work in the universe, but it does not provide us with knowledge of why the universe is ultimately the

way it is, nor can it inform us about the purpose or meaning of its existence.

(2) Our definition affirms that science is a way of *knowing*. By the pursuit of authentic science we do indeed come to understand better the physical universe in which we live. Authentic science is not simply an esoteric game but a way to understand the world better. We construct scientific models that tell us, in part, what the world is like. They do not tell us what the world is, but they are able to give us valid insights into some aspects of reality.

(3) Science is an activity carried out by *human beings*. It is not a perfect enterprise free from the foibles of humanity.

(4) Science is based on human *interpretation* of the evidences and observations made in the scientific pursuit of understanding. This is the theoretical aspect of science in which scientists try to find out how their data and observations can be described as simply as possible in a single framework. A complete treatment of this claim must recognize the interaction between the hypothesis guiding the experiments and the interpretation of the results. No "fact" ever provides us with its own interpretation. In some way, every experimental "fact" is "theory-laden," and the scientist must strive to take into account the complexities of the interpretational task. He usually does this by constructing, in as neutral a mode as possible, progressively more demanding experiments to test the hypotheses and theories being used.

(5) Science, by definition, is concerned with *natural* categories, categories that can be described within the mechanistic perspective of science. It is precisely this limitation that also marks the strength of scientific descriptions and understandings. Science does not limit itself to natural categories because of some prejudice against supernatural descriptions, but because it must limit the scope and the content of authentic science to a well-defined and testable range. We acquire a great freedom once we appreciate two closely related truths: (a) Science does not and cannot provide answers to questions of ultimate meaning, purpose and primary causes; and (b) there are insights into reality that cannot be obtained

by scientific investigation. (But this in no way represents a negative assessment of the validity or the value of such insights.)

(6) Evidence acceptable as scientific must be accessible to public testing. Private visions, insights and revelations do not provide the basis for a scientific description.

(7) Science proceeds by interpretation of *sense data* obtained from *interaction* with the world. Science is limited to certain kinds of questions and areas of human experience that can be tested. This comprises an important set of categories for human life and experience, but by no means does it comprise all that human beings would like to know or need to know.

If we adopt this definition for authentic science, we can recognize a few basic characteristics of such an endeavor. It is impossible to do science without a faith commitment to a number of fundamental *presuppositions*—that the world is understandable through rational processes of the human mind; that natural phenomena are reproducible; that patterns of order can be sought and found, and that there is a physical reality that does not depend ultimately on us. The scientist succeeds as a scientist to the extent that he maintains an *impersonal* relationship with the *objects* of his investigation; this limits the ability of science to deal fully with the interpersonal dimensions of human life. It causes necessary distinctions to be made, for example, between research psychology and clinical psychology. The former follows a scientific (scientist/object) pattern, whereas the latter incorporates a large measure of interpersonal interactions (scientist-as-person/person).

Even when scientists act from the best of motives and are successful in achieving their goals, the *ambivalence* of all human activity asserts itself; every time we increase our capability for good by increasing our knowledge, we simultaneously increase our capability for evil. Science is *ethically silent:* It has no way of defining the good. Its function is to tell us "what is," not "what ought to be." The great ethical fallacy is to identify the two.

There are activities that look like science, use the terminology of science and claim the authority of science, but that violate the basic integrity of authentic scientific activity at a fundamental level. They are counterfeit science, commonly called *pseudoscience.* Pseudoscience springs from three identifiable sources: (a) bad science, in which the basic guidelines of authentic science are neglected or ignored; (b) claims of scientific achievement that exceed the capabilities of science—for example, the derivation of ethics from science; (c) attempts to arrive at scientific conclusions under pressure from a philosophical, metaphysical, religious, or political ideology that defines from the beginning what the results must be.

Authentic Theology

We limit our discussion in this paper to authentic theology in the Christian tradition and seek a definition of such theology to compare with the foregoing definition of authentic science. By the term "authentic theology," we mean a way *of knowing based on the human interpretation of the Bible and human experience in relationship with God.* Once again we may consider the implications of these various terms.

(1) To say that Christian theology is a way of knowing is to affirm that it is not the only way of knowing.

(2) Christian theology is also a way of *knowing.* It *is* commonly said that to believe that theology is a way of knowing is nothing more than a matter of faith. This assertion is acceptable if we recognize that it is a matter of faith to believe that any activity provides us with authentic knowledge (i.e., valid insight into the nature of reality); the proposition is as true of science as it is of theology. Both rest upon presuppositions, both provide evidence and both require a faith commitment before genuine involvement is possible.

The main difference between science and theology is the kind of knowledge that each gives. Science primarily answers questions about "how" something happens; theology primarily answers questions about "why" something happens, what the purpose and meaning of the events are, and what are its ultimate causes. Science establishes as wide a gap as possible between the observer and the observed, whereas theology deals with the realm of human experience, in which we enter into relationships with other persons, making ourselves vulnerable in the process.

(3) Christian theology is based on *human* interpretation. As long as human beings seek to understand a verbal revelation (oral or written), there is no other possibility. Christians believe that God made the world and inspired the Bible, but it is human beings who react with His revelation in the world to do science and with His revelation in the Bible and their experience to do theology.

(4) Christian theology is based on human *interpretation*. Just as "facts" in science never provide their own interpretations, so Bible passages and experiences do not provide their own unambiguous interpretations. The claim to believe only what "the Bible says" is, in fact, an impossibility; we are unable to believe anything except an interpretation (our own, or someone else's) of what the Bible says. This does not denigrate the inspiration, authority or trustworthiness of the Bible; it simply affirms the necessity of human communication. It does not imply that the meaning of the Bible and our experience is up-for-grabs, a relativistic area in which anyone can make an equally valid judgment. In both science and theology we take as a matter of faith that there is an appropriate set of interpretational principles (hermeneutics) that must be followed to obtain valid insights from our study of the natural world in science (authentic science) or of the Bible and our experience in theology (authentic theology). If our scientific understanding and our theological understanding appear to conflict, it is not "science vs. the Bible," as if science required interpretation but the Bible does not, but rather science (as a human interpretation following appropriate rules) vs. theology (another human interpretation following appropriate rules). There are, of course, spiritual resources available to help us in any interpretation—resources that are given to us as individuals and as a community.

(5) Christian theology is based on human interpretation of *the Bible*. Christians accept the Bible as a trustworthy

source of God's revelation to us. Thus the Bible is more like the love letter of a friend than a manual on how to make a machine. From our interpretation of the Bible, we want to come to know what God wishes to say to us. Traditional advice on biblical interpretation involves three questions: (a) What does the passage say? (b) What did the passage mean when it was written? (c) What does the passage mean to us today? To answer these questions a set of interpretational principles, commonly called hermeneutics, has been developed: (a) the principle of progressive revelation over time; (b) the importance of the situation and conditions under which the words were originally written; (c) recognition of the wide variety of human literary styles involved in the Bible; (d) the general practice of understanding questionable passages in terms of clear passages and the biblical revelation as a whole; (e) the appreciation of God's total revelation both in the created universe and in the Bible, so that authentic scientific interpretations of His work, as defined here, cannot ultimately contradict authentic theological interpretations of His verbal and historical revelation, as defined here; and (f) consideration of both deductive and inductive approaches to the Bible, so that neither approach alone dominates our interpretation.

(6) Christian theology is based on human interpretation of the Bible and *human experience*. Theology is not a scholarly investigation of esoteric problems in an ideal world, but a practical application of biblical understanding to our world. Although experience may be highly subjective, we must think carefully about a proposed biblical interpretation that regularly violates human experience.

Theology tries to provide guidelines for contemporary events and experiences on which the Bible is silent by extrapolating consistently beyond the biblical revelation on which it is based. In this area the guidance of the Holy Spirit is vital. Theology must also deal with the significance of scientific findings. The meaning of events within science can be dealt with by scientific interpretation itself, but the meaning of events beyond science can be dealt with only by theology. The modern scientific paradigms such as relativity, quantum mechanics and cosmology all provide occasions for speculation in the hazardous business of seeking to derive theological insights from scientific theories. It is the task of theology to relate these non-scientific, supposedly theological insights to the biblical revelation.

Consistent with the foregoing characteristics of authentic Christian theology, we can summarize a few of the adjectives that describe it. Such theology is *personal,* because it is concerned primarily with the relationship of human beings to God and to each other. Christianity at its core is not a theology but a relationship; not a philosophy of life but a love between a person and God; not a set of rules but a personal commitment that turns rules into joy and service into privilege. The fundamental act of a Christian is to commit him/herself to God in an existential act of trusting faith. This in itself is not theology, but theology then clarifies the significance of this commitment to living for God. Theology can be studied as if it were science, but it cannot be lived unless it is practiced like marriage. Like science, theology is also *ambivalent,* capable of being used as much for evil as for good, and as capable of being distorted or adapted for self-centered human needs as of being lived for the glory of God and the welfare of human beings. Theology finds *the basis for ethics* not in some relativistic human choice or in some misguided attempt to derive values from science but in the character and will of God. Finally, authentic Christian theology provides us with the foundation for *a worldview and a life.* Seeing God as the Creator, Revealer and Redeemer provides an understanding of the relationship between God and the world, a proper perspective on sin and evil in the world and guidelines for a new life in which Christians seek to glorify God by their words and deeds, demonstrating what it means to be citizens of God's kingdom while still being citizens of earth.

There is also a parallel between pseudoscience and *pseudotheology.* Pseudotheology (a) may simply be bad theology based on interpretations of the Bible and experience that violate guidelines of hermeneutics; (b) may attempt to do things that authentic theology cannot do, such as deriving scientific mechanisms from theology; or (c) may attempt to use theology in an effort to establish or justify a particular philosophical or religious ideology previously chosen.

We may summarize the common features of both science and theology as follows:

- Both science and Christian theology are based on faith commitments: a faith commitment to the intelligibility of the world and the "possibility" of doing science, and a faith commitment to God as most clearly revealed in the Person of Jesus Christ.
- Both science and theology provide us with partial descriptions of part of reality.
- The defense of authentic science is closely coupled with the defense of authentic theology. If one of these comes under serious attack or attempted reformulation, the other suffers with it.
- Insofar as the descriptions of science are compatible with the actual physical world, and insofar as the descriptions of theology are compatible with the actual relationships that describe our life in and with God, both provide true and valid insights that need to be integrated.
- In general these insights provide different kinds of information that deal with the same reality. Once again, integration of the two insights in the individual person or community is the crucial response.

Pattern 1: Science Has Destroyed the Possibility of Faith

Science and theology tell us the same kinds of things about the same things. When scientific and theological descriptions conflict, one must be right and the other wrong. In this encounter science always proves to be the winner.

This is perhaps the most commonly held view of the interaction between science and Christian faith. This view is part of the subconscious structure of our whole culture and the unspoken assumption of secular society around the world. This pattern argues that Christian faith as expounded historically through Christian theology has become impossible in the present scientific day, a relic of a less knowledgeable past. Whether it is Freud claiming that God is only an anthropocentric projection, or Marx claiming that Christianity is the opiate of the people, the thrust is and has been for centuries the same: No informed, modern person can possibly continue to accept the mythological claims of biblical Christianity.

V. Y. Frenkel[5], for example, argues that there is a simple and inevitable sequence of development: (1) Every religion starts with fear of the unknown, but, as it becomes somewhat more mature and less needed for that purpose, it becomes a religion of morality to prescribe the ethical "do's and "don'ts" of a society; (2) when it is realized that the attempt to direct the moral sensitivities of a relativistic society is neither effective nor ultimately possible, a cosmological religion develops in which the personal attributes of God are replaced by impersonal concepts such as the "spirit of the universe"; (3) finally, when this last attempt to sustain religion has run its course, only atheism is left.

Many arguments are advanced to defend the thesis that belief in the historic Christian faith is no longer intellectually respectable or psychologically acceptable. Perhaps the most common of these is the argument that modern scientific understanding has made God unnecessary. In the past, when human beings were ignorant of scientific explanations for the phenomena observed in the world, they were quick to assign God (or many gods) as the necessary and sufficient cause. Now that we know what really happens, we don't need God anymore. This argument does strike directly at a common but fundamentally false conception of God held by many Christians: God's presence and activity in the world are made known primarily by His direct action in those areas where we are ignorant of any scientifically describable mechanism.

This is the "God of the gaps" position that seeks apologetic strength by establishing the existence of areas in which we are, and by definition must, remain unable to provide any scientific descriptions. This is a fundamentally mistaken view of the biblical revelation of the nature of God and His activity in the world, which sees God as active in all phenomena—the natural that can be described scientifically as well as the supernatural that cannot. In the biblical view the whole universe depends moment-by-moment for its very existence on the continuing free activity of God, Who is the Ground and Foundation of existence itself. To argue that the God of the Bible—as contrasted with the "God" of some institutionalized religions—has become unnecessary is fundamentally to misunderstand the biblical revelation.

A second argument advanced in support of the thesis (that science has destroyed the possibility of accepting the historic Christian faith) claims that scientific understanding of natural phenomena has made belief in the "supernatural" impossible. But this argument is based on the mistaken assumption that "natural" and "supernatural" are mutually exclusive descriptions, that "supernatural" means an act of God, whereas "natural" means an event that is not related to God's activity. The problem is closely related to the "God of the gaps" issue described above. It is resolved by recognizing that events in the world can be considered simultaneously both from a natural perspective (what is the scientific description of the mechanisms involved?) and from a supernatural perspective (what is the meaning and purpose of this event; how does it relate to God and ultimate reality?). To be complete, a description of events in the world must include both natural and a supernatural contexts.

A third reason often advanced for modern science's supposed impeachment of Christianity's credibility is that science has shown that Christian faith is *only*. . . . (and this can be followed by any number of possible descriptions) a psychological experience, another human religion, a sociological phenomenon, etc. The fallacy here is that science, by its very nature, cannot proclaim that something is *only*. . . . Science can give us descriptions of what is, but the claim that a scientific description ultimately invalidates all other descriptions results from philosophical extrapolation, not from the legitimate consequences of authentic science. Science itself knows no *only*.

Related to the above misunderstandings of the relationship between God and the world is the objection that, while the Bible talks about miracles happening, today we know scientifically that miracles are impossible. Such an objection is based on the unjustified conclusion that science is the only possible way to obtain knowledge and insight into truth. Because miracles are events that, by definition, may not be describable scientifically, this perspective demands that they not be possible. But such a view is not based on science. It is based on a particular philosophical extrapolation beyond science. Science shows us that miracles would not be expected, not that it is impossible for them to occur.

A second objection to miracles relates to their apparent call for God to intervene in an otherwise orderly and well-behaved world in order to pull off some kind of magic act that violates natural laws. But, again, this objection is based on a faulty view of the relationship between God and the world. The biblical view delivers us from this dilemma: The continuing existence of the world depends upon God's free activity; natural laws do not prescribe what will happen but are human descriptions of God's normal activity; God's free activity in a miracle is not qualitatively different from God's free activity in sustaining natural phenomena. Miracles are not arbitrary violations of natural laws but appropriate evidences of God's free activity in revealing Himself.

Pattern 2: Faith Is to Be Upheld in Spite of the Findings of Science

Science and theology tell us the same kinds of things about the same things. When scientific and theological descriptions conflict, one must be right and the other wrong. In this encounter, the theological descriptions always have priority.

In this pattern, possible threats of science against faith are warded off by holding up theological interpretations as the only ones relevant for a Christian. This pattern may not be often advanced in the scholarly literature, but its significance for Christians and Christian culture cannot be underestimated. Those who feel that theology needs to be upheld over science in this modern scientific day most often seek to find a scientific framework in which to make their case against the science that proves troublesome to them; such advocates would be found in another of the patterns to be described here. But we should not forget that a large Christian constituency has no interest in science whatsoever, either apologetically or as an area worthy of extended interaction. This subdivision of Christians adopts a fundamentally anti-intellectual stance with respect to faith and effectively seeks to separate itself and its society from the influences of a world dominated by science.

In this framework the important questions and issues of life have only supernatural answers, and meaningful scientific descriptions will never be found. If science appears to disagree with these theological interpretations, so much the worse for science, which is clearly either incompetent or, more likely, deliberately antireligious. The primary orientation of this pattern is to ignore science and to discourage participation in science. Often, young people brought up in this environment are led to believe that a career in science is not something that any Christian should contemplate. The important things in life are spiritual, and they have nothing in common with science and its earthly concerns.

Sometimes Christians who adhere to this pattern become involved with the interaction between science and Christian faith by undertaking efforts to make theology the ultimate guide for acceptable science. The attempt is made to determine by theology which theories in science are consistent with Christian faith and which are not, or even to reformulate science so that its format can be dictated by theology.[6] When this happens, there is always the pitfall of sacrificing scientific integrity for the sake of apparent theological credibility, thus producing a pseudoscience.

In a world in which the successes of science are well established, it appears that this pattern will be unable to survive very long. Its demise may be accompanied by considerable loss of faith among its proponents. Those committed to it will find themselves squeezed into a smaller and smaller "God of the gaps" position, particularly if they seek to witness to the world around them.

Pattern 3: Science and Faith Are Totally Unrelated: Neither One Can Say Anything About the Other

Science and theology tell us different kinds of things about different things. There is no common ground between them. Science has absolutely nothing to say about theology, and theology has absolutely nothing to say about science. Conflict is impossible.

Although description of this pattern probably requires the least elaboration, this does not mean that it has few advocates. It could even be argued that this is one of the most common patterns in everyday life. It is, after all, an attempt to eliminate the conflict that plays such a dominant role in the first two patterns. Science and theology are put into separate airtight compartments, so that no interaction between them is possible; such an approach is judged to be the "safest" way to handle the problem.

For many people, it has become convenient to think in a secular, cultural and scientifically-related way during six days of the week and then, discontinuously, on the seventh day, to think in a religious and theologically-related way for the purposes of a worship service or a gathering of those professing faith. If the attitudes followed during the six days contradict the attitudes held on the seventh day, it does not matter. During the week we can act as if the world were five billion years old, but on the seventh day we can also act as if it were only ten thousand years old. Neither position has an actual claim on basic reality; they are an example only of unrelated statements.

In recent years the position that science and theology cannot, by definition, interact at all has been a major theme of "neo-orthodox" theology, spearheaded by such notable theologians as Karl Barth. In this case, one might argue that the desire to defend and preserve the perceived truths of Christian theology in the midst of a threatening scientific climate has led to a pattern that seems to promise immunity for theology. It is, however, difficult to maintain a vital position in which the significance of science and theology for each other is simply ignored. In practice, it is likely that indifference and apathy to the issues may well be the most common result.

Pattern 4: Science Provides the Rational Basis That Demands Faith

Science and theology tell us the same kinds of things about the same things. The scientific descriptions of the world provide such overwhelming evidence of the truth of the Bible and Christian theology that we have no choice but to believe them.

This pattern accepts the modern conviction that science is the prime defender and revealer of the truth and seeks to build an apologetic for the faith based on science. It expresses a reaction against the non-rational and anti-intellectual emphases of Pattern 2 and attempts to marshal all the social prestige enjoyed by science in defense of the Faith. It is the pattern of an appreciable subgroup of Christians who desire to bring to bear the most powerful elements of their modern armory against the popular attacks on Christianity in the name of science. It emphasizes a logical, systematic, intellectual defense of conservative Christian biblical interpretation so compelling that non-Christians would be convinced on the basis of this evidence alone to become Christians.[7,8]

If science has called the authenticity and authority of the Bible into question, then an attempt is made to show that the Bible can be defended scientifically, that the Bible revealed scientific truth long before it was discovered scientifically, and that the integrity of the Bible can be demonstrated objectively by showing how every apparent interaction with the descriptions of modern science can be harmonized with the biblical record. Although it is doubtful that anyone would openly claim that he or she could prove the validity of the Christian faith by logical or scientific approaches, this pattern comes closest to such a claim.

The marshalling of evidence that supports the reasonableness of the Christian faith and the trustworthiness of the biblical revelation is indeed a worthy attempt. It can be an effective witness to help those under the impression that all modern science contradicts Christianity to see that this simply is not the case. The destruction of caricatures is always a valuable achievement.

But the methodology of this pattern is troublesome for two fundamental reasons. First, it makes science the ultimate judge and arbiter of truth and reliability in an area where such a position for science is not justified. There is a strong desire to set forth "objective evidence" in such a convincing way that a faith commitment itself almost becomes unnecessary. There appears to be no place for a personal response to Christ's love, only for an intellectual response to scientifically testable evidence. So strong is the commitment to "science" that proponents of this position frequently contend that miraculous events properly should be considered as part of a scientific description, thus uniting them with advocates of Pattern 6 in arguing for a change in the definition of authentic science and its built-in limitations.

Second, this pattern gives far too little significance to the nature of the revelation actually given to us in the Bible, choosing to assume instead that it is the same type of communication that we might expect to obtain by reading a daily newspaper or textbook. Among the most questionable are those arguments based on the existence of "prescience" in the Bible. Almost everything we know about the nature of the biblical revelation from its own character and purposes, everything we understand from the relevance of progressive revelation, everything we would ascribe to the actual purpose and meaning of the Bible, argues against hidden pre-scientific insights resulting from special revelation thousands of years ago. This is more like an argument from mysticism or magic than it is a faithful understanding of the nature of communication between God and human beings.

Advocates of this pattern frequently miss the importance of "human interpretation" in both science and theology. Instead of recognizing that there are no "self-interpreting facts," they would argue the contrary. But any student of the philosophy of science knows that facts do not provide their own meaning and that every experiment is itself "theory-laden." To deny this is to reject the very qualities that characterize authentic science as human interpretation of observations. But such arguments also commonly misunderstand the essential role of human interpretation in biblical interpretation.

Pattern 5: Science Provides the Philosophical Structure in Which Faith Needs to Be Redefined

Science and theology tell us the same kinds of things about the same things. Traditional biblical theology must be thoroughly redefined and rewritten in order to be consistent with the developments of modern science.

Whereas Pattern 4 sought to justify traditional conservative Christian theological interpretation by showing that it was scientifically defensible, this pattern argues for a new definition of theology to make it consistent with the results of modern science.[9-12] It is the general position of a considerable number of Christians who, being well-versed in science, feel the need to alter traditional theological positions to bring them more into harmony with the philosophical implications suggested to them by modern science. One might argue that in Pattern 4 scientific reasoning was put into the service of theological convictions, whereas in Pattern 5 new theological formulations are proposed in order that they might be consistent with an interpretation of the results of modern science. This approach is based either on (a) the effort to reconstruct Christian theology in categories that are acceptable to a modern scientific worldview, or (b) to argue for a major new insight and revelation of God coming to us through the models and descriptions of modern science. There is often only a thin line that separates Pattern 5 from Pattern 6, which calls for a radical revision of both science and theology in the future to form one common view.

One of the issues that relates to several of these patterns is "natural theology," the attempt to derive theological concepts from the scientific investigation of the natural world. In Pattern 3, in which natural theology is seen to constitute a scientific threat to theology, the thrust of theological apologetics is to deny any validity to natural theology. As is so often the case, this effort has been carried to such an extreme that Romans 1:20 has been seen as having virtually no content concerning the natural evidence for the existence and power of God. The opposite extreme, in which scientific descriptions are seen as providing the basis for a theological revolution as in Pattern 5, or in which both scientific and theological descriptions are rewritten to provide a new synthesis as in Pattern 6, base their principal arguments on what might be called "natural theology." Pattern 7 attempts to avoid the polar extremes of the response to "natural theology."

In assessing advocates of this pattern, it is difficult to determine whether they intend their rhetoric to be taken literally or as a form of poetic overstatement; in more extreme cases of the former, there could even be considerable overlap with Pattern 6. There can be no debate that certain theological models have changed as scientific understanding has increased, primarily because faulty models, which were later shown to be inappropriate interpretations, were originally adopted as apparently reasonable interpretations of the Bible. The problem is aggravated by those who, following Pattern 4, insist that certain biblical models for the physical world be taken as actual scientific descriptions. When these models break down under the development of scientific understanding, it appears that the biblical revelation itself needs to be altered drastically, whereas in fact we have realized the fallacy in our caricature of a biblical picture.

Our new insights into the vast size and perplexing properties of the universe and our new perspectives on its physical structure and interactions, brought to us through such modern theories as quantum mechanics and relativity, impress on us what we should have realized all along: Our God is far greater than we could ever imagine. Classical determinism, our simplistic way of thinking of Him, is inadequate in the universe that we begin to see more clearly through applications of quantum physics. Scientific research shows us with ever more wonders the fantastic ways in which God acts in the universe. But, as we learn more and more about the way in which God acts, we do not learn anything that challenges the basic revelation of God as the loving Father of our Lord Jesus Christ, who died for our sins on the cross.

Nor does this increased scientific knowledge create any significant differences in our meaning or expression of the fundamental characteristics of the Christian life: love, joy, peace, patience, kindness, goodness, faith, gentleness, self-control, mercy, compassion, forgiveness, redemption and regeneration. This returns us to the problem of understanding the statements of advocates of Pattern 5: Are they only reacting to the increase in our scientific understanding with excessive language that proclaims the greatness of God, or are they really proposing that Christian theology needs to be totally revolutionized because of this growth in scientific understanding?

So-called "scientific theology" usually supposes that biblical categories of thought are hopelessly unacceptable to the modern scientific mind, that religious beliefs are wholly products of human activity, and that, in the final analysis, it is knowledge and understanding that save. The task therefore is to reconstruct biblical categories and translate them into acceptable scientific categories. What is envisioned is frequently described in such dramatic terms as a "new Reformation" or "reformulation" of religious concepts to bring them into line with contemporary scientific descriptions, or a "new paradigm." All these expectations call for a reinterpretation of biblical theology to make it consistent with contemporary science.

This task may result, for example, in seeing Nature as God, the natural system as the Kingdom of God, science as truth, evil as nonviable, and salvation as the human quest for survival. Usually sin is no longer a meaningful category to be mentioned, and since there is no sin, there is no need for a savior from sin. Theology constructed in this way, being shaped by current scientific descriptions and not by authentic biblical or experiential interpretation, can be nothing other than pseudotheology.

Pattern 6: Both Science and Faith Need to Be Redefined So That an Appropriate Synthesis Can Be Achieved

Science and theology should tell us the same kinds of things about the same things, but the present status of science and theology makes this impossible. What is needed, therefore, are radical transformations of science and theology into new approaches compatible with one another and a new understanding of reality.

Becoming dissatisfied with the continuing apparent conflicts between science and theology, this pattern looks with visionary hope toward the time when science and theology will have grown into one coherent discipline. This view has attracted advocates ranging from the moderate to the extreme and from sound Christian positions to New Age doctrines.[10-15] At its best, this pattern envisions a growing awareness of the similarities between scientific and theological descriptions and a continued recognition of their legitimate differences; at its worst, it calls for a radical change in both science and theology, thus denying the characteristics of authentic science and authentic theology upon which their effectiveness and trustworthiness depend.

A mystical convergence of science and theology in the future does not necessarily speak of the fulfillment of authentic science and authentic theology. If such a convergence does occur, it may well be because we have lost both authentic science and authentic Christian theology. Nowhere is this more evident and more challenging than in those cases where pseudoscience and pseudotheology have been joined together in an effort to synthesize a new relationship between science and theology, a great new transformation to occur in the not-too-distant future, spoken of in glowing terms: a transformation in which science and theology will join together, their conflicts will end, and the two will become one marvelous and mystical celebration of the human spirit. Such a movement claims the authority of science but actually rests upon a particular philosophical or religious interpretation of science not derived from authentic science. The case for this new paradigm that calls for a redefinition of science to accommodate dimensions of life not previously included in our definition of authentic science and a thorough re-thinking of our theology in light of science, abounds in poetic language and dramatic claims. Upon inspection, however, it turns out that these claims are simply not true. Here are some specifics:

- It is not true that modern science is demonstrating to us the nature of the eternal order that underlies the universe.
- It is not true that modern science is showing us spiritual dimensions of reality previously unknowable.
- It is not true that the developments of modern science have contributed or can contribute in any major way to our spiritual understanding.
- It is not true that modern science has become the basis for human assurance that God made us and cares about us.
- It is not true that the earth is a living organism with an earth spirit.
- It is not true that all matter has a non-material center characterized by intelligence.

Much of the language of this pattern is indistinguishable from New Age thinking, an uncritical acceptance of Eastern Monism. It is important, therefore, to appreciate the great temptation that such thinking poses for modern religious believers immersed in a scientific world. The subtlety of language, the ease of shifting from one perspective to another, the charm of incorporating new visions constructed from pseudoscience and pseudotheology, are all very much a part of the challenge that Christians face in the future.

When we read in Christian literature such phrases as "the development of the sphere of the spirit expanded by modern science," "a new order in which science will enrich our spiritual understanding," or "a new understanding of spiritual truths based upon discoveries of modern science," we ought to reflect on the similarity between these words and those of New Age advocates. Christians will wish to be very cautious that statements of theirs that may sound like these will not be mistaken for the class of assertions being advanced in support of New Age thinking. They will wish to be very careful in maintaining clearly the definitions of authentic science and authentic spiritual thinking.

Many of the foregoing claims are supposed to be based on insights gained from the "new science" (a term which usually refers to relativity and quantum mechanics), but in reality they are little more than an *ad hoc,* semi-poetic construction. They speak in mystical terms about the findings of modern science having shown the reality of a "spirit" intrinsic to all reality. But, as a matter of fact, scientific descriptions have not shown any such thing; by their very nature they are intrinsically incapable of giving information about the existence or nonexistence of "spirit." In fact, consideration of the effects on human society that have been brought into prominence by scientific and technological developments strongly suggests that the trend is toward depersonalization of human beings, not toward recognition of a nonmaterial, spiritual quality.

Contrary to frequently-heard claims, physicists are not telling us that there is an innate "intelligence" present in each atom of matter. There may well be people saying such things, but they are philosophers or theologians who are mistakenly seeking some kind of apparent foundation in science for their own preconceived faith commitments. They are attempting a grand synthesis of pseudoscience and pseudotheology. The strongest advocates of this pattern have adopted the viewpoint of Eastern Monism and have then sought to find support in particular interpretations of modern science.

Pattern 7: Faith and Science Provide Complementary Insights into Reality That Need to Be Integrated

Science and theology tell us different kinds of things about the same things. Each, when true to its own authentic capabilities, provides us with valid insight into the nature of reality from different perspectives. It is the task of individuals and communities of individuals to integrate these two types of insight to obtain an adequate and coherent view of reality.

At the end of this sequence of possible patterns for relating science and faith, we come to the one, with its appropriate limitations and openness, that seems to demonstrate the most consistent relationship to the characteristics of authentic science and authentic Christian theology.[16-24] It is the perspective of complementarity—the holding of both scientific and theological descriptions together, recognizing their differences and appreciating their similarities, and making an effort to integrate them into one whole picture—that does justice to both as insights into the nature of reality. Effective complementarity demands insights from authentic science and authentic theology, rejects inputs from pseudoscience and pseudotheology and proceeds to the task of integrating these insights, all the while recognizing that science and theology give us different kinds of descriptions of the same reality.

It is important to recognize that complementarity is not simply a matter of preference, as though there might well be a choice better than complementarity. It is a matter of necessity in many areas of communication. Complementarity is not a cop-out but an effort to respect the integrity of different, authentic insights into the nature of reality.

There are two basic reasons derived from the nature of communication that make complementary descriptions necessary: (a) the limitations imposed on us when we try to describe something that is unknown in the terms of that which is known; and (b) the use of descriptions drawn from different areas of experience to describe the same event or phenomenon.

Whenever we attempt to characterize something unknown, something that is not part of our regular experience, we have no choice available to us except to describe the unknown in terms of what is known to us. Since such a single description can never be complete, our understanding of the unknown can never be completely accurate. We are, however, aided if we have available to us two or more attempts to describe the unknown from different perspectives of human endeavor. In both science and theology, for example, we are involved with the expression of what things are *like,* employing similes, metaphors, analogies, models, and pictures.

Scientific descriptions commonly consist of *models* of the world being observed and described. These models do not describe the world fully or with complete accuracy, but we believe (as a matter of personal scientific faith) that the better the model is—i.e., the more it corresponds to our perceptions of the world and allows us to predict new perceptions that can be tested—the more completely it images for us what reality is *like* (not what reality is). Such models change as we gain new information and formulate new pictures and ways of looking at things that agree more fully with our new information. For this reason, it makes no sense to speak about God revealing to us a "true scientific model" in the Bible; the very nature of communication and revelation makes such communication impossible.

This condition is not unique to scientific descriptions. Theological descriptions also make use of models (or metaphors) to reveal to us what God is like and what His relationship to the world is like. God Himself is pictured for us in the Bible under the models of Father, King, Husband, Bridegroom, and even Hen. This means, for example, that there are attributes of fatherhood that give us valid insights into some of the qualities of the character of God; it certainly in no sense implies that God is wholly like a human father or that our human concept of fatherhood is adequate to describe the actual characteristics of God. Similarly, the central biblical doctrine of atonement is presented to us under various models: healing, wholeness, redemption, reconciliation, sacrifice, legal substitution, and victory. No one of these models does full justice to the ultimate mystery of atonement; yet we have a more complete description of God's activity in this event if we include the insights of all of these models than if we include the insights of only one or two.

Thus we often find it both expedient and necessary to use more than one metaphor to give a number of possible different perspectives on the unknown, providing thereby a more complete representation than would any single metaphor alone. Particular models or metaphors give particular insights, but, of necessity, each conveys only partial and incomplete insights into the nature of reality. Therefore, when we use more than one model, it is common to use scientific metaphors to describe scientific issues and theological metaphors to describe theological issues. For example, in science we find that complementary descriptions of an electron as a particle and as a wave are used depending on the type of experiment we perform to measure it. In theology we find the complementary descriptions of God/human relationships as Divine Sovereignty and human responsibility, again dependent on the perspective we are adopting and the type of questions we are asking. In all such cases it is critical that a meaningful question be asked in order to get a meaningful answer.

Sometimes complementary descriptions drawn from different realms of discourse and experience are applied to the same event. This can happen within different levels of scientific investigation, as, for example, with descriptions drawn from both chemistry and psychology to describe psychological aspects of whole human beings. It can also happen when scientific and theological descriptions are given for the same event or phenomenon. Healing can be described appropriately as both antibiotic defense against infection and the healing activity of God. To eliminate one description or the other decreases our understanding of the whole process; both are needed. Although we do not yet have all the information necessary, it is likely that the origin of life can be appropriately described in terms of physical, chemical and biological processes and, at the same time, in terms of the creative activity of God bringing something new into being. To be able to give a description in scientific categories by no means makes unnecessary, invalid or meaningless a complementary description of the same event in theological categories. The opposite is also true: having a theological description does not rule out the significance of a scientific description.

Other situations requiring the integration of complementary descriptions from science and theology are not difficult to find. Some of the most illustrative of these have to do with different kinds of descriptions of a human being and human relationships. To speak of a human being as the product of "genes" is to use scientific language; to speak of the same human being as a living "soul" is to use theological language. Both descriptions are valid; neither can be ignored. If the description of "soul" is abandoned in favor of a description only of "genes," the human being is reduced to an organic machine. If the description of "genes" is abandoned in favor of a description of "soul," the human being becomes a kind of dualistic "ghost in the machine." A complementary approach recognizes that "genes" describes a human being on the biological level, whereas "soul" describes a human being on the theological level. One way of integrating them that does not do violence either to authentic science or to authentic theology is to see the soulful properties of a human being as emergent properties of the whole, resulting from the particular patterned interactions of the biological parts in accordance with the creative activity of God.

Specific examples can also be drawn in the area of ethical issues concerned with the beginning and ending of life. Each of these must be informed by insights drawn from the biological and psychological scientific areas, and from biblical perspectives on the value of human personhood.[25]

As important as the recognition of what "complementarity" claims is the recognition of what it does claim.

- Complementarity is not equivalent to the compartmentalization of Pattern 3. It is true that each description in a complementary set can be totally complete on its own level of description without leaving gaps on that level for the other discipline to fill and without demanding some kind of conflict. But complementarity recognizes that valid insights from science and theology each deal with the same reality and must be integrated. It does not hold the two different insights to be totally unrelated, without interaction or effects on one another.
- Complementarity does not make the claim that no aspect of theology is or should be affected by science, or that no aspect of science is or should be affected by theology. It does maintain that science is incapable of providing

the foundation for ethics or knowledge about the relationship between God and human beings and that theology is incapable of providing mechanistic information about the "how" questions of the physical universe. But it also freely recognizes, as discussed earlier, that growth in scientific understanding of the way in which God has actually created the world can affect the form of theological models that had been formed from cultural frameworks of the past. Complementarity also freely recognizes that theological insights can affect one's choice of problems in the physical sciences, or even one's choice of an integrating, descriptive model in the more culturally-related sciences of psychology or sociology, in which worldview can play as large a role as research results.

- Complementarity is not a thoughtless acceptance of contradiction, paradox or dualism. It is a recognition of those circumstances in which two or more different but valid insights are available to describe and understand something beyond the abilities of known models to encompass. If it is possible by more complete understanding to remove the contradiction, resolve the paradox or eliminate the dualism, then this course of action must be taken. But if this is not possible in a particular case, then the full benefit of integrating complementary insights is manifest.

Conclusions

We will walk a philosophical tightrope in the years ahead between these various patterns of relating science and Christian faith. We need to be prepared to defend authentic science and to recognize and contest those claims made in the practice of pseudoscience. And we need to be prepared to defend authentic Christian theology and to recognize and contest those claims made in the practice of pseudotheology. Finally, we need to bring together the complementary insights provided by authentic science and authentic theology and to integrate them into our lives, thoughts and actions.

In this way we can most effectively live out what it means to be faithful disciples of Jesus Christ in all of life.

Notes

(References cited in this paper are meant to be illustrative, not exhaustive.)

1. R. H. Bube, *The Encounter Between Christianity and Science* (William B. Eerdmans Publishing Co., 1968).
2. R. H. Bube, *The Human Quest: A New Look at Science and Christian Faith* (Word Press, 1971).
3. R. H. Bube, *Science and the Whole Person* (American Scientific Affiliation, 1985).
4. R. H. Bube, "How Can a Scientist Be a Christian in Today's World?" in *Can Scientists Believe?* N. Mott, ed. (James & James, 1991), 109–120.
5. V. Y. Frenkel, "Some Remarks on Scientists and Religion by a Simplicio of Our Time," in *Can Scientists Believe?* N. Mott, ed. (James & James, 1991), 121–127.
6. See, for example, H. M. Morris and J. C. Whitcomb, Jr., *The Genesis Flood* (Presbyterian and Reformed Publishers, 1961); P. E. Johnson, *Darwin on Trial* (InterVarsity Press, 1991).
7. J. P. Moreland, *Scaling the Secular City: A Defense of Christianity* (Baker Book House, 1987).
8. J. W. Montgomery, ed., *Evidence for Faith: Deciding the God Question* (Probe Books, 1991).
9. R. W. Burhoe, "The Human Prospect and the 'Lord of History,'" *Zygon,* 10 (1975): 299–375.
10. R. J. Russell, "Christian Discipleship and the Challenge of Physics: Formation, Flux and Focus," *Perspectives on Science and Christian Faith,* 42 (1990): 139–154; R. H. Bube, "Reflections on Christian Discipleship and the Challenge of Physics,"*Perspectives on Science and Christian Faith,* 43 (1991): 193.
11. R. J. Russell, "Theological Implications of Physics and Cosmology," in *The Church and Contemporary Cosmology,* J. B. Miller and K. E. McCall, eds. (Carnegie Mellon University Press, 1990), 247.

12. F. Capra and D. Steindl-Rast with T. Matus, *Belonging to the Universe* (Harper and Row, 1991).
13. J. Templeton and R. L. Herrmann, *The God Who Would Be Known* (Harper & Row, 1989).
14. M. Dowd, *The Meaning of Life in the 1990s* (Living Earth Christian Fellowship, 1990).
15. J. White, *The Meeting of Science and Spirit: Guidelines for a New Age* (Paragon House, 1990).
16. H. J. Van Till, *The Fourth Day* (William B. Eerdmans Publishing Co., 1986).
17. J. Polkinghorne, *Reason and Reality* (Trinity Press, 1991).
18. I. Barbour, *Issues in Science and Religion* (Prentice-Hall, 1966).
19. D. MacKay, *The Clockwork Image* (InterVarsity Press, 1974).
20. D. MacKay, *Human Science and Hurnan Dignity* (Hoddern and Stoughton, 1977).
21. D. MacKay, *The Open Mind* (InterVarsity Press, 1988).
22. R. J. Berry, ed., *Real Science, Real Faith* (Monarch Publications, Ltd., 1991).
23. R. H. Bube, "Reductionism, Preductionism and Hierarchical Emergence," *Journal of the American Scientific Affiliation,* 37 (1985): 177.
24. R. H. Bube, "The Relationship between Scientific and Theological Descriptions," *Journal of the American Scientific Affiliation,* 38 (1986): 154.
25. R. H. Bube, "Of Dominoes, Slippery Slopes, Thin Edges of Wedges and Camels' Noses in Tents: Pitfalls in Christian Ethical Consistency," *Perspectives on Science and Christian Faith,*42 (1990): 162.

Creation Science and Methodological Naturalism?

J. P. Moreland

J. P. Moreland is Professor of Philosophy in the Talbot School of Theology at Biola University. With degrees in chemistry, theology and philosophy, he has published over 25 articles in magazines and journals, including the *American Philosophical Quarterly, Philosophy and Phenomenological Research, Grazer Philosophische Studien,* the *Australasian Journal of Philosophy,* and the *Journal of the Evangelical Theological Society.* He has also authored or co-authored eight books, including *Scaling the Secular City* (1987), *Christianity and the Nature of Science: A Philosophical Investigation* (1989), *Does God Exist? The Great Debate* (1990), *The Life and Death Debate: Moral Issues of Our Time* (1990), and *Immortality: The Other Side of Death* (1992) and is editor of *The Creation Hypothesis: Evidence for a Designer,* to be released by Intervarsity Press in 1994.

For some time now, notes Tom Morris, editor of *Divine and Human Action,* many Christian intellectuals, especially theologians, have accepted theological antirealism.[1] Theological antirealism is the notion that it is futile to bring one's Christian theism to bear on the intellectual task of developing a constructive worldview about metaphysical questions concerning the existence and nature of reality.

Fortunately, Morris also notes, theological realism has made a strong comeback in the field of philosophy, and currently a number of Christian thinkers are doing metaphysics and epistemology (the study of knowledge) in light of the commitments that are implicit in a Christian worldview. The same thing cannot be said, however, when it comes to natural science. A number of models have been formulated to integrate science and theology, including the following:[2]

(1) Science and theology are concerned with two distinct realms of reality (the natural and supernatural) and/or science and theology are governed by very different objects (e.g., the material universe and God) and can only be defined in relation to them.

(2) Science and theology approach the same reality but do not directly interact. They complement each other, but they adopt very different standpoints, ask and answer very different kinds of questions, and use very different standards of knowledge (e.g., objectivity and logical neutrality in science, personal involvement and commitment in theology).

(3) Science generates a metaphysic in terms of which theology is then formulated.

(4) Theology provides a context wherein the presuppositions of science (understood in a realist way) are most easily justified.

(5) Science and theology are interacting approaches to the same reality that can be in conflict or agreement to varying degrees of strength. They can be compatible, but they can be mutually exclusive.

It is possible to embrace one or more of these models, but only Position 5 allows direct interaction, conflict, and mutual reinforcement. But currently most intellectuals who focus on these issues reject Position 5 and embrace the popular but (in my opinion) unsupportable view that concepts of God or a direct miraculous act of God should play no role in the scientific enterprise. It is widely believed that natural science and theology mix like oil and water, namely, not at all. Theological antirealism pervades natural science, manifesting itself in an approach that limits the relationship of science and theology to Positions 1–4 above, with Position 2 being especially popular. Applied to the question of origins, this theological antirealism entails any form of "theistic science" is a contradiction, because theistic science is *not* a science. Rather, it is religion masquerading as science.[3]

It is beyond the scope of this essay to attempt to define "theistic science" to everyone's satisfaction, even if such a thing were possible (which I seriously doubt). In its broadest sense, theistic science is a research program committed to the following propositions: (1) God, a personal agent of great power and intelligence, has purposefully created and designed the world through direct primary agent causation and indirect secondary causation and has intervened directly in its development at various times (including prehistory, i.e., history prior to the arrival of human beings); (2) the commitment expressed in Proposition 1 can appropriately enter into the very fabric of scientific practice and the use of scientific methodology.

Proposition 1 is the more important of the two, for unless one embraces some form of scientism, one can rationally believe it regardless of whether 2 is true. The two propositions taken together, however, constitute the essence of theistic science. I will be offering a limited defense of the controversial thesis that 1 and 2 are both true.

Progressive creationism, "Young-Earth" creation science and a number of other theories propose details consistent with the general research program of theistic science. Regarding theistic science (he addresses one version of it, but his comments apply to other versions as well), Michael Ruse claims that "even if scientific creationism were totally successful in making its case as science, it would not yield a *scientific* explanation of origins. Rather, at most, it could prove that science shows that there can be *no* scientific explanation of origins."[4] Elsewhere, Ruse states that "The Creationists believe the world started miraculously. But miracles lie outside of science, which by definition deals with the natural, the repeatable, that which is governed by law."[5]

Interestingly, a significant number of Christian scholars have made similar claims.[6] For example, philosopher Paul de Vries and scientist Howard J. Van Till have argued that natural science must presuppose *methodological naturalism*, leaving concepts like God or direct acts of God outside the boundaries of natural science. By "natural science" what is meant is the scientific endeavors called physics, chemistry, geology, astronomy, biology, and related fields.[7] Thus theistic science is fundamentally misguided because it has a faulty philosophy of science and an improper view of how science and theology should relate to each other.

I wish to criticize the claim that methodological naturalism constitutes natural science, taking de Vries and Van Till as representatives of the claim. In my view, theistic science *is* a science, and there is nothing about the nature of natural science that should exclude theological or philosophical concepts. A detailed defense of my view is obviously too involved to be attempted here. Rather, in what follows, I will discuss some important preliminary considerations, state and criticize the positions of de Vries and Van Till, suggest how the notion of God can, or perhaps, should, enter into natural science, and look at three main criticisms of this position.

Preliminary Considerations

Consider the following propositions:

(1) By its very nature, natural science must and should adopt methodological naturalism.

(2) Theistic science is a religion, not a science.

(3) The concepts of God and miraculous, primary causal acts of God are not appropriate to natural science.

It is important to remember that these claims are not first order claims *of* science about some scientific phenomenon. Rather, they are second order philosophical claims *about* science. They take a vantage point outside of science and refer to science itself as their subject. Thus these claims should be evaluated within the field of philosophy, especially philosophy of science. Scientists are not experts on these questions, and when they comment on them, they do so as philosophers, not as scientists.

Second, we need to distinguish three different types of theory changes that can happen as science develops. Part (and perhaps all, according to Kuhn and other antirealists) of the history of science involves theory replacement—episodes in which earlier theories are abandoned in favor of later ones. There are at least three different types of theory replacements. First, a new theory may replace an old one, which although still considered a scientific theory is now considered inadequate. An example would be the change from phlogiston chemistry to oxygen chemistry. Let us call this type of theory change TC_1.

Second, there are replacements in which a new theory supplants an old one, and the scientific community comes to value different "epistemic virtues," i.e., different kinds of justification and support for scientific theories. For example, scientists value theories that are simple, empirically accurate, predictively successful, fruitful for guiding new research, capable of solving their internal and external conceptual problems, and given to using certain types of explanations and not others (e.g., "appeal to efficient and not final causes").

Sometimes a theory change occurs in such a way that the abandoned theory, though still considered scientific, is judged to have become unacceptable and its "epistemic virtue" is no longer regarded as good, or at least not as good as was previously thought. For example, the shift from classical to quantum models of matter can be seen to involve a shift from "all events have causes to which one must appeal in explaining those events" to "all events do not have causes, and one need not cite a cause as an explanation of a particular event." Similarly, the shift from vital force theories of organisms to more mechanistic or physicalist views of organisms involved an abandonment of the old theories as well as the elevation of a new standard of support: "reject explanations of living processes in terms of vital forces, fluids or final causes." Here the abandoned theory is still considered scientific, but the theory change is an occasion for a rearrangement of epistemic virtues. These theory changes are of both first and second order, since the analysis of the relative merits of epistemic virtues is partly philosophical in nature. Let us call this type of theory change TC_2.

Finally, there are theory changes in which the replaced

theory is not merely abandoned but is no longer thought to have been a scientific theory in the first place. Here the discarded theory does not pass from being a good scientific theory to an unacceptable scientific theory. Rather, the theory passes from being an apparently good scientific theory to never having been a scientific theory or, at least, to no longer being regarded as scientific. It is sometimes thought that the shift from creationist theories to Darwinism is a prime example.[8] Let us call this type of theory change TC_3.

More is claimed for a TC_2 shift than for a TC_1 shift, and more still for a TC_3 shift. It is one thing to claim that an old theory is not as good as a new theory. It is a stronger claim to assert that a kind of support valued by an old theory is no longer as good as one valued by a new theory. The new theory may be better than the old one for other reasons. Even if the claim is true for this specific theory replacement, it may not be true in other areas of science or in other theories in the same area of science. It is an even stronger claim to assert that the abandoned theory was never science to begin with and should no longer be regarded as such in light of the new theory. It is, in fact, a radical position to claim that practitioners of an abandoned theory, which they and advocates of rival scientific theories took to be scientific (how else could they take themselves to be advocates of rival scientific theories?), were not even practicing science. Surely the burden of proof is on anyone making such a strong claim.

There is a third preliminary consideration worth mentioning. If someone is going to state that some feature is part of the essence of natural science or is a necessary condition for it, then it becomes impossible to practice natural science if that feature is not present. That is, given our human sensory and intellectual faculties, there is no possible world in which natural science is practiced and the feature in question is not present.

Science Presupposes Methodological Naturalism

A Clarification of Methodological Naturalism

Let us call the view under consideration "methodological naturalism." Two main advocates of methodological naturalism have been Paul de Vries and Howard J. Van Till.[9] Methodological naturalism, as they present it, has four central defining features:

(1) *The goal of natural science:* According to de Vries, the goal of natural science is "to place events in the explanatory context of physical principles, laws, fields" (388). Explanations refer only to natural objects and events, not to the personal choices and actions of human or divine agents. According to Van Till, "The 'epistemic' goal of the natural sciences is to gain knowledge of the intrinsic intelligibility discernible in the physical properties, behavior and formative history of the physical world in which we live. The principal forms of this knowledge are the results of empirical investigation and the product of scientific theorizing about the composition, structure, behavior, and history of the physical systems we observe." (136).

(2) *Methodological naturalism vs. metaphysical naturalism:* De Vries claims that "the natural sciences are committed to the systematic analysis of matter and energy within the context of methodological naturalism" (389). Within natural science, answers are sought to questions within nature, within the non-personal created order. For example, in describing how two charged electrodes separate hydrogen and oxygen gas when placed in water, the "God hypothesis" is both unnecessary and out of place. Science is irrelevant to the question of the existence of God because the God question is totally outside the domain of natural science and its adoption of methodological naturalism. By contrast, metaphysical naturalism is a philosophical perspective that denies the existence of God. Methodological naturalism and metaphysical natural-

ism are totally separate things, and the former has no bearing at all on the latter.

Van Till's views are similar to those of de Vries. According to Van Till, the object of natural scientific study is "the physical universe—no more, no less. It is the world of atoms and of the subatomic particles constituting them. It is the world of things made of atoms" (127–8). "The object of scientific investigation must be empirically accessible: there must be some way to interact with it physically" (128).

While the entire physical universe is the object of study, not all of its qualities or aspects are within the domain of scientific inquiry. The natural sciences study the physical universe with its constituent parts, focusing on the physical properties of physical objects, the physical behavior of a physical system, or the formative history of the universe and its inhabitants—that is, of physical systems. "Only those qualities that are *intrinsic* (i.e., wholly resident within the empirically accessible physical universe) are included within the domain of scientific inquiry" (131). Questions about transcendent issues (e.g., ultimate origins, which require a consideration of beings or agents that transcend the physical universe, the governance of the universe) lie completely outside the domain of natural science.

(3) *Natural scientific explanation:* To the best of my knowledge, neither de Vries nor Van Till offers a complete, explicit statement of his views regarding scientific explanation in the natural sciences. Nonetheless, an implicit model of explanation emerges from what we have already seen. For de Vries, "science does not merely describe events" (388); more importantly, the main—perhaps only—goal of science is to seek explanations of natural phenomena by answering how-questions. An answer to a how-question will describe regular, empirically observable patterns in the natural world (e.g., the relationship among pressure, temperature and volume of a gas) and explain them in terms of a natural mechanism. These explanations refer to real entities and processes in the natural world and give true, or approximately true, descriptions of these entities and processes.

Van Till's views are similar to de Vries' but diverge in one slight, but important respect. Van Till seems to agree that scientific laws and theories must be understood in realist ways, and he sees it as a large, perhaps major, focus of science to answer how-questions by describing mechanisms and processes that tell us how physical behaviors and formative histories are generated. In contrast to de Vries, however, Van Till also emphasizes the fact that science does not merely explain how phenomena take place, but also establishes the existence of the phenomena themselves and describes what they are. Natural science answers what-questions as well as how-questions and, for Van Till, the former do not appear to be mere means or occasions for doing the latter.

(4) *A complementarian view of integration and agency:* Finally, de Vries and Van Till both hold to a complementarian view of the relationship between natural science and theology. According to this view, science and theology are two completely separate levels of study that either focus on different realms of reality or provide complementary views of the same area of reality by asking and seeking to answer very different sorts of questions. In particular, de Vries and Van Till apply complementarity to human and divine agency and action. For example, de Vries analyzes the act of raising one's hand to vote at a club meeting (389–90). At the level of natural science, a complete account of such an act could be given in terms of brain states, neurons, etc. Such an account would be true and complete at that level of explanation. A complete, non-interacting description of that event could be given at another level by appealing to the individual's purposes and reasons for voting as he did.

Van Till's views are similar. Both he and de Vries agree that personal agency and action (divine or human) fall completely outside the domain of natural science and involve a level of description that complements the scientific description of the physical aspects of agency and action. Since the scientific description is complete within its own level (i.e., the description explains all aspects of this phenomenon that fall within the domain of natural science), descriptions of personal agency and action do not directly interact with it. No inferences are allowed to go from one level of description to another.

Critique of Methodological Naturalism

Keep in mind what de Vries and Van Till are asserting. They are attempting to show that theological concepts (e.g., "God" or "direct acts of God") are outside of the boundaries of natural science. To show this, their characterization of natural science must describe the very essence, or at least necessary conditions, of natural science. They offer the four features of methodological naturalism listed above as necessary conditions for natural science; that is, natural science for humans is impossible in the absence of these features. This is a strong claim and, in my view, is implausible.

Consider first the goal of science as stated in methodological naturalism. De Vries and Van Till both assume scientific realism in their characterizations the goal of science. Now scientific realism may be, in fact, true. If, however, the goal of natural science is stated in realist terms and presented as a necessary condition for natural science, then the stated antirealist goals of science (e.g., to make useful predictions or harmonize with observations) become impossible. They are logically inconsistent with natural science. This view is simply false. Antirealist treatments of the goals of natural science are philosophies of science; they may be true. If natural science is consistent with antirealist statements of the goals of natural science, then a realist interpretation of those goals cannot be a necessary condition for natural science.

Furthermore, it is implausible to claim that natural science has only one goal. A number of goals have been offered for scientific theory formation, use, and testing: construction of theories that are: (1) simple (yet capable of various interpretations); (2) empirically accurate; (3) predictively successful; (4) internally clear and consistent; (5) useful in solving external conceptual problems raised by other disciplines, e.g., theology, metaphysics or logic; (6) fruitful in guiding new research; and (7) free of certain kinds of explanatory devices.[10] In addition, these goals are capable of both realist and antirealist interpretations. For the realist, the presence of one or more of these goals signals that a theory is true or approximately true. For the antirealist, the presence of these goals merely shows that the theory is rational, solves problems, and so forth. I conclude, then, that methodological naturalism's statement of the goal of science is inadequate.

Methodological naturalism's statement of methodological naturalism itself must also be judged inadequate. One minor point is that de Vries identifies naturalism with physicalism (388). But this will not do. Roughly, in this context, naturalism is the denial of the existence of God and the assertion that the things that make up reality exclude superhuman personal agents. But one could be a naturalist without being a physicalist, by embracing Platonic forms or abstract objects like sets. One could also be a physicalist and not a naturalist (e.g., if one held that God was a physical object). Second, and more importantly, methodological naturalism's characterization of the methodological stance of natural science fails, because its alleged status as a necessary condition for natural science renders alternative characterizations logically impossible. For example, it is at least possible and surely consistent with science that science could be understood purely in terms of phenomenalism. Some of these approaches to science deny the existence of a material universe and reduce statements about physical objects to statements about private mental sense data. If such views are even possible philosophies of science, then the existence or study of matter cannot be a necessary condition for natural science.

Furthermore, if anti-realist philosophies of science are true, then there probably *is* no world of atoms or subatomic particles.[11] These are useful fictions. Even if we grant the existence of atoms, surely it is consistent with natural science to view events as real and atoms as fictions or logical constructs.[12] Methodological naturalism fails to allow for this possibility. And while we are on the subject of atoms, to which atoms is Van Till referring? Dalton's, Thomson's, Newton's, Bohr's, the atoms of quantum theory, or of some future model? The point I am making is two-fold. First, atomism is not a theory but a research program, i.e., a family of theories. Although Van Till would require that it offer a conception of natural science and define necessary conditions for natural science, it cannot. As a research program, it is too vague.

Second, some anti-realist views hold that the history of science is a history of replaced, not refined, theories, that earlier theories did not refer to real entities at all, and, by a pessimistic induction, modern theories do not refer to real entities either. In short, there is no such thing as an atom, but only an atom-in-theory-T, and this observation complicates Van Till's appropriation of "the world of atoms" in a way that renders it inadequate as a necessary condition for natural science.

More could be said, but perhaps enough has been offered to cause us to pause and observe an important lesson derived from our treatment of the goal and method of science according to methodological naturalism.[13] Recently, Larry Laudan has shown that attempts to draw a line between science and non-science or pseudo-science (by stating a set of necessary and sufficient conditions for something to count as science), are rooted in a desire to identify beliefs that are "'sound' and 'unsound,' 'respectable' and 'cranky,' or 'reasonable' and 'unreasonable.'"[14] Such attempts are rooted in polemical battles which, for one reason or another, try to show that a practice based on a particular worldview is not really science at all.

Now this is clearly the explicit goal in the methodological naturalism of de Vries and Van Till, however laudable their motives and intentions may be on other grounds. To state criteria that exclude some practice from natural science, one needs to state the very essence of natural science, or at least necessary conditions for it, and go on to assert that the target in question, in this case theological concepts like "God" or "direct acts of God," fails to embody the necessary conditions for natural science. The problem with all such attempts is that they are either too broad or too narrow; to date, no plausible line between science and non-science or pseudo-science has ever been drawn satisfactorily.[15]

I have tried to show that certain features of methodological naturalism are too narrow. In their attempts to state necessary conditions for natural science that exclude theological concepts from its domain, they excluded too much. In my view, Laudan's advice applies to methodological naturalism: "If we would stand up and be counted on the side of reason, we ought to drop terms like 'pseudo-science' and 'unscientific' from our vocabulary; they are just hollow phrases that do only emotive work for us. As such, they are more suited to the rhetoric of politicians and Scottish sociologists of knowledge than of empirical researchers."[16]

If what I have argued so far is correct, then we can draw, at least tentatively, an initial conclusion about the use of theological concepts as found in, say, theistic science. Note first that theistic science has been regarded by scientists and philosophers of science as a scientific theory (or better, as a research program that contains a family of scientific theories) for some time. In a highly regarded study of Darwin and creationism, Neal C. Gillespie notes that various versions of creationism were widely seen as scientific theories prior to and during the Darwinian revolution.[17]In a similar vein, Philip Kitcher asserts:

> Moreover, *variants* of Creationism were supported by a number of eminent nineteenth-century scientists—William Buckland, Adam Sedgwick and Louis Agassiz, for example. These Creationists trusted that their theories would accord with the Bible, interpreted in what they saw as a correct way. However, that fact does not affect the scientific status of those theories. Even postulating an unobserved Creator need be no more unscientific than postulating unobservable particles. What matters is the character of the proposals and the ways in which they are articulated and defended. The great scientific Creationists of the eighteenth and nineteenth centuries offered problem-solving strategies for many of the questions addressed by evolutionary theory.[18]

The shift from creationism to evolutionary theory was first and foremost an example of TC_1, not TC_3, and it is the latter that is implicit in methodological naturalism. Now, as we saw earlier, the burden of proof is squarely on the shoulders of those who would justify a TC_3 from a TC_1 type of theory. In the absence of an acceptable line of demarcation between science and non-science or pseudo-science, or even of a set of necessary conditions for science, this burden of proof has not been met.

We may initially and tentatively conclude, then, that methodological naturalism, at least as it is presented by de Vries and Van Till, has not successfully prevented theological concepts from entering into the very fabric of science. More specifically, however poor the theories of theistic science are as first order paradigms, they cannot be faulted as non-science or pseudo-science merely by citing the fact that they contain theological concepts. I cannot rule out the possibility that some more adequate, forthcoming version of methodological naturalism will be successful. But because of the difficulties inherent in drawing an adequate line of demarcation between science and non-science or pseudo-science, I am skeptical about the prospects of this happening.

However, the matter need not be left here. There are two other features of methodological naturalism: natural scientific explanation and complementarity of integration and agency. Rather than focusing directly on these aspects of methodological naturalism, it will be more useful to address them through a brief discussion of how theological concepts like "God" or a "direct act of God" can be appropriate parts of natural science. In what follows, I will try to give a "better picture"[19] of how theological concepts figure into the practice of science than the one offered by methodological naturalism, though I readily admit that the "picture" to follow needs more details and refinements.

Theological Concepts and the Fabric of Natural Science

Theological Concepts and External Conceptual Problems

Scientific laws and theories typically involve observational concepts and their associated terms (e.g., "is red," "sinks"), as well as theoretical concepts and their associated terms (e.g., "is an electron," "has zero rest mass"). Often, scientists try to solve both empirical and conceptual problems.[20] Roughly, an empirical problem is a puzzlement about an observation of some scientific datum that strikes us as odd and in need of an explanation. For example, what is the precise movement of the tides and why do they move as they do?

Frequently, scientists try to solve conceptual problems, which come in two types: internal and external. Internal conceptual problems arise when the concepts within a theory are defective in some way, e.g., vague, unclear, contradictory, or circularly defined. External conceptual problems arise for a scientific theory when it conflicts with a rationally well-founded doctrine of another theory, regardless of the discipline with which that theory is associated. Natural science has always interacted with other fields of study in complicated ways that defy a simple characterization.

An external conceptual problem tends to count against a given scientific theory, because part of the practice of science is to make sure that a scientific theory solves its problems, external conceptual problems included. Thus, external conceptual problems counter the complementarity model of the relationship between science and theology, because in these cases science directly interacts with another discipline (like philosophy or theology) in an epistemically positive or negative way. For example, Darwin and many of his followers have advocated a physicalist understanding of living organisms, including human beings.[21] Paul Churchland's remark is typical:

> The important point about the standard evolutionary story is that the human species and all of its features are the wholly physical outcome of a purely physical process. . . . If this is the correct account of our origins, then there is neither need, nor room, to fit any nonphysical substances or properties into our theoretical account of ourselves. We are creatures of matter. And we should learn to live with that fact.[22]

If someone had good philosophical or theological reasons to reject physicalism, then these reasons would provide external conceptual problems for any version of naturalistic evolutionary theory (and most modern versions are naturalistic because, as Churchland correctly notes, they include the view that the only mechanism responsible for our appearance is a physical process). Here is another example. According to David Hull:

> The implications of moving species from the metaphysical category that can appropriately be characterized in terms of 'natures' to a category for which such characterizations are inappropriate are extensive and fundamental. If species evolve in anything like the way that Darwin thought they did, then they cannot possibly have the sort of natures that traditional philosophers claimed they did. If species in general lack natures, then so does *Homo sapiens* as a biological species. If *Homo sapiens* lacks a nature, then no reference to biology can be made to support one's claims about "human nature." Perhaps all people are "persons," share the same "personhood," etc., but such claims must be explicated and defended *with no reference to biology*. Because so many moral, ethical and political theories depend on some notion or other of human nature, Darwin's theory brought into question all these theories. The implications are not entailments. One can always dissociate "*Homo sapiens*" from "human being," but the result is a much less plausible position.[23]

Again, if someone has good philosophical or theological reasons to believe in the existence of human nature or the moral or political theories grounded in human nature, these would provide external conceptual problems for naturalistic versions of evolutionary theory. Note carefully Hull's acknowledgement that the relationship between evolution and the notion of "human nature" is not an entailment relation. It is logically possible to hold the two in complementarity. But Hull correctly points out that, epistemically speaking, two propositions can relate to one another in important ways other than logical consistency. This point is captured in the two examples of external conceptual problems—non-physicalist views of living organisms (including humans) and the existence of human nature and the moral/political theories grounded in it.

In sum, if there are philosophical or theological arguments against some scientific notion, e.g., physicalism as applied to human beings and their actions, evolutionary theories of origins, the idea that events can come-to-be without causes, the notion that the universe has already endured an actually infinite past, and so on, then these problems tend to count against scientific theories that entail such notions, because solving these external conceptual problems is a scientific and intellectual requirement of those theories.

Science has never exhausted the rational, nor has science ever been a discipline or set of disciplines intellectually isolated from direct interaction, mutual reinforcement, or competition from other fields of study, especially philosophy and theology. External conceptual problems provide a window for intellectual issues from other fields to enter the very fabric of science when it comes time to assess a scientific theory for its problem-solving effectiveness, because part of that assessment will include the presence of external conceptual problems.

Methodological naturalism does not leave room for external conceptual problems and, thus, is a revisionary account of the way science has been practiced and an inadequate model for how science ought to be practiced. I do not know why external conceptual problems have been left out of the methodologically naturalistic account of natural science. Perhaps de Vries and Van Till believe that the history of science is a series of TC_2 events that justify reading natural science in a way that eliminates the solution of external conceptual problems from the practice of science. In other words, it may be that their reading of the history of science shows that solving external conceptual problems has not been as valuable as other epistemic virtues (e.g., making successful predictions, being empirically accurate) that are more in keeping with methodological naturalism. Because to my knowledge they do not raise this issue, I can only speculate about the matter. But if their account of methodological naturalism includes something like this, then it is clearly inadequate. For one thing, some current scientific theories (or research programs) do try to solve external conceptual problems—evolutionary epistemology and ethics come readily to mind.

More importantly, examples of TC_2 changes do not justify reading those changes in TC_3 ways. That is, even if we grant that the history of science justifies placing external conceptual problems at the bottom of our ladder of epistemic goals for a scientific theory, that does not justify the notion that solving external conceptual problems is not even a part of science. If one allows such external conceptual problems, then the complementarity model is inadequate—external conceptual problems illustrate cases where science and theology do not merely complement each other but actually interact and compete. As we have seen, external conceptual problems allow theological and philosophical issues to enter into the very fabric of natural science.

A Model of Theological Concepts and the Formation, Use and Testing of Theories in Natural Science

We can extend and enrich our discussion of external conceptual problems by looking at specific ways that theological concepts can figure into the practice of natural science. Again, I can only offer a sketch of these issues here, but I hope that will be sufficient to suggest ways of supplying details that show the inadequacies of methodological naturalism. There is no single way that theological concepts have entered and should enter into the practice of science. But here are different aspects of an admittedly sketchy model:

(1) By stimulating the desire to think God's thoughts after Him and be a good steward of His creation, theology can provide the scientist with extra motivation to do science. And, arguably, Christian theology justifies science itself by providing the most reasonable worldview for scientific presuppositions. These points are consistent with methodological naturalism.

(2) Theology can provide external conceptual problems (e.g., that human life arose in the Middle East) for certain scientific

theories (e.g., those that postulate the beginning of human life in Asia).

(3) Theology solves certain internal conceptual problems that are difficulties for naturalistic theories (e.g., illegitimate spectator interference in pre-biotic soup experiments in order to overcome the probability against life having arisen by chance).

(4) Theology can provide pictures of what was and was not going on in the formation of some entity (e.g., the universe, first life, the basic kinds of life, man, and for some, the geological column).[24] These pictures can serve as guides for new research (e.g., by postulating that a purpose will be found for vestigial organs). They yield predictions that certain theories will be falsified (e.g., theories of natural selection working at the level of macroevolution, theories entailing a universe without beginning) and certain discoveries made (e.g., gaps in the fossil record, fixity of created "kinds").[25]

Part of scientific methodology includes the psychology of discovery. While there is no established procedure for scientific discovery, scientists often use tacit knowledge from a domain of scientific study to generate sample conceptual structures for discussion and analysis. However, some conceptual structures are derived from "the top down"—that is, from a prior commitment to a broader metaphysical view of reality (which can, in turn, come from theology), and can be used to guide research and make predictions. In such cases, a philosophical or theological theory can answer what-questions: (1) what an entity is, e.g., living organisms are not reducible to properties or physical entities; (2) what caused an event, e.g., first life was directly created by a primary causal act of God; or (3) what historical sequence actually took place, e.g., human beings arose in the Middle East. The answers can, in turn, be supported or falsified by scientific attempts to discover the truth about those what-questions.

For example, evolutionary theory and theistic science may have very different pictures of how some phenomenon came to be. According to theistic science, a series of naturalistic mechanisms did not lead from a pre-biotic soup of inorganic chemicals to the appearance of life on earth. Thus theistic science can yield statements that guide research and predict that a gap will exist where God's primary agent causal activity occurred and that various models of intervening mechanisms will prove false. Further, theistic science suggests that living things should show certain features bearing the stamp of intelligent design.[26]

(5) The notion of God as an intelligent designer and/or primary causal agent can explain certain phenomena (e.g., the origin of life or the information in DNA) that science can investigate.[27] It is simply false to assert that scientists explain things merely by using natural laws. Scientists also explain by citing causal entities, processes, events, or actions. For example, cosmologists explain certain aspects of the universe by citing the Big Bang as a single causal event.[28]

Some branches of science, e.g., the search for extra-terrestrial intelligence, archeology, forensic science, psychology, and sociology, use personal agency and the desires, willings, intentions, awarenesses, thoughts and beliefs of agents to describe the causal entities, processes, events, or actions that they cite as explanations for certain phenomena.[29] For example, Richard DeCharms claims that "A scientific concept of self that does not encompass personal causation is inadequate."[30] Thus, there is nothing non-scientific about appealing to personal agency in a scientific explanation, and it is this insight that creationists express in their view of theistic science.

It may be objected that such appeals are permissible in the human sciences but not in the so-called natural sciences like biology or paleontology. This response clearly begs the question by smuggling methodological naturalism into an attempt to define and classify examples of "natural science." If, in fact, certain phenomena are best explained by an intelligent creator/designer model, or even if such explanations are merely logically possible, then biology, paleontology, and other fields will not be "natural" sciences in the methodologically naturalistic sense. And clearly, classification of a science as "natural" in the methodological sense should follow arguments about the data and not use question-begging, arbitrary legislations to eliminate other views by definition.

If fact, such question-begging legislations can and have hurt science by ruling out of court important options for explaining data. This is clearly the case in psychology. In its heyday, behaviorism rejected internal mental states and agency by reducing them to publicly observable behavior. The positivism and/or physicalism lurking behind the scenes of such legislations hurt psychology, and recent developments in that field have made progress precisely because the notion of the self, along with related concepts, have once again been used in psychological explanation. This methodologically naturalist straightjacket would deny the same freedom of movement to biology and paleontology.

We are now in a position to evaluate methodological naturalism's model of naturalistic scientific explanation, which seems to limit scientific methodology to answering how-questions with naturalistic mechanisms (de Vries) or to overemphasize this aspect of scientific methodology (which may be implicit in Van Till). I would argue that science answers what—questions even when it cannot answer how—questions. That is, it is a legitimate part of the business of natural science to establish a phenomenon even if it either cannot or cannot yet give a naturalistic mechanism to explain how that phenomenon came or comes about.

For example, scientists had established certain facts about the death of the dinosaurs before there was any universal agreement as to what mechanism was responsible for their deaths. Furthermore, science assumes the existence of ultimate causal entities, processes, events and actions, for which no mechanism or how—question is even possible. The initial conditions of the Big Bang, the values of the ultimate constants of nature (e.g., the universal gravitational constant), and the existence and properties of ultimate particles (if there are any) could be taken as things that would be ultimates for science. According to some, all science could do is establish these phenomena. Because they are ultimates, there would be no mechanism more basic than they that could answer a how—question explaining them. In science, ultimates explain other things, but they themselves, as ultimates, are givens without explanation.

If theology implies that a gap exists between two events and that the later event results from God's primary agent-causal activity and from intelligent design, then establishing scientific implications and predictions from these assumptions and marshalling scientific evidence for and against them can be genuine parts of natural science, even if no natural mechanism exists to answer a how-question. Some of these predictions make strong assertions about what will not be the case if a certain theory is true. Since they describe phenomena not permitted by the theory, they, can, in principle, be proven false.[31]

To be sure, the origin of life would not be entirely open to natural scientific investigation (some of the issues, such as why God acted to create in the first place), would be strictly theological, but this does not imply that the phenomenon would not fall within the domain of science at all. Advocates of methodological naturalism seem preoccupied with how—questions and regularly recurring phenomena (e.g., electrolysis experiments) for which natural mechanisms complement theological concerns and the secondary causal activity of God. But this partial picture does not exhaust natural science, as we have seen.[32]

The same may be said of the complementary view of divine agency. When God acts through secondary causes (e.g., when regularly recurring events generated by natural mechanisms are in view), then theology may legitimately be seen as complementary to science. But such a picture allows only for state-to-state causation, i.e., a state of affairs causes another state of affairs (the effect). For example, the moving of one billiard ball causes the moving of a second billiard ball on contact.

When God acts as a primary cause, however, He acts as an agent cause.[33] I cannot attempt a detailed sketch of agent causation here, but the important thing about agent causation is this: the cause of an action (e.g., raising my arm, voting for an election, directly creating first life) is the agent itself, and not a state of affairs in the agent. There is no set of prior conditions inside or outside the agent that guarantees the effect. The agent must exercise his or her causal powers and simply act.

This means that in states of affairs produced by agent causes (the hand being raised, life being created) there will be a gap between the effect and the state of affairs that existed prior to that effect.[34] When I raise my arm, the state of affairs in me at the physical level just prior to the action (say, in my brain and central nervous system) will not be sufficient to cause my arm to raise, and the physical state of affairs correlated with my arm being raised will not be smoothly continuous with that prior state of affairs. A similar observation could be made for cases of God's primary causal agency, and the resulting gaps (e.g., between inorganic materials and first life) can, at least in principle, be scientifically detectable.[35]

In sum, complementarity has an inadequate view of agency and agent causation and as a result fails to see that the effects of God's primary agent-causal activity could leave scientifically detectable gaps.

This, then, is a brief sketch of how theological concepts like "God" or "a direct act of God" can be integrated within natural science. It may be helpful at this point to offer a short response to three objections that are frequently raised against the type of picture I am advocating as a contrast to methodological naturalism.

Criticisms of the Model

Objection 1: This model utilizes an inappropriate "God of the gaps" strategy. One appeals to God merely to fill gaps in our scientific knowledge of naturalistic mechanisms. These gaps are used apologetically in natural theology to support Christian theism, but, since scientific progress is making these gaps increasingly rare, this strategy is not a good one.

Reply: First, the model does not limit God's causal activity to gaps. Moreover, as Plantinga has argued, theistic science need not have any apologetic aim at all.[36] Even if it does, creationists need not limit their apologetic case to gaps. The model merely recognizes a distinction between primary and secondary causes (however much this needs further refinement) and goes on to assert that primary causes could have scientifically testable implications.

Second, it is not to cover our ignorance that the model attempts to explain in light of God and His activities. It makes the appeal only in the presence of good theological or philosophical reasons, e.g., in cases such as the origin of the universe, first life, or basic "kinds" of life, for which certain theological or philosophical considerations would cause us to expect a gap in nature where God has acted through primary causation.

Third, even if the gaps in naturalistic scientific explanations are getting smaller, this fails to prove that there are no gaps at all. It begs the question to argue that just because most alleged gaps turn out to be explainable in naturalistic terms, therefore all alleged gaps will turn out this way. After all, what else would one expect of gaps but that there would be few of them? Gaps due to primary divine agency are miracles, which are in the minority for two reasons. First, God usually operates (acknowledging the need for further clarity regarding this notion) through secondary causes; primary causal gaps are His extraordinary, unusual way of operating and, by definition, will be few and far between. Second, the evidential or sign value of a miraculous gap arises most naturally against a backdrop where the gaps are rare, unexpected and have a religious context (e.g., there are positive theological reasons to expect their presence).

Finally, scientists, creationists and non-creationists alike, have made a distinction between "empirical" and "historical" science, and this distinction is helpful for answering the God of the gaps problem. Roughly, empirical science is an approach to the world that focuses on repeatable, regularly recurring events or patterns in nature (e.g., the relationship among pressure, temperature and volume in a gas). By contrast, historical science focuses on past events that are not repeatable (e.g., the origin of the universe, first life, various kinds of life).

Advocates of this distinction claim that appealing to God is legitimate in historical science but not in empirical science because the former deals with cases in which theology leads us to expect God's primary causal activity, while the latter deals with God's secondary causal activity.[37] It could be argued that most cases in which an appeal to God has been made to cover for our ignorance of a gap it involves issues of empirical, not historical, science. Thus when those gaps are filled by naturalistic mechanisms, the conclusion to draw is not that one should never appeal to God to explain some scientifically discoverable phenomenon, but rather that such appeals should be limited to cases in historical science, precisely because the distinction between historical and empirical science captures the differences between primary and secondary causation.

Moreover, the distinction between empirical and historical science suggests a way to respond to an objection recently raised by David Hull. According to Hull, science has no choice but to embrace methodological naturalism and reject theological notions within science, because once scientists "allow reference to God or miraculous forces to explain the first origin of life or the evolution of the human species, they have no way of limiting this sort of explanation."[38]

Hull's criticism is a red herring and wide of the mark. For one thing, Christian advocates of theistic science do not see God as capricious, nor do they appeal to purposeful causal acts of God willy-nilly or merely to cover ignorance, but only when they have good theological or philosophical reasons for doing so. Second, it could be claimed that such appeals to divine action should be limited to certain areas within historical science (where theological or philosophical reasons suggest that such appeals are legitimate) and not used in empirical science. Thus it is simply false and misleading to claim, as Hull does, that once this sort of thing is allowed there is no way to stop it.

Objection 2: God's direct creation of life cannot be directly observed and, in any case, the claim that God did something by a primary causal action would always be empirically equivalent to an alternative explanation—that an undiscovered natural mechanism accounts for the phenomenon in question. Thus, such a claim cannot be tested empirically and, therefore, falls outside the bounds of natural science.

Reply: The role of observation and empirical testability in natural science is extremely complicated. For our present purposes, however, three brief points can be made. First, individual propositions in natural science are not tested against experience piecemeal, but rather, entire sets of propositions or groups of theories are tested for an empirical implication. A specific proposition (this magnetic field has such and such properties) may be empirically untestable, even in principle. If it is embedded in a theory or set of theories with testable results, however, the proposition can be an appropriate part of a theory of natural science. Similarly, the statement "God directly created first life" may not be empirically testable by itself, but it does have empirical implications when embedded in a network of other propositions.

Second, van Fraassen has shown that a potentially infinite number of different scientific theories can explain a given set of empirical data. Some philosophers who have held that all meaningful statements could be confirmed by observation and experiment have tried to reduce all scientific statements to statements about private sense perceptions. There is no empirical difference between their reductions and alternative theories that speak of real material objects and those that make metaphysical claims about occult entities, natures, and unobservable processes thought to cause certain observed phenomena. Observational data have not confirmed or refuted any of these different accounts. One of two empirically equivalent theories cannot be ruled out as a scientific theory just because it utilizes unobservable metaphysical entities.

Third, if two theories—A and B—are empirically equivalent and A solves internal or external conceptual problems better than B, then, all things being equal, A is to be preferred to B. If A involves an appeal to God and primary causes to explain, say, the origin of life, and B is the claim that there is an undiscovered natural mechanism, then A would be preferable to B, all things being equal, if A solves theological and philosophical problems not solved by B.

Objection 3: Explaining some phenomenon by a direct, primary causal act of God is not fruitful for guiding new research and yielding new empirically testable hypotheses in other areas of investigation. The idea violates the principle that "a scientific theory ought to be fruitful in guiding new research." Thus the practice of explaining something by an appeal to God's direct causation is not a scientific practice and should be excluded from natural science. As Richard Dickerson put it, "The most insidious evil of supernatural creationism is that it stifles curiosity and therefore blunts the intellect."[39]

Reply: First, something can be true without being fruitful. An appeal to God's primary causal activity could give a true explanation of some scientific phenomenon (the origin of the universe) without suggesting new lines of research.

Second, even if we grant that theistic scientists' use of theological concepts has not fruitfully suggested new lines of research (and this need not be granted), all that follows from this is that theistic scientists need to do more work developing their models, not that their models are not part of natural science.[40]

Third, an appeal to fruitfulness in the cases we are considering begs the question and represents a naive understanding of fruitfulness as a criterion for assessing the relative merits of rival hypotheses. Two rivals may solve a problem differently by depicting the phenomenon in question differently. Copernicus solved the motion of the planets by placing the sun in the center of the universe. Ptolemy solved that motion by a complicated set of orbitals with smaller orbitals. Each solution was different (and not necessarily of equal effectiveness).

Furthermore, the standards for what counts as a "good" solution may be determined differently by the competing models. Thus, often (though not always) the model itself, not its rival, sets the standards for adequacy in problem solving. Creationists and evolutionists do not need to attempt to solve a problem, say, a gap in the fossil record, in precisely the same way, nor do they need to employ the same types of solutions or value the same theory characteristics in their solutions. Creationists may elevate the epistemic virtue "solve theological or philosophical internal and external conceptual problems" above the epistemic virtue "offer solutions yielding fruitful lines of new research." There is nothing unscientific about this at all, and it is question-begging to claim that a criterion of "fruitfulness" set by one theory (say, the search for evolutionary mechanisms) should be most important for a rival theory, and that, if it is not, the rival is not even science.

Sometimes one rival will consider a phenomenon basic and not in need of a solution. It may, therefore, disallow questions about how or why that phenomenon occurs and thus hardly can be faulted for not being fruitful in suggesting lines of research on mechanisms that, according to the theory, do not exist. As Nicholas Rescher has pointed out: "One way in which a body of knowledge S can deal with a question is, of course, by *answering* it. Yet another, importantly different, way in which S can deal with a question is by disallowing it. S disallows [Q] when there is some presupposition of Q that S does not countenance: given S, we are simply not in a position to raise Q."[41] For example, motion was not natural in Aristotle's picture of the universe and thus examples of motion posed problems in need of explanation. In Newton's picture of the universe, however, uniform linear motion is natural, and only changes in motion pose problems in need of solution. Suppose a Newtonian and an Aristotelean are trying to solve the observational problem of how and why a particular body is moving in uniform linear motion. To solve the problem, the Aristotelean must tell how or why the body is moving, but the Newtonian can disallow the need for a solution by labeling the phenomenon as a basic given for which there cannot be a more basic mechanism to solve a how—question.

Similarly, for creationism, certain phenomena, like the origin of life or gaps in the fossil record, are not problems in need of solution beyond an appeal to the primary causal agency of God. They *are* problems for evolutionary theory, and fruitful lines of research for new mechanisms must be sought. However, it is naive and question-begging to fault creationists for not developing fruitful problem-solving strategies for such gaps. Because these phenomena are basic for creationists, such strategies are simply disallowed. In this case, it is enough for creationists to use theological notions to guide research for scientific tests that will establish the phenomena predicted by the theological constructs. Once the what-question is answered, no mechanistic how-question arises.[42]

It would seem, then, that while it is a major part of the practice of natural science, methodological naturalism does not adequately capture all of natural science. Its widespread acceptance by scientists may be due in part to the increasing specialization of the training that scientists undergo. The modern scientist is often out of touch with other areas of science, and he or she is usually unfamiliar with philosophy in general and the history and philosophy of science in particular. Since methodological naturalism is a philosophical view, this lack of familiarity is problematic. I am speculating here and, in any case, this observation does not apply to de Vries or Van Till. Nevertheless, in spite of its popularity, I conclude that (1) methodological naturalism, at least as presented by Paul de Vries and Howard J. Van Till, is inadequate as an entire model of natural science; (2) there is a "picture" of science (which needs further development) that allows theological concepts like "God" and "a direct act of God" to enter into the very fabric of natural science; and (3) certain standard objections against this "picture" fail. Recently, Alvin Plantinga has challenged Christian scholars to develop a "Theistic Science" that stands in sharp contrast to the view of science that adopts methodological naturalism.[43] This essay has been an attempt to second that challenge.

Notes

1. Thomas V. Morris, ed., *Divine and Human Action* (Cornell University Press), 3–4.
2. See A. R. Peacocke, "Introduction," in *The Sciences and Theology in the Twentieth Century,* ed. by A. R. Peacocke (University of Notre Dame Press, 1981), xiii-xv.
3. John Wiester and Phillip Johnson have suggested this term to me, although it has been used by Alvin Plantinga and others.
4. Michael Ruse, *Darwinism Defended* (Addison-Wesley, 1982), 322.
5. Ruse, *Darwinism Defended,* 322; cf. David Hull's review of Phillip Johnson's *Darwin on Trial* in *Nature,* 352 (August 8, 1991), 485–86.
6. For a recent lively debate involving Alvin Plantinga, Howard J. Van Till, Pattle Pun, and Ernan McMullin on the scientific status of creationist theories, see *Christian Scholar's Review,* (September 1991).
7. See Howard J. Van Till, Robert E. Snow, John H. Stek, Davis A. Young, *Portraits of Creation* (William B. Eerdmans Publishing Co., 1990), 127.
8. Cf. David L. Hull, *The Metaphysics of Evolution* (State University of New York Press, 1989), 62–75.
9. See Van Till, *Portraits of Creation;* Paul de Vries, "Naturalism in the Natural Sciences: A Christian Perspective," *Christian Scholar's Review,* 15 (1986), 388–96. All references in the text are to these two sources. See also, Howard J. Van Till, Davis A. Young, Clarence Menninga, *Science Held Hostage* (InterVarsity Press, 1988).
10. See J. P. Moreland, *Christianity and the Nature of Science* (Baker Book House, 1989), 95–98.
11. Cf. Larry Laudan, *Progress and Its Problems* (University of California Press, 1977); *Science and Values* (University of California Press, 1984); Bas C. van Fraassen, *The Scientific Image* (Oxford University Press, 1980).

12. For an example of this, see Eugene Fontinell, *Self, God and Immortality* (Temple University Press, 1986).
13. Van Till's claim that methodological naturalism focuses only on those qualities that are intrinsic (wholly resident within the empirically accessible physical universe) is difficult to sustain because, as a Platonist, I would argue that there is no such thing as a property that is wholly "resident" in the physical universe. Indeed, in my view, no property is itself physical, though a property may be "physical" in the sense that it can (or, perhaps, can only) be exemplified by a physical object. See J. P. Moreland, "How to Be a Nominalist in Realist Clothing," *Grazer Philosophische Studien*, 39 (1991), 75–101. Van Till seems oblivious to these problems.
14. Larry Laudan, "The Demise of the Demarcation Problem," in *Physics, Philosophy and Psychoanalysis*, ed. by R. S. Cohen, L. Laudan (Dordrecht, Holland: D. Reidel, 1983), 119.
15. For more on this, as well as the literature surrounding this discussion, see J. P. Moreland, *Christianity and the Nature of Science*, 19–42, 218–34.
16. Laudan, "The Demise of the Demarcation Problem," 125.
17. Neal C. Gillespie, *Charles Darwin and the Problem of Creation* (University of Chicago Press, 1979), especially chapters 1–2.
18. Philip Kitcher, *Abusing Science: The Case Against Creationism* (MIT Press, 1982), 125.
19. Saul Kripke, *Naming and Necessity* (Harvard University Press, 1972), 93–94.
20. See Laudan, *Progress and Its Problems*. Laudan combines his analysis of the place of empirical and conceptual problems in science with anti-realism. But these two theses are distinct, and one need not embrace anti-realism to recognize the fact that empirical and conceptual problems have been a significant part of the business of science throughout its history, although one's interpretation of the precise nature of that role will be informed by one's stand on the realism/anti-realism controversy.
21. Cf. Howard E. Gruber, *Darwin on Man: A Psychological Study of Scientific Creativity* (University of Chicago Press, 1974), 201–17; D. M. Armstrong, *A Materialist Theory of Mind* (Routledge

& Kegan Paul, 1968), 30; Arthur Peacocke and Grant Gillett, eds., *Persons and Personality* (Basil Blackwell, 1987), 55.

22. Paul Churchland, *Matter and Consciousness* (MIT Press, 1984), 21.

23. David Hull, *The Metaphysics of Evolution* (State University of New York, 1989), 74–75.

24. Theology (and philosophy) can also provide a metaphysical picture of what some entity is, and this can serve as part of a model for scientific investigation. Thus, both David Wiggins and Richard Connell have shown that philosophical arguments in support of viewing living organisms as genuine substances—things possessing natures, falling under natural kinds and maintaining unity and sameness through change—provide materials for (1) a rejection of any scientific or other tendency to reduce living organisms to either mere heaps, Lesniewskian sums, space-time worms, or property-things; and 2) a search for more specific substance-determining capacities and principles of individuation by biologists or other scientists. See David Wiggins, *Sameness and Substance* (Harvard University Press, 1980), 117–119; Richard Connell, *Substance and Modern Science* (University of Notre Dame Press, 1988). E. Mayr has argued that Darwinian evolution is hard to square with an essentialist, substantial view of living organisms. See *Populations, Species and Evolution* (Harvard University Press, 1970), 4. Thus, if philosophical or theological arguments exist for viewing living organisms as substance-things, these can serve as external conceptual problems for standard evolutionary orthodoxy.

25. There are some affinities between my picture of theological concepts in science and Nicholas Wolterstorff's notion of a theological control belief. See Nicholas Wolterstorff, *Reason within the Bounds of Religion* (William B. Eerdmans Publishing Co., 1984).

26. For a survey of different kinds of design-like properties, see J. P. Moreland, *Scaling the Secular City* (Baker Book House, 1987), 44–56.

27. The notion that personal agency, intention, and so forth, can be part of scientific explanation is ambiguous. It can either mean that certain phenomena that are accessible to scientific discovery, falsification and verification are best explained by

personal agency, or it can mean that there is a scientific explanation for the personal action itself. The former is what I mean by claiming that an intelligent designer can be used in scientific explanation. The latter is false and is, I believe, what Roderick Chisholm had in mind when he claimed that there would be no complete scientific account of human beings (since human action is not done by state-to-state causation but by agent causation.) My view is that personal agency (human or divine) can be at least scientific, but I do not believe that it is only scientific.

28. I am indebted to Mark D. Hartwig and Stephen C. Meyer for pointing out this example to me.
29. Cf. Richard DeCharms, "Personal Causation, Agency and the Self," in *The Book of the Self: Person, Pretext and Process,* ed. by Polly Young-Eisendrath and James Hill (New York University Press, 1987), 384–403; M. Brewster Smith, "Perspectives on Selfhood," *American Psychologist,* 33 (December 1978), 1053–1063.
30. DeCharms, "Personal Causation, Agency and the Self," 18.
31. I owe this point to Stephen C. Meyer and Mark D. Hartwig.
32. Recall Ruse's claim, cited earlier, that if Scientific Creationism were successful in making its case, it would not yield a scientific explanation of origins, but rather would prove that there is no scientific explanation of origins. Even if we grant Ruse this point, it would follow that Scientific Creationism is not science only if we were to grant the further point that science is exhausted by the practice of explanation (and a specific sort of explanation at that, i.e., a covering law model of explanation or a realist causal-model type of explanation that can use only naturalistic concepts as part of its model). But, as we have seen, there is no good reason to grant this further point.
33. For more on agent action, state-to-state causation and agent causation, see William P. Alston, "God's Action in the World," in *Evolution and Creation,* ed. by Ernan McMullin (University of Notre Dame Press, 1985), 197–220; William Rowe, "Two Concepts of Freedom," *Proceedings of the American Philosophical Association,* Supplementary Volume 61 (Sept. 1987), 43–64; Stewart C. Goetz, "A Noncausal Theory of Agency," *Philosophy and Phenomenological Research,* 49 (December 1988), 303–316; Roderick Chisholm, *On Metaphysics* (University of Minnesota

Press, 1989), 3–15; John Bishop, *Natural Agency* (Cambridge University Press, 1989).

34. I am using "agency" and "agent causation" to stand for two different views: (1) agents as substances cause their own actions; (2) agents as substances simply act by exercising their causal powers; such acts are uncaused and done for reasons. Either approach leaves room for genuine agency and libertarian freedom and contrasts with state-to-state causation. Recently, Dennis M. Senchuk has argued for wholes with emergent properties that, qua wholes, can feedback causal action to their parts. See his "Consciousness Naturalized: Supervenience Without Physical Determinism," *American Philosophical Quarterly,* 28 (January 1991), 37–47. Unfortunately, Senchuk's view is still deterministic because he only allows for state-to-state causation and not agency as I am using it here. For a treatment of how dualism and agent causation relates to the first law of thermodynamics, see Robert Larma, "Mind-Body Interaction and the Conservation of Energy," *International Philosophical Quarterly,* 26 (September 1986), 277–85.

35. This point is made repeatedly by Phillip Johnson, who asks in a number of different ways what it is that God actually did to bring the world and life into existence. See his *Darwin on Trial* (Regnery Gateway, 1991).

36. Alvin Plantinga, "Evolution, Neutrality and Antecedent Probability: A Reply to McMullin and Van Till," *Christian Scholar's Review,* 21 (September 1991), 86–87.

37. An exception to this rule would be in cases where there are theological or philosophical reasons for thinking that God acts directly and by means of primary agent-causal ways in a regular way, e.g., in regeneration.

38. David Hull, review of Phillip Johnson, *Darwin on Trial,* in *Nature,* 352 (August 8, 1991), 485–86.

39. Richard E. Dickerson, "The Game of Science: Reflections After Arguing with Some Rather Overwrought People," *Perspectives on Science and Christian Faith,* 44 (June 1992), 137.

40. It may be thought that creationism has been around a very long time and that creationists have had more than enough time to develop their models. But I do not think that this is the case. It is certainly true that creationism has been around a

"very long time" if we regard it as a research program. But more specific creationist theories get refined and replaced from time to time, and it seems to me that current creationist theories, while sharing important features with creationist theories of, say, the nineteenth century, still have important new features that justify the claim that more time is legitimately required for modern creationists to develop their contemporary models.

41. Nicholas Rescher, *The Limits of Science* (University of California Press, 1984), 22.

42. It should be added that some appeals to fruitfulness actually distort an intellectual issue. For example, William Bechtel argues that of two views regarding the relationship between mental states and brain states—the two are different but correlated (property or substance dualism); or the two are identical (type or token identity physicalism)—the identity thesis can be judged as the superior position based on the fruitfulness of the scientific research program that follows from it. See *Philosophy of Mind* (Lawrence Erlbaum Associates, 1988), 101–103. This recommendation distorts the proper order of analysis regarding the mind/body problem (philosophy is more basic and important than is science), and in any case, whatever research program the identity thesis generates, the same research program, perhaps with very minor modifications, could be generated from the dualist correlation position.

43. Alvin Plantinga, "When Faith and Reason Clash: Evolution and the Bible," *Christian Scholar's Review*, 21 (September 1991), 29–31.

When Faith and Reason Meet

Howard J. Van Till

Howard J. Van Till is chairman of the Department of Physics and Professor of Physics and Astronomy at Calvin College, where he has been a faculty member for a quarter of a century. With numerous articles and reviews to his credit, he is the author of *The Fourth Day: What the Bible and the Heavens are telling us about the Creation* (1986), and co-author of *Science Held Hostage: What's Wrong with Creation Science AND Evolutionism* (1988) and *Portraits of Creation: Biblical and Scientific Perspectives on the World's Formation* (1990).

Adversaries, Isolationists or Allies?

Those of us who pay attention to the way in which North American Christians view natural science are painfully aware that the present state of affairs leaves considerable room for improvement. And the responsibility for effecting that improvement must, I submit, be shared equally by scientists and Christian believers. What about those of us who belong to both communities? Double responsibility would seem to be our lot; perhaps that accounts for my personal efforts in this arena.

I am a Christian believer who is trained in physics and astronomy. Having been nurtured within a heritage that assumes careful thought and sincere faith to be allies, I have become increasingly frustrated by the adversarial framework of the resurgent creation-evolution debate. Hence, during the past decade I have committed the majority of my professional effort to clarifying the discussion of the proper rela-

---

A version of this essay appeared as "Is Special Creationism a Heresy?" *Christian Scholar's Review* 22, 4 (June 1993). Reprinted by permission.

tionship of natural science to Christian belief. Clearly, my project is far from finished.

Much of the public discussion of this topic is cast in the framework of a perceived tension (some would call it a warfare) between faith and reason. Those who side with faith might argue that humble Christian faith is sure to hold the position of virtue over the pride and arrogance often associated with human reason. On the other hand, those who side with reason might argue that a carefully reasoned evaluation of well-crafted theories based on empirical investigation is sure to be superior to positions dogmatically held on the basis of faith alone (especially when faith is perceived to be no more than a blind confidence in some traditional authority). In this adversarial atmosphere, those of us who wish to be at once faithful to the Christian heritage and reasonable in our evaluation of scientific theories face a difficult task. Is it possible to resolve the tension? What ought to happen when faith and reason meet? Should they engage in heated battle? I think not. Should they instead turn their backs on one another, each proceeding in blissful confidence of the other's irrelevance? I do not find that response any better than warfare. As I see it, the only path toward growth in understanding of these issues is the one on which faith and reason stroll side by side in earnest and constructive dialogue—each desiring to learn from the other. What follows, then, is intended to be a small contribution to that conversation.

Macroevolution Under Attack

Several years ago I published a book that the publishers chose to title *The Fourth Day.* It featured a lengthy but more informative subtitle: *What the Bible and the Heavens are telling us about the Creation.* In this book I explored the relationship of biblically-informed Christian beliefs and empirically-informed scientific theories regarding the formative history of the physical universe. Scientific considerations were focused almost exclusively on the evolution of those inanimate objects and structures of interest to astronomy and cosmology—planets, stars and galaxies. On only one or two pages did I make passing reference to the possibility of biological evolution, noting that, in principle, I had no objections to it on either scientific or theological grounds. But guess which pages are by far the most often cited by anxious critics?

The possibility of common ancestry among all of God's creatures is evidently a frightening and distasteful concept to millions of North American Christians. Many treat the macroevolutionary paradigm, which envisions an uninterrupted genealogical continuity from the first life-forms to us, with an unreasoned, ill-informed and sometimes ill-mannered hostility that will ultimately be self-defeating. In the present context, however, I need say no more about that kind of stance.

I would prefer to address instead the more persuasively formulated skepticism toward Darwinism that such persons as Phillip Johnson (Professor of Law, University of California at Berkeley) and Alvin Plantinga (Professor of Philosophy, Notre Dame University) have articulated.[1]

My first question is, why the skepticism? Why do the majority of North American Christians treat the macroevolutionary paradigm with such skepticism?[2] The answer to this question of motivation is probably far more complex than any one of us might imagine, but let us consider a brief list of likely factors.

(1) Does today's skepticism toward the macroevolutionary paradigm stem primarily from the reasoned judgment that there is insufficient empirical support for this concept, or perhaps that the evidence even undercuts it? Much of contemporary anti-evolutionary rhetoric is directed toward the goal of establishing this thesis—and we must admit that, as with all scientific theories, the data provide less than exhaustively conclusive evidence for evolutionary models. Nonetheless, I am not personally convinced that this is the primary reason that critics reject this particular concept. I suspect that other factors are playing more decisive roles.

(2) Does today's skepticism toward the macroevolutionary paradigm, a paradigm characterized by natural processes and

genealogical continuity, stem from the judgment that the Bible, taken at face value, requires its believers to picture creation as a series of irruptive acts in time—commonly labeled "miraculous interventions"—that break the continuity of natural phenomena? Or, to rephrase the question, is evolution—even "theistic" evolution"—when judged by biblical and historic Christian standards, a heresy? Many people genuinely believe this to be so (and I must respect their sincerity), but critics like Johnson and Plantinga insist that their skepticism toward evolutionary continuity is not at all based on biblical literalism. In any case, however, I shall soon argue that representative and highly respected shapers of early Christian thought favored a picture of the world's formative history that was marked, not by a series of irruptive interventions in the course of time, but by a continuity of natural phenomena. Hence, for persons who have been exposed to the thought of Patristic writers like St. Basil and St. Augustine, the question might be, Is *special creationism* a heresy?

(3) Does today's skepticism toward the macroevolutionary paradigm stem from the judgment that it is merely the product of the naturalistic worldview being foisted upon modern Western culture by an anti-theistic intellectual establishment? On this question, credentialed skeptics like Johnson and Plantinga appear to join the young-earth creationists in hearty agreement that the popularity of the evolutionary paradigm is nothing more than the consequence of naturalistic propaganda. We are, they say, the unwary victims of a grand hoax perpetrated by the pompous preachers of metaphysical naturalism.

I must admit that Johnson, Plantinga and others are correct in calling attention to the vocal advocates of naturalism who stridently assert that if the common ancestry thesis is true then there is "nothing left for a creator to do,"[3] or that "Darwin made it possible to be an intellectually fulfilled atheist."[4] But how should Christians and other theists respond to such bold assertions? Many have responded by rejecting the concept of evolutionary continuity, the concept on which Dawkins and company base their apologetic claims for the enhanced credibility of atheism.

My own response, however, is quite different. Like the critics of contemporary Darwinism, I judge that the phenomena of random mutation and natural selection by themselves are conceptually insufficient to account for the formative history of the present array of life-forms.[5] On the other hand, for reasons that will soon become apparent, I find nothing inherently objectionable in the concept of genealogical continuity. But while we need not, in my estimation, reject the concept of common ancestry, we do have every right to reject the Dawkinsian leap from the *common ancestry thesis* to the *no Creator thesis,* because the latter simply does not follow from the former.

(4) Finally, might the contemporary skepticism toward the macroevolutionary paradigm have grown largely out of an apologetic fear that naturalism could be correct in asserting, "If there are no gaps, then there is no need for a creator"? I suspect that this fear may be far more important as a motivating factor than most skeptics would care to admit. For Christian theists, however, the good news is that this apologetic fear, although it may have become common during the past few centuries, is entirely unwarranted and would most likely have been soundly rejected by such early Christian theologians as St. Basil and St. Augustine.

Of Gaps and God

In order to prepare ourselves to see the contemporary relevance of the way in which St. Basil and St. Augustine pictured the creative activity of God, let us begin with the following question: according to historic, biblically-informed theism, what sort of a Creation did God bring into being at the beginning? It was a rationally intelligible world, because the Creation is called to declare the glory of its rational and thoughtful Creator, and because God has prepared our minds to perceive that glory. It was an orderly world, because the orderliness of the Creation bears witness to the Creator's sense of order and coherence.

What kind of order was it? Ancient and medieval cosmologies commonly incorporated the concept of static hierarchical order in both the celestial and terrestrial realms. In the realm of life-forms, not only did they think it possible to order the whole array of creatures hierarchically from lowest to highest, or from simplest to most complex, but they also assumed that beings on one rung of the ladder of "kinds" were so different from those on the next that no conceivable natural process could transform one kind into another. They sought to assemble cosmic history from the individual histories of each kind of creature acting within the permanently fixed boundaries of its being.

Of course that cosmological picture has been replaced by another. The static hierarchy of planetary and celestial spheres has been replaced by the dynamic picture of an expanding universe in which chemical elements, galaxies, stars and planets have a formative history. New forms and structures of matter appear in the course of time as the products of ordinary physical processes that the disciplines of astrophysics and cosmology are coming, we believe, to understand progressively better.

This historical appearance of new forms is found also in the arena of living creatures. Contrary to the assumptions that shaped the ancient and medieval world-picture with its static hierarchy of forms, the array of creatures we see today was not always present. The first life-forms to appear were relatively simple; today both simple and complex forms are present and remarkably diverse. Numerous forms that once thrived are now extinct.

How might these successive life-forms be related? If one insists that differences in ontology (being) or morphology (structure) are too great to be bridged by ordinary creaturely processes, then the pathway of genealogical continuity would have to be ruled out.

What could be put in its place? In the time of St. Basil and St. Augustine (4th and 5th centuries, A.D.) the concept of a spontaneous generation of each kind posed few problems. Now, of course, such a picture would be unthinkable. Instead, many of my fellow Christians now seem to prefer the concept of "special creations" by miraculous divine interventions" in the course of the world's formative history.

In the context of our present knowledge about the temporal succession of life-forms over a multi-billion-year span of time, however, appealing to the concept of special creation leads to a profoundly significant implication concerning what sort of world the Creator brought into being: *the economy of this created world must be developmentally incomplete.* That is to say, the whole system of creaturely capacities (what matter and material systems are capable of doing) must be characterized by built-in barriers or deficiencies in its developmental system that require the Creator to perform extraordinary creative acts in the formative history of the world to cause new forms of life (including the first form of life) to appear at the times indicated in the paleontological record.

Hence, the concepts of special creation and gaps in the developmental system of the created world go hand-in-hand. Here, then, is the perceived apologetic link between gaps and God: Creation's developmental economy includes gaps that only the miraculous interventions of God the Creator could bridge.

Of St. Basil, St. Augustine and Functional Integrity

Those who defend a special creationist picture of God's creative work often appeal to the biblical formula, "Let there be.... and it was so," presuming this formula to certify unequivocally that the Creator's commands were effected *immediately*—both in the sense of "without delay in time" and in the sense of "without employment of ordinary creaturely powers." There is, however, a different way to understand the same biblical language. Recall, for instance, the following texts from Genesis 1 that report the expression of God's will for the formation of living creatures:

> v. 11 Let the earth make itself green with grass, with seed-bearing plants, with fruit trees bearing fruit according to their types with their seed in them on the earth.

v. 20 Let the waters swarm with swarming things, living creatures, and let birds fly about over the earth across the firmament of the heavens.

v. 24 Let the earth produce living creatures according to their types: cattle, creeping things, and wild animals according to their types. [translation by Gordon J. Wenham]

In each case the Creator calls upon earthly material to do something. The sovereign King of Creation speaks, and Creation must respond. The earth must make itself green with grass, plants and trees. The waters must give rise to the swarming activity of sea creatures. The earth must produce cattle, creeping things and wild animals. The Creator does not speak words of magic that have coercive or manipulative power over earthly material, but words of royal edict that call upon the earth and water to use their resident capacities—the gifts of active being that the Creator has already given them—to produce the plants and animals that the Creator had in mind.

This is a Creation endowed with *functional integrity.* The Creator has equipped it to do whatever He calls upon it to do. It suffers no gaps or deficiencies in its economy that need to be bridged either by words of magic or by the Creator's direct manipulation. This "doctrine of Creation's functional integrity," as I wish to call it, has deep roots in the history of Christian theology. I make no pretense here of offering an exhaustive or disinterested historical review of the relevant literature, but for the limited purpose of illustrating the point, let us look briefly at two relatively early Christian theologians, St. Basil of Caesarea (330–379) and St. Augustine of Hippo (354–430).

St. Basil's HEXAEMERON[6]

In the judgment of many, "St. Basil's work on the *Hexaemeron* is one of the most important Patristic works on the doctrine of creation.[7] Delivered as a series of nine homilies, this work has the style of material spoken to inspire praise of the Creator, not the style of a treatise written to be subjected to philosophical or theological scrutiny; its central concern is the meaningful relationship between God and mankind, not the relationship of natural philosophy and Christian theology. Nevertheless, I find it an instructive exercise to examine St. Basil's homilies for their general concept of the nature of the created world and the character of God's creative activity. For our limited purposes, we may set aside numerous details that St. Basil articulated in the conceptual vocabulary of Aristotelian science in order to focus on broad principles and important presuppositions.

Consistent with the way in which early Christian theologians had come to articulate the doctrine of creation, St. Basil affirms his conviction that the existence of the world is neither eternal nor self-caused. Rather, the effective will of a transcendent Creator, who created the world we see from nothing, provided both the origin of the world's existence and its beginning in time. Therefore, whatever the visible world's properties and capacities may be, these must be seen as endowments freely and thoughtfully contributed by the Creator alone—St. Basil can conceive of no other source.

Summarized as succinctly as possible, St. Basil's picture[8] of creation is one in which God, by the unconstrained impulse of his effective will, instantaneously called the substance of the entire Creation into being at the beginning and gave to the several created substances the harmoniously integrated powers to actualize, in the course of time, the wonderful array of specific forms that the Creator had in mind from the outset. God's primary act of creation produced both matter and the forms it was later to attain. In contrast to those philosophers who spoke of a creator adding form to preexistent matter, St. Basil says: "But God, before all those things that now attract our notice existed, after casting about in his mind and determining to bring into being that which had no being, imagined the world such as it ought to be, and created matter in harmony with the form which He wished to give it" (II.3). Reflecting on the earth's initial lack of adornment with grass, cornfields or forests, St. Basil notes that, "Of all this nothing was yet produced; the earth was in travail with it in virtue of the power that she had received from the Creator. But she was waiting for the appointed time and the divine order to bring forth" (II.3).

In St. Basil's judgment, harmony, balance and provision for all future needs are characteristics of the created world that deserve our profound appreciation. Both fire and water, for example, are necessary for the economy of terrestrial life as we know it. But these two elements (as understood in St. Basil's day) must be provided in correct proportions so that neither one will consume the other. Observing the comfortable balance that appeared to prevail between these two contending substances, St. Basil says that we owe "thanks to the foresight of the supreme Artificer, Who, from the beginning, foresaw what was to come, and at the first provided all for the future needs of the world" (III.5). From this it follows, of course, that the Creator need make no special adjustments at some later date to compensate for inadequate provision at the beginning. "He who, according to the word of Job, knows the number of the drops of rain, knew how long His work would last, and for how much consumption of fire he ought to allow. This is the reason for the abundance of water at the creation" (III.5).

Because each element is called upon to contribute its natural activity to the functional arrangement and operation of the created world, St. Basil must make clear that even these natures are the products of God's creative word, not manifestations of any powers independent of God. "Think, in reality, that a word of God makes the nature, and that this order is for the creature a direction for its future course" (IV.2). Why, for instance, does water flow from higher to lower places? Says St. Basil, "It was ordered that it should be the natural property of water to flow, and in obedience to this order, the waters are never weary in their course" (IV.3).[9]

St. Basil sees the divine command recorded in Gen. 1:11, "Let the earth bring forth grass . . . ," as God empowering the earth for all time to assemble and sustain all manner of plant life. This command from God "gave fertility and the power to produce fruit for all ages to come" (V.1). In several ways St. Basil expresses his conviction that, although the Creator's word is spoken in an instant, the Creation's obedient response is extended in time. "God did not command the earth immediately to give forth seed and fruit, but to produce germs, to grow green, and to arrive at maturity in the seed; so that this first command teaches nature what she has to do in the course of the ages" (V.5). In language that seems almost to anticipate modern scientific concepts St. Basil goes on to say that, "Like tops, which after the first impulse, continue their evolutions, turning themselves when once fixed in their centre; thus nature, receiving the impulse of this first command, follows without interruption the course of the ages, until the consummation of all things" (V.10). Later, speaking against the Manicheans, St. Basil emphasized that the earth did not simply uncover things already living within it, but that it was empowered by God to produce what was not yet a realized form. "He who gave the order at the same time gifted it with the grace and power to bring forth" (VIII.1). This is consistent with an earlier comment on the Holy Spirit's activity in creation: "The Spirit . . . prepared the nature of water to produce living beings" (II.6).

In his reflections on the words, "Let the earth bring forth the living creature," St. Basil speaks eloquently of the Creation actively carrying out the effective will of the Creator. "Behold the word of God pervading creation, beginning even then the efficacy that is seen displayed today, and will be displayed to the end of the world! As a ball, which one pushes, if it meet a declivity, descends, carried by its form and the nature of the ground and does not stop until it has reached a level surface; so nature, once put in motion by the Divine command, traverses creation with an equal step through birth and death, and keeps up the succession of kinds through resemblance, to the last" (IX.2).

Consistent with the world picture of his day, St. Basil, of course, envisions no historical transformation of these varied kinds; at the same time he offers no theological objection whatever to the concept of spontaneous generation of living creatures from earthly substance alone. For instance, "We see mud alone produce eels; they do not proceed from an egg, nor in any other manner; it is the earth alone which gives them birth. 'Let the earth produce a living creature'" (IX.2). St. Basil apparently envisions the first appearance of each kind of living creature as having occurred in like manner, the earth having been endowed from the beginning with all of the powers necessary to realize physically the whole array of life-forms created in the mind of God. The elements of the world, which God created from nothing at the beginning, lacked none of the capacities that they would need in the course of the ages to bring forth what God intended. The economy of the created world was, from the outset, complete—neither cluttered with things that had no useful function nor lacking any capacity integral to its function. In St. Basil's words, "Our God has created nothing unnecessarily and has omitted nothing that is necessary" (VIII.7).

I shall close this brief survey of St. Basil's *Hexaemeron* by calling attention to the high value that St. Basil placed on the systematic investigation of the created world. In his discussion of the fourth day of the creation narrative St. Basil soundly condemns the foolishness of astrology (especially for its unwarranted extrapolation from stellar configurations to human destinies), but he has words of praise for the proper science of astronomy. "[T]here are many other discoveries about the size and distance of the sun and the moon to which any one who will make a serious study of their action and of their characteristics may arrive by the aid of reason" (VI.11). Furthermore, speaking against basing one's concept of celestial bodies on superficial appearance alone, St. Basil says that, "We must not then measure the moon with the eye, but with reason. Reason, for the discovery of truth, is much surer than the eye." (VI.11). This reason was not isolated from observation, to be sure, but was stimulated and constrained by observation in the manner that St. Basil himself exemplified. Reason was not the adversary of faith, but rather its constructively informative partner.

St. Augustine's DE GENESI AD LITTERAM[10]

In his work, *De Genesi ad litteram, The Literal Meaning of Genesis,* St. Augustine provides an extensive commentary on the first three chapters of Genesis. His goal is to demonstrate a one-to-one correspondence between the text of these chapters and what actually took place in the creative work of God; in fact, this is precisely how he defines the term "literal" in this endeavor.[11] In contrast to modern biblical literalism, however, St. Augustine shows no disdain for interpreting certain words and phrases in early Genesis in a figurative sense, but even these figurative readings are firmly bounded by the controlling assumption that Genesis 1–3 is "a faithful record of what happened" (1.1.1).

In constructing his literal reading, St. Augustine makes extensive use of the analogy of Scripture; he often decides the meanings of words or phrases in Genesis by comparing them with other relevant texts. St. Augustine is equally insistent, however, that the literal meaning derived in this way may never stand in contradiction to one's competently derived knowledge about "the earth, the heavens, and the other elements of this world," knowledge that one rightfully "holds to as being certain from reason and experience" (1.19.39). In a tone that leaves no doubt concerning his attitude, St. Augustine soundly reprimands those Christians who defend interpretations of Scripture that any scientifically knowledgeable non-Christian would recognize as nonsense. "Reckless and incompetent expounders of Holy Scripture bring untold trouble and sorrow on their wiser brethren when they are caught in one of their mischievous false opinions and are taken to task by those who are not bound by the authority of our sacred books" (1.19.39).

For a number of reasons, St. Augustine, like St. Basil, concludes that God created "all things together" in one initial, all-inclusive and instantaneous creative act. The six-day structure of the narrative conveys something other than a succession of temporal periods to be placed on the human calendar. For St. Augustine the days represent both a topically ordered set of divine revelations to the angels (2.8) and a textual accommodation to the limited powers of comprehension of those who now read the Scriptural account (4.33.52). Furthermore, the number six has a mathematical significance as a "perfect" number, a number that is the sum of its factors [6 = 1x2x3 and 6 = 1 + 2 + 3] (4.2).

The initial and simultaneous creation of "all things together," reported to us within the literary framework of a six-day narrative, should not be taken to mean that all created things suddenly materialized in mature form at the beginning. With considerable labor and repetition, St. Augustine developed a rather sophisticated program of interpretation by which he sought to distinguish what took place at the beginning from what took place in the course of time. In the beginning, according to St. Augustine, God called into being all created substance and all creaturely forms. At this beginning all created forms existed both in the mind of God and in the formable substances of the created world. In the formable substances, however, the creaturely forms existed only potentially, not actually. Although the creaturely forms were not yet actualized in visible, material beings, these forms were there potentially in the powers and capacities, called by St. Augustine "causal reasons" or "seed principles," with which the Creator had originally endowed the created substances. In summary, the material of the created world, initially created in an unformed but formable state, has possessed from the outset a full spectrum of causal reasons that enable it, in the course of time, to give material forms to all of the creatures to which the mind of God originally gave conceptual form.

Perhaps we should let St. Augustine speak for himself on this issue. "But from the beginning of the ages, when day was made, the world is said to have been formed, and in its elements at the same time there were laid away the creatures that would later spring forth with the passage of time, plants and animals, each according to its kind" (6.1.2). "In all these things, beings already created received at their own proper time their manner of being and acting, which developed into visible forms and natures from the hidden and invisible reasons which are latent in creation as causes" (6.10.17). " ... [W]hat He had originally established here in causes He later fulfilled in effects" (6.11.19). Finally, "... some works belonged to the invisible days in which He created all things simultaneously, and others belong to the days in which He daily fashions whatever evolves in the course of time from what I might call the primordial wrappers" (6.6.9).

Lest we be tempted to infer that St. Augustine is thereby proposing a macroevolutionary scenario in which these emerging life-forms are genealogically related in a continuous line of descent with modification, we must immediately note that he in fact offers no scientific theory regarding material mechanisms and no suggestion whatsoever of any historical modification of the created "kinds." Consistent with the world-picture of his day, St. Augustine envisioned each unique "kind" of creature to have been individually conceptualized in the Creator's initial act of creation and independently actualized as the causal reasons functioned to give material form to the conceptual forms created at the beginning. Standing in the tradition of a hierarchically structured cosmos populated with fixed kinds of creatures, St. Augustine had good reason to envision the independent creation and formation of each kind. Further, without any knowledge of genetic variability or of the temporal succession of life-forms over a multi-billion-year span of time, St. Augustine had no basis for questioning either that tradition or the concept of spontaneous generation. St. Augustine made appropriate use of both his heritage and the conceptual vocabulary of his time.

I wish to draw attention, however, not to the details of St. Augustine's portrait of God's creative work as articulated in the vocabulary of his day, but to one of his underlying presuppositions concerning the character of the created world: the universe was brought into being in a less than fully formed state but endowed with capacities to transform itself, in conformity with God's will, from unformed matter into a marvelous array of structures (e.g., dry land separating from oceans) and life-forms. In other words, St. Augustine envisioned a Creation that was, from the instant of its inception, characterized by *functional integrity.* Every category of structure, creature and process was conceptualized by the Creator from the beginning but actualized in time as the created material employed its God-given capacities in the manner and at the time that the Creator intended from the outset.[12]

St. Augustine envisioned a created world that the Creator had endowed with a functionally complete economy. When the Creator said, "Let the earth bring forth . . .," the earth had no right to reply, "Do it yourself, God, for by your omission I am lacking the capacities to do what you ask." Instead, the earth was able to bring forth simply by employing the God-given capacities of its creaturely being—no gaps, no deficiencies in Creation's economy, no need for God to overpower matter or to act in the same manner as creature in order to make up for capacities missing in the economy of the created world.

From Functional Integrity to Evolutionary Creation

I am well aware that for many persons the term "evolutionary creation" may appear to be an oxymoron of the highest order. Having been told by biblical literalists and philosophical materialists alike that we must choose *either* creation *or* evolution, how can we view a term like "evolutionary creation" as anything but double-talk?

Nonetheless, our reflections on Patristic portraits of God's creative work would serve well as a basis for giving substantive meaning to this term. In the Christian tradition, to see the world as a Creation is to see it as something that owes both its existence and its economy to the free and effective will of its Creator. As such, the title "Creation" by itself provides no clues concerning either the story line or the details of its formative history. For clues of this sort we must, I believe, go directly to the created world and employ the best of empirical science.[13]

By employing the term "evolutionary" in this context I mean to call attention to a prevalent feature in the story line of Creation's formative history—a feature contributed by modern science. As I would use the term, it simply calls attention to the idea of continuous historical development for both physical structures (galaxies, stars, planets) and life-forms as part of the normal operation of the created world. Given the discovery of structural relationships, genetic variability and temporal succession of species among life-forms, the concept of evolutionary continuity would soon surface as worthy of both empirical and theoretical investigation.

This concept of evolutionary creation emphatically would not constitute a radical departure from the historic Christian doctrine of creation. Although the details of an evolutionary creation scenario might differ significantly from those of traditional independent creation scenarios, I see no strain at all at the level of fundamental doctrine.[14]

On the contrary, I would argue that if one were to begin with the doctrine of Creation's functional integrity (as we described it in our review of St. Basil and St. Augustine), add the empirical discovery of the temporal succession of life-forms and disallow the concept of spontaneous generation (mud to eels, for instance), then one would have the broad concepts of genealogical continuity and descent with modification nearly at hand. Add to this the successes of geology, astronomy and cosmology in reconstructing the continuous formative histories of earth, stars, galaxies, elements and space-time—each of which presupposes the functional integrity of the universe—and the portrait of an evolutionary creation is practically ready for framing and display in the narthex of one's local church.[15]

As scientifically informed Christians seeking to articulate our faith in the twentieth century, we would offer this portrait as our attempt to capture the vision of a universe brought into being from nothing and pregnant with potentialities conceived in the mind of the Creator. In a manner rich with both pattern and novelty, both continuity and freedom, both coherence and contingency, some of these latent potentialities would be actualized in the course of time—galaxies and galagos, stars and starfish, planets and planaria, hulking quasars and human beings.

Given only our knowledge of atoms and atomic behavior, I believe that we would have no right to expect the formation of such awesome structures and wondrous creatures, but yet—by God's thoughtful provision of these potentialities from the beginning of space and time until the present—these awesome wonders have been achieved, not by matter apart from God, but by matter created and enabled by God to accomplish what he intended. Admittedly, our development of the doctrine of Creation's functional integrity has emphasized the absence of gaps in the created world's developmental economy, but we must also note that the concept of Creation's gapless economy does not in any way entail the requirement that the Creation is either independent of God or closed to interaction with him. Functional integrity is *not* equivalent to absolute autonomy. To recognize the functional integrity of the Creation does not entail reducing the Creator either to the remote God of deism or to the unnecessary god of atheism.[16]

And what about miracles? Would they be disallowed or downgraded in a Creation marked by a gapless economy? Not at all. In fact, the status of miracles would be elevated. Special creationist scenarios appear to require numerous "miraculous divine interventions"—mandatory supplements to the incomplete economy of the created world. Without them there would be no way to bridge the gaps conceived to be characteristic of Creation's developmental history. In a Creation marked by functional integrity, however, miracles would no longer be obligatory; instead, they would be voluntary acts of God freely performed for their special revelatory or redemptive value.

Some persons assert that the concepts of common ancestry and evolutionary continuity steal all creative power from the Creator and give it instead to molecular matter. But no molecule, not even DNA, can *create* a new creature. At most, DNA can use its capacity for variation to explore what might be called "possibility space," and thereby *discover* novel forms that are viable in the environment at hand.[17] And why is possibility space so richly arrayed with viable structures and connecting pathways if not because the Creator chose thoughtfully and intelligently to provide these potentialities from the beginning?

Other persons say that if one cannot capture purpose

in the impersonal descriptions of molecular mechanisms, then no purpose is there, or anywhere. Such talk, I say, is nonsense. Even molecular randomness is well within the reach of the Creator's purposive employment. Randomness at one level is no enemy of either pattern or purpose when examined within an enlarged arena of consideration.[18] Discussions of purpose always require a context larger than physics, chemistry or biology. Instead of jumping from the recognition of random molecular variations to the conclusion of purposelessness, I am inclined to propose that these variations may be essential to the achievement of God's purposes for the formative history of the created world.

Some persons say that genealogical continuity and the thesis of common ancestry leave no gaps for special acts of miraculous intervention to bridge. I say, Good! That forces me to stand humbly before my Creator with an even greater sense of awe. Try to imagine what creativity would be required to bring into being a world with such thoughtfully conceived capacities that it could travel from a big-bang beginning to the universe of stunning structures and complex creatures now present along the pathway of coherence and continuity—no shortcuts, no gaps bridged by *ad hoc* special effects. That may require more creativity than the human mind can imagine, but who are we to impose human limits on God?

From the Dialogue of Faith and Reason to Conclusions

Finally, what conclusions might we draw from all that we have considered so far? What might we identify as the product of this brief meeting of faith and reason? I would propose the following as two especially important summary statements:

(1) The modern special creationist picture of God's creative work as a series of "divine miraculous interventions" in the course of time does *not* comport with the vision of Patristic scholars like St. Basil and St. Augustine. Hence, the rhetoric that treats special creationism as if it were an inviolable

"deliverance of the faith" is simply indefensible, and this needs to be more widely known both within and outside of the Christian community.

(2) We ought *not* to treat the fundamental presupposition of the macroevolutionary model—that a wholeness unbroken by gaps or deficiencies characterizes the developmental economy of the physical universe (including the historical stream of life-forms)—as if it were the adversary of the Christian doctrine of creation, but rather as a vision that is wholly consistent with the historic doctrine of Creation's functional integrity. Hence, the rhetoric that treats all evolutionary scenarios as if they were by nature subverters or defeaters of the faith is simply indefensible, and this needs to be more widely known both within and outside of the Christian community.

What, then, is our answer to the provocative (some might say excessively polemical) question used as the subtitle for this essay? Must we conclude that special creationism is a heresy? Have we made a case for such a strong charge as this? I judge that we have not. Although the modern special creationist scenario for Creation's formative history may lack convincing biblical, theological or empirical warrant, the charge of heresy seems inordinately strong. While many of us may deeply regret the way that special creationism's anti-evolution rhetoric has come to be popularly associated with Christian belief, thereby placing many persons in the painful position of having to choose between intellectual integrity and Christian faith, the charge of heresy still strikes me as excessive. I am convinced that special creationism should be rejected, but I am not asking that it be condemned.

The formative history of the world we know as God's Creation is far richer in wondrous phenomena than our imagination or theorizing will ever be able to capture. Nonetheless, I expect that we will be able to grow in our knowledge and understanding of some of these phenomena, and that in this endeavor we will be immensely aided by the doctrine of Creation's functional integrity—a vision regarding the character of the universe that has already proved to be one of the most fruitful concepts ever employed in our scientific enterprise.

Notes

1. See, for instance, Phillip Johnson's *Darwin on Trial* (InterVarsity Press, 1991) and Alvin Plantinga's essay, "When Faith and Reason Clash: Evolution and the Bible," in *Christian Scholar's Review,* 21,1 (September 1991): 8–32.
2. See the statistics from a recent Gallup Poll as reported in *U.S. News & World Report,* December 23, 1991, 59.
3. Sentiments to this effect may be found in the works of Carl Sagan, Stephen Hawking, William Provine, P. W. Atkins, and others who present the concept of evolution in the framework of a naturalistic worldview.
4. Richard Dawkins, *The Blind Watchmaker* (W.W. Norton and Co., 1986), 6.
5. Mutation and selection may be essential components of the dynamic processes of evolutionary development, but these processes in themselves cannot account for the rich array of genetic possibilities. Processes such as these may provide the connective pathways from one viable life-form to another, but neither the existence of those potential life-forms nor the effectiveness of the connective processes is self-explanatory. The world of life-forms and transformational processses is far richer than one would have any right to expect on the basis of naturalism alone. Hence, in contrast to those who speak as if the concept of evolutionary continuity provides affirmation for naturalism or defeat for theism, I find that the concept of evolution begs for an explanation far more grand than naturalism can supply.
6. The *Hexaemeron* by St. Basil the Great, Archbishop of Caesarea, in *Nicene and Post-Nicene Fathers,* second series, VIII, trans. Blomfield Jackson (1894, reprint, William B. Eerdmans Publishing Company, 1989). Subsequent references to this work will be identified by homily number (I-IX) and numbered section.
7. George Dragas, "St. Basil's Doctrine of Creation," in EKKLESIA kai THEOLOGIA, 3 (1982): 1079–1132.
8. I find it essential to distinguish between the *doctrine* of creation (theological in focus) and a *picture* of creation—a conceptual

depiction of the particular historical scenario through which God's creative activity became manifest in time.

9. St. Basil does, however, appear to show some inconsistency on this point. He envisions God's command as having suddenly created earthly basins as the place where the waters should be gathered to form seas (see IV.4). While this may permit water to act in accord with its nature, does it not require a rather drastic violation of the nature of earth?
10. St. Augustine, *The Literal Meaning of Genesis,* trans. John Hammond Taylor, *Ancient Christian Writers,* 41–42, (Newman Press, 1982). Subsequent reference to this work will be identified by book, chapter and section numbers.
11. Although I find many of St. Augustine's theological perspectives fruitful, I would be so bold as to suggest that, given the nature of the text, this particular interpretative goal may be unattainable.
12. St. Augustine went so far as to argue that even miracles (like the transformation of water into wine) should be seen, not as divinely imposed violations of causal reasons, but as manifestations of material substances exercising—albeit in an unusual manner—the powers originally given to them by God. To St. Augustine, it appears, the idea that water had been given the capacities to transform itself into wine seemed no more extraordinary than the idea that mud had been given the capacity to produce eels. We might also note here that the interpretative goal of St. Augustine—to formulate a one-to-one correspondence between the text of Genesis 1–3 and the historical particulars of what took place—becomes especially difficult to square with his doctrine of Creation's functional integrity when he deals with the text regarding the formation of Eve from the rib of Adam.
13. Although I stand with the historic Christian Church in believing that the early chapters of Genesis do refer to an authentic history of God's creative activity, I am also convinced that we are not warranted in treating this biblical literature as a chronicle of historical details that are directly relevant to scientific reconstructions of Creation's formative history. For more on this, see my *The Fourth Day: What the Bible and the Heavens are telling us about the Creation,* (William B. Eerdmans Publishing Company, 1986), especially chapters 1–5.

14. See note 8.
15. The term "functional integrity of the universe" is meant to include not only the usual principle of universality (physical laws do not vary by time and place) but also the idea of the universe's gapless economy. Some authors assert that scientific theorizing based on these principles employs "methodological naturalism" or "provisional atheism." I find these terms offensively misleading because they imply that a naturalistic (and thereby atheistic) worldview provides a sufficient basis for the principles in question. I do not believe that it does. As I see it, naturalism is free to presuppose these principles, but it has no basis for any claim that they are either self-evident or derivable from naturalistic "first principles."
16. Skeptics of evolution appear convinced that the only basis for favoring the concept of genealogical continuity over the concept of special creation is that it provides proponents of naturalism with an intellectually satisfying answer to the question, "How did this vast array of life-forms come to be?" In the minds of both skeptics of evolutionary continuity and proponents of naturalism the macroevolutionary paradigm effectively eliminates the need for divine action of any sort. Hence, they conclude, the macroevolutionary paradigm strongly favors naturalism over theism. I strongly contest this conclusion. One goal of this essay has been to demonstrate that, contrary to popular rhetoric, the concept of genealogical continuity may be seen as an empirically stimulated outgrowth of the historic Christian doctrine of creation, and that it therefore offers no apologetic advantage whatsoever to the proponents of naturalism.
17. One might draw a useful analogy from chaos theory: The dynamically changing state of a physical system traces out a path through "phase space" (the set of all possible states for that system). Distributed throughout this phase space are "attractors" which lead the system to spend most of its time near certain special states. By analogy, it is conceivable that biological species, families, and other categories could represent attractors in a genetic phase space. Employing the conceptual vocabulary of chaos theory, one could sensibly discuss the possibilities of both variability (that descendants might occupy a different point in genetic phase space than did their ancestors)

and stasis (the tendency of populations to linger in the vicinity of genomic attractors) without fear of contradiction.

18. Let me offer a simple illustration of this point. The molecular motions of the air in one's sitting room are characterized by a high degree of randomness. Nonetheless, we may purposefully employ that very randomness to maintain a windless environment at a stable and comfortable temperature. If, then, we humans are able to employ random processes to accomplish our purposes, could not the Creator do the same?

The Star of Bethlehem: Science of the Ancients

Craig Chester

Craig Chester is a founding member and current president of the Monterey (California) Institute for Research in Astronomy (MIRA), the only private American professional observatory established in this century. As a software consultant, he has worked on a variety of U.S. Navy and U.S. Air Force projects, developing ground equipment and software tools for satellite communications. He holds a Ph.D. in astronomy from Case Western Reserve University.

Given the nature of the other essays in this volume, the relevance of a chapter on the Star of Bethlehem may not be immediately apparent, but it is a subject that presents an interesting perspective on God's relationship to His created universe. In its own way, this story may be as important as the creation/evolution debate in illuminating the relationship between science and theology.

The Story of the Star in the East

Someone once observed, "The universe is composed of stories, not atoms." The Star of Bethlehem is certainly a story (as is most of the Bible, first and foremost). It is a mystery and a puzzle, involving not only theology and astronomy, but also history and even astrology.[1] It is an attempt of men to understand not the universe at large, but specific events, or "What I Saw."

What do we know about the Star of Bethlehem? The popular conception is summarized in the Christmas carol:

> We three kings of Orient are/Bearing gifts we traverse afar,
> Field and fountain, moor and mountain/ Following yonder star.
> O star of wonder, star of night/ Star with royal beauty bright,
> Westward leading, still proceeding/ Guide us to thy perfect light.

We all know these lines as the story of the Star, which is fine—except for the fact that almost everything in it is wrong. The actual New Testament account of the Star of Bethlehem comes from the second chapter of the Gospel of Matthew (told here in the Revised English Bible translation):

> Jesus was born at Bethlehem in Judaea during the reign of Herod. After his birth astrologers [Magi] from the east arrived in Jerusalem, asking, "Where is the newborn king of the Jews? We observed the rising of his star, and we have come to pay him homage." King Herod was greatly perturbed when he heard this, and so was the whole of Jerusalem. He called together the chief priests and scribes of the Jews and asked them where the Messiah was to be born. "At Bethlehem in Judaea," they replied, "for this is what the prophet wrote: 'Bethlehem in the land of Judah, you are by no means least among the rulers of Judah; for out of you shall come a ruler to be the shepherd of my people Israel.'"
>
> Then Herod summoned the astrologers to meet him secretly, and ascertained from them the exact time when the star had appeared. He sent them to Bethlehem, and said, "Go and make a careful search for the child, and when you have found him, bring me word, so that I may go myself and pay him homage."
>
> After hearing what the king had to say they set out; there before them was the star they had seen rising, and it went ahead of them until it stopped above the place where the child lay. They were overjoyed at the sight of it and, entering the house, they saw the child with Mary his mother and bowed low in homage to him; they opened their treasure chests and presented gifts to him: gold, frankincense, and myrrh. Then they returned to their own country by another route, for they had been warned in a dream not to go back to Herod.

What is your initial reaction to this story? It seems to me that it is not a fabulous tale. That is, it does not conjure up fantastic details or images, and it is told in a rather mundane fashion, not at all like a fable. It is also the only account we have of it in our Bible. Later, various non-canonical sources did elaborate on it. Books like the Protevangelium of James and an epistle of Ignatius say this star was the brightest star in the sky, brighter than all other stars combined, even including the sun and the moon, which bowed down before it. But Matthew is very matter-of-fact.[2]

The Historical Perspective

To understand this story, we must view it in the context of its time. Who were these Magi? Where did they come from? Magi is the plural of Magus, the root of our word magic; "court astrologer" is probably the best translation. "Wise men" is also a good term, descriptive of the esteem in which they were widely held. The group of Magi in question (it is the Christmas carol, not Matthew, that refers to three of them) came "from the east." They might have been Zoroastrians, Medes, Persians, Arabs, or even Jews. They served as court advisors, making forecasts and predictions for their royal patrons based on their study of the stars, about which they were quite knowledgeable. Magi often wandered from court to court, and it was not unusual for them to cover great distances in order to attend the birth or crowning of a king, paying their respects and offering gifts. It is not surprising, therefore, that Matthew would mention them as validation of Jesus' kingship, or that Herod would regard their arrival as a very serious matter.[3]

When might these Magi have appeared in Judaea? Obviously, determining the story's date is important if we are to look for astronomical connections. We might assume that it was around 1 B.C. or 1 A.D., since that is when, by conventional reckoning, Jesus was born. But the calendar these dates are based on was set by the Roman monk Dionysius Exiguus in the year 525 A.D., long after the fact. Scholars writing in the first and second centuries A.D. asserted that

Jesus was born between what we now call 4 B.C. and 1 B.C. They were living much closer to the event and had access to thousands of historical records in many excellent libraries, and their opinions probably should be given much more weight than has been common.

How about the time of the year? The best clue is a passage in the Book of Luke:

> And there were in the same country shepherds abiding in the fields, keeping watch over their flock by night.

If the reference to "fields" is accurate—not pastures or holding pens—we might guess at a date in late summer or early fall, for it was customary for farmers to allow sheep and cattle to graze the stubble in the fields following the harvest. This clue is suggestive, but hardly definitive.

One difficulty in seeking a precise date is the fact that Matthew reports two separate sightings, possibly separated by a substantial time. First the Magi saw the Star rising *en anatole,* best translated as "rising in the east," the ancient technical term for an achronychal rising, when an object rises at sunset and is visible all night. After they come to Jerusalem—we do not know how long that took, and there is no indication that the Star was in any way involved with the journey—they see the Star again as they travel the few miles to Bethlehem:

> there before them was the star they had seen rising, and it went ahead of them until it stopped above the place where the child lay.

There was no need for a bright or supernatural guiding light to find Bethlehem from Jerusalem; it lies just five miles south on the main road. There is a reference to the "house" rather than to a stable or manger, and there is no mention of an infant (*brephos* in the Greek) but of a *paidion,* or toddler, indicating that some months may have elapsed since the birth itself.

What are the astronomical possibilities? This question has been asked many times since the Christian apologist Origen first raised it around 250 A.D. It is safe to say that every astronomical event known to have occurred during, say, the decade of interest has at some point been proposed as the Star of Bethlehem.

The key point to answering this question is to note that it is not just *any* astronomical event that is of interest. We can restrict our inquiry to those appearances that would have had astrological significance to the Magi, who declared:

> "We observed the rising of *his* star, and we have come to pay him homage."

An astrological event may not have been very obvious at all; certainly it was not obvious to Herod. Had it been an incomparably bright object, as later writers thought, there would be numerous written records of it. It is much more plausible that the Star of Bethlehem went unnoticed by all but a few experts such as the Magi.

The Death of Herod

A major key to the chronology is the date of the death of Herod, who figures prominently in our story. Herod was alive when the Star of Bethlehem appeared and the commonly quoted date for his death is 4 B.C.[4] Thus dates of 7 B.C. through 4 B.C. are often given for the birth of Jesus. The political events of this period are best known from the writings of Josephus Flavius, the Jewish historian who lived from 37 A.D. to about 95 A.D. His testimony has always been considered vital in determining these dates. But the accounts of Josephus and the entire history of this period have been reassessed recently, with important new results, by Ernest Martin, whose book, *The Star that Astonished the World,* has become the authoritative source on the subject.[5]

According to Josephus, on the night of a lunar eclipse Herod executed two rabbis. They were accused of inciting some young men to climb up on the wall and tear down the golden eagle that the king had ordered placed on the gate to the Temple in Jerusalem. This eagle was, of course, an abomination to the Jews because it was a graven image. Soon Herod himself died and was buried. One of his sons inherited his throne, shortly after which Passover was celebrated.

It was long believed that the lunar eclipse in question occurred on March 13, 4 B.C. But this was only a partial eclipse (40 percent total) and fairly hard to detect. And it occurred only 29 days before Passover. Here is what would have had to happen in those 29 days:

Herod was sick at the time of the execution of the rabbis and his condition worsened almost immediately. He was treated for a time by his physicians, to no avail. Herod then decided to pack up the royal household and move to Jericho to take the baths. He tried the baths unsuccessfully for some days and then returned to Jerusalem. Believing that he would soon die, Herod came up with a diabolical plan to insure that all of Israel would mourn his death, in spite of his unpopularity. He commanded the leading men from around the country to come to Jerusalem; there he imprisoned them in the Hippodrome and ordered the army to execute them as soon as he was dead. Israel would indeed mourn.

In the meantime, word arrived from Rome that Herod had the Emperor's permission to execute his rebellious son Antipater and he promptly complied. Five days later he died, but not before decreeing that his was to be the largest funeral ever held in the history of the world. His body was embalmed. The army was assembled to carry his body in the funeral procession to a burial site some 25 miles away. The soldiers walked in bare feet, as was required when in mourning, traveling one mile a day. A legate from Rome, where word of Herod's death had been received, arrived to protect the royal treasury. Finally, Herod's son Archelaus was crowned king and had time to issue a few decrees prior to the celebration of Passover.

The 29 days between the eclipse of 4 B.C. and the following Passover simply do not allow enough time for all of this to have happened. A minimum of ten weeks would have been required. But, on January 10, 1 B.C., there was a total lunar eclipse visible in Palestine, and it occurred twelve and and a half weeks before Passover. As Martin points out, there are other compelling reasons to regard 1 B.C. as the true date of Herod's death. For example, the War of Varus, known to have followed Herod's death, can be redated to 1 B.C., where it fits the other known facts perfectly.

If we conclude that Herod did die in the spring of 1 B.C., we are free to add the years 3 B.C. and 2 B.C. to our search for the Star of Bethlehem. What was happening then? The year 2 B.C. marked the 25th anniversary of Caesar Augustus' rule and the 750th anniversary of the founding of Rome. Huge celebrations were planned. The whole empire was at peace. The doors of the temple of Janus were closed for only the third time in Roman history. To honor their emperor, the people were to rise as one and name Augustus *pater patriae,* or "Father of the Country." Now, getting the people of an empire to do something spontaneously requires a great deal of organization. And so an enrollment, or census, was ordered:

> In those days, a decree went out from Caesar Augustus that all the world should be enrolled.... And all went to be enrolled, each to his own city.

This enrollment, described in the Gospel of Luke, which brought Joseph and Mary to Bethlehem, has always been a mystery since no regular taxation census occurred at this time. But the *pater patriae* enrollment fits perfectly.

The Astronomical Perspective

What astronomical events, possibly in the years 3 or 2 B.C., might have been related to the Star of Bethlehem?

Novae have been suggested, the unexpected, sudden brightening of a star from invisibility into a bright object for a period of days or weeks. There is no historical record of such a nova, nor is it clear what a nova's astrological significance would be. Comets are candidates, for they appear sporadically, move, and even seem to point down to the earth. (This was Origen's choice.) But the recorded comets around this time, even Halley's Comet in 12 B.C., were not very impressive; astrologically, they were considered ominous. Meteors and fireballs are even less likely candidates.

Conjunctions of planets have long been considered good possibilities. A conjunction is a close apparent approach between two celestial objects. Technically speaking, a conjunction occurs at the moment when both objects have the same celestial longitude; one is due north of the other. The closer the objects are, the more visually impressive is the event and the more significant astrologically. In 3 B.C. and 2 B.C., there was a series of close conjunctions involving Jupiter, the planet that represented kingship, coronations, and the birth of kings. In Hebrew, Jupiter was known as *Sedeq* or "Righteousness," a term also used for the Messiah.

In September of 3 B.C., Jupiter came into conjunction with Regulus, the star of kingship, the brightest star in the constellation Leo. Leo was the constellation of kings, and it was associated with the Lion of Judah. The royal planet approached the royal star in the royal constellation representing Israel. Just a month earlier, Jupiter and Venus, the Mother planet, had almost seemed to touch each other in another close conjunction, also in Leo. Then the conjunction between Jupiter and Regulus was repeated, not once but twice, in February and May of 2 B.C. Finally, in June of 2 B.C., Jupiter and Venus, the two brightest objects in the sky save the sun and the moon, experienced an even closer encounter when their disks would have appeared to touch; to the naked eye they became a single object above the setting sun. This exceptionally rare spectacle could not have been missed by the Magi.

In fact, we have seen here only the highlights of an impressive series of planetary motions and conjunctions fraught with a variety of astrological meanings, involving all the other known planets of the period, Mercury, Mars, and Saturn. The astrological significance of these impressive events must surely have been seen by the Magi as the announcement of the impending birth of a great king of Israel.

September 11, 3 B.C. is perhaps the most interesting date of all. Not only was Jupiter very close to Regulus in the first of their conjunctions, but the sun was in the constellation of Virgo (of obvious symbolism), together with the new moon, in a configuration that fits a plausible interpretation of a passage in the Book of Revelation describing the birth of a male child who is to be the ruler of the universe. Significantly, September 11, 3 B.C., also marked the beginning of the Jewish New Year, traditionally regarded as the anniversary of Noah's landing after the Great Flood.

But if the planet Jupiter was the Star of Bethlehem, or was a component of the events that triggered the visit by the Magi, how do we view the final appearance of the Star on their journey to Bethlehem? It would have been in the southern sky, though fairly high above the horizon. Could it have stopped over Bethlehem?

The answer is yes. The word "stop" was used for what we now call a planet's "stationary point." A planet normally moves eastward through the stars from night to night and month to month, but regularly exhibits a "retrograde loop." As it approaches the opposite point in the sky from the sun, it appears to slow, comes to a full stop, and moves backwards (westward) through the sky for some weeks. Again it slows, stops, and resumes its eastward course. It seems plausible that the Magi were "overjoyed" at again seeing before them, as they traveled southward, *His* star, Jupiter, which, at its stationary point was standing still over Bethlehem. We do know for certain that Jupiter performed a retrograde loop in 2 B.C. and that it was stationary on December 25, interestingly enough, during Hanukkah, the season for giving presents.

What Room for God?

Where has this search for the Star of Bethlehem taken us? There has been much discussion in the other essays in this volume about the "God of the gaps"—finding God in the gaps between the portions of some subject that we feel we understand scientifically. It seems to me that this is a dangerous position, for science by definition cannot admit to such gaps and must search continually to fill them with its understanding, and will often succeed in so doing. Here the situation is different. The question is: What *meaning,* what room for God, do we find in the events that we know to have occurred?

If we have correctly identified the Star of Bethlehem, the science is clear and simple. Keplerian orbits of planets[6] are quite predictable, so that we can deduce quite accurately what the sky looked like two thousand years ago. Even the ancient Magi understood apparent planetary motions quite well. Predictions of the conjunctions of 3 and 2 B.C. were made 400 years prior to the birth of Christ and they were in error by only a few days. There is no need to invoke God or divine miracles to explain what happened in the heavens above Judaea. Natural laws are sufficient.

But is this kind of sufficiency really enough for us? The significant question raised here is not what happened, but *why* it happened. What does it mean? Was Matthew right in seeing this event as divine confirmation of a central moment in God's plan for mankind? What room is left for God, not as an agent filling in the gaps between what we can understand as physical causes, but as the creator of purpose? And was God's purpose fulfilled by the great celestial dance that we call the Star of Bethlehem?

These questions are examples of the kind of decisions we are faced with daily. No theologian can say, in a way convincing to a scientist, that some event required an act of God outside natural law. Similarly, no scientist can say that some event was *merely* (a dangerous word) an act of natural law working itself out with no other meaning. That is, no one is forced to believe that what happened in the heavens two thousand years ago was a simple, natural event devoid of meaning. The Star of Bethlehem is an excellent example of an event that occurs right at the intersection of Christianity and science, in a world created by a God who chose to institute natural laws but who nevertheless continues to carry out His own purposes.

Notes

1. My background is astronomy. I also took some fascinating courses in Biblical studies at Harvard Divinity School, but I do not pretend to be an expert of any sort. It should also be noted that I am not presenting any original research in this essay. Many scholars, including scientists, theologians and historians, have studied the Star of Bethlehem.
2. It has been suggested that this is a commentary by Matthew, always found of referring to Old Testament prophecies, on Balaam's oracle in the Book of Numbers that "a star shall come forth out of Jacob and a scepter shall rise out of Israel." It would be uncharacteristic of Matthew to refrain from pointing out this prophecy explicitly, had he had it in mind.
3. The Hebrew prophet Daniel, himself a member of the Magi, foretold that a king of kings would come forth from Israel. The Roman emperor Nero was even advised, on the strength of this prophecy, to move his capital to Jerusalem.
4. The reference is to Herod the Great. It was his son Herod Antipas who executed John the Baptist and who ruled at the time of the Crucifixion.
5. Ernest Martin, *The Star that Astonished the World* (ASK Publications, 1991). See also, John Mosley, *The Christmas Star* (Griffith Observatory, 1987).
6. Johannes Kepler (1571–1630) was the German astronomer who discovered the physical laws describing planetary orbits.

What Is Darwinism?

Phillip E. Johnson

Phillip E. Johnson is the author of one of the most discussed books of recent years, *Darwin on Trial* (1991), which takes issue with Darwinian evolutionary theory. An attorney with degrees from the University of Chicago and Harvard, he gained his early legal experience as a law clerk to justices on the California Supreme Court and the U.S. Supreme Court and as deputy district attorney (with duties as criminal trial prosecutor) in Ventura County, California. Since 1968, he has also served as a professor of law at the University of California-Berkeley.

There is a popular television game show called "Jeopardy," in which the usual order of things is reversed. Instead of being asked a question to which they must supply the answer, the contestants are given the answer and asked to provide the appropriate question. This format suggests an insight that is applicable to law, to science, and indeed to just about everything. The important thing is not necessarily to know all the answers, but rather to know what question is being asked.

That insight is the starting point for my inquiry into Darwinian evolution and its relationship to creation, because Darwinism is the answer to two very different kinds of questions. First, Darwinian theory tells us how a certain amount of diversity in life forms can develop once various types of complex living organisms are already in existence. If a small population of birds happens to migrate to an isolated island, for example, a combination of inbreeding, mutation and natural selection may cause this isolated population to develop characteristics different from those possessed by the ancestral population on the mainland. When the theory is understood in this limited sense, Darwinian evolution is uncontroversial and has no important philosophical or theological implications.

Evolutionary biologists are not content merely to explain how variation occurs within limits, however. They aspire to answer a much broader question: how complex organisms like birds, flowers and human beings came into existence in the first place. The Darwinian answer to this second question is that the creative force that produced complex plants and animals from single-celled predecessors over long stretches of geological time is essentially the same as the mechanism that produces variations in flowers, insects and domestic animals before our very eyes. In the words of Ernst Mayr, the dean of living Darwinists, "trans-specific evolution [i.e., macroevolution] is nothing but an extrapolation and magnification of the events that take place within populations and species." Neo-Darwinian evolution in this broad sense is a philosophical doctrine so lacking in empirical support that Mayr's successor at Harvard, Stephen Jay Gould, once pronounced it in a reckless moment to be "effectively dead." Yet neo-Darwinism is far from dead; on the contrary, it is continually proclaimed in the textbooks and the media as unchallengeable fact. How does it happen that so many scientists and intellectuals, who pride themselves on their empiricism and open-mindedness, continue to accept an unempirical theory as scientific fact?

The answer to that question lies in the definition of five key terms. The terms are *creationism, evolution, science, religion,* and *truth.* Once we understand how these words are used in evolutionary discourse, the continued ascendancy of neo-Darwinism will be no mystery, and we need no longer be deceived by claims that the theory is supported by "overwhelming evidence." I should warn at the outset, however, that using words clearly is not the innocent and peaceful activity most of us may have thought it to be. There are powerful vested interests in this area that can thrive only in the midst of ambiguity and confusion. Those who insist on defining terms precisely and using them consistently may find themselves regarded with suspicion and hostility, and even accused of being enemies of science. But let us accept that risk and proceed to the definitions.

The first word is *creationism,* which means simply a belief in creation. In Darwinist usage, which dominates not only the popular and professional scientific literature but also the media, a creationist is a person who takes the creation account in the Book of Genesis to be true in a very literal sense. The earth was created in a single week of six 24-hour days no more than 10,000 years ago; the major features of the geological column were produced by Noah's flood, and there have been no major innovations in the forms of life since the beginning. It is a major theme of Darwinist propaganda that the only persons who have any doubts about Darwinism are "Young-Earth" creationists of this sort, who are always portrayed as rejecting the clear and convincing evidence of science to preserve a religious prejudice. The implication is that citizens of modern society face a choice that is really no choice at all. Either they reject science altogether and retreat to a pre-modern worldview, or they believe everything the Darwinists tell them.

In a broader sense, however, a creationist is simply a person who believes in the existence of a *creator* who brought about the existence of the world and its living inhabitants in furtherance of a *purpose.* Whether the process of creation took a single week or billions of years is relatively unimportant from a philosophical or theological standpoint. Creation by gradual processes over geological ages may create problems for Biblical interpretation, but it creates none for the basic principle of theistic religion. And creation in this broad sense, according to a 1991 Gallup poll, is the creed of 87 percent of Americans. If God brought about our existence for a purpose, then the most important kind of knowledge to have is knowledge of God and what He intends for us. Is creation in that broad sense consistent with *evolution?*

The answer is "absolutely not," when "evolution" is understood in the Darwinian sense. To Darwinists, evolution means *naturalistic* evolution, because they insist that science must assume the cosmos to be a closed system of material causes and effects that can never be influenced by anything outside of material nature—by God, for example. In the beginning, an explosion of subatomic particles created the cosmos, and, undirected, naturalistic evolution produced everything that followed. From this philosophical standpoint it follows deductively that from the beginning no intelligent purpose guided evolution. If intelligence exists today it is only because it has itself evolved through purposeless material processes.

A materialistic theory of evolution inherently must invoke two kinds of processes. At bottom the theory must be based on chance, because that is what is left when we have ruled out everything involving intelligence or purpose. Theories that invoke *only* chance are not credible, however. One thing that everyone acknowledges is that living organisms are enormously complex—far more so than, say, a computer or an airplane. That such complex entities came into existence simply by chance is clearly less credible than that they were designed and constructed by a creator. To back up their claim that this appearance of intelligent design is an illusion, Darwinists need to provide some complexity-building force that is mindless and purposeless. Natural selection is by far the most plausible candidate.

If we assume that random genetic mutations provided the new genetic information needed, say, to give a small mammal a start towards wings, and if we assume that each tiny step in the process of wing-building gave the animal an increased chance of survival, then natural selection ensured that the favored creatures would thrive and reproduce. It follows as a matter of logic that wings can and will appear as if by the plan of a designer. Of course, if wings or other improvements do not appear, the theory explains their absence just as well. The needed mutations did not arrive, or "developmental constraints" closed off certain possibilities, or natural selection favored something else. There is no requirement that any of this speculation be confirmed by either experimental or fossil evidence. To Darwinists the ability to imagine the process is sufficient to confirm that something like that must have happened.

Richard Dawkins calls the process of creation by mutation and selection "the blind watchmaker," by which he means that a purposeless, materialistic designing force substitutes for the "watchmaker" deity of natural theology. The creative power of the blind watchmaker is supported only by very slight evidence, such as the famous example of a moth population in which the percentage of dark moths increased during a period when the birds were better able to see light moths against the backdrop of smoke-darkened trees. This example may show that natural selection can do something, but not that it can create anything not already in existence. Even such slight evidence is more than sufficient, however, because evidence is not really necessary to prove something that is practically self-evident. The existence of a potent blind watchmaker follows deductively from the philosophical premise that nature had to do its own creating. There can be argument about the details, but if God was not in the picture, something very much like Darwinism simply has to be true, regardless of the evidence.

That brings me to my third term, *science*. As we have already seen, Darwinists assume that naturalistic principles fully explain the history of the cosmos and its life forms. This reflects a philosophical doctrine called scientific naturalism. Said to be a necessary consequence of the inherent limitations of science, scientific naturalism transforms the limitations of science into limitations upon reality in order to maximize the explanatory power of science and its practitioners. It is, of course, entirely possible to study organisms scientifically on the premise that they were all created by God, just as scientists study airplanes and even works of art without denying that these objects are intelligently designed. The problem with allowing God a role in the history of life is not that science would cease, but rather that scientists would have to acknowledge the existence of something important that is outside the boundaries of natural science. For scientists who want to be able to explain everything—and "theories of everything" are now openly anticipated in the scientific literature—this is an intolerable possibility.

The second feature of scientific naturalism that is important for our purpose is its set of rules governing the criticism and replacement of a paradigm. A paradigm is a general theory, like the Darwinian theory of evolution, which has achieved general acceptance in the scientific community. The paradigm unifies the various specialties that make up the research community and guides research in all of them. Thus zoologists, botanists, geneticists, molecular biologists, and paleontologists all see their research as aimed at fleshing out the details of the Darwinian paradigm. If molecular biologists see a pattern of apparently neutral mutations that have no apparent effect on an organism's fitness, they must find a way to reconcile their findings with the paradigm's requirement that natural selection guides evolution. They can do this by postulating a sufficient quantity of invisible adaptive mutations, which are deemed to be accumulated by natural selection. Similarly, if paleontologists see new fossil species appearing suddenly in the fossil record and remaining basically unchanged thereafter, they must perform whatever contortions are necessary to force this recalcitrant evidence into a model of incremental change through the accumulation of micromutations.

Supporting the paradigm may even require what in other contexts would be called deception. As Niles Eldredge candidly admitted, "We paleontologists have said that the history of life supports [the story of gradual adaptive change], all the while knowing it does not."[1] Eldredge explained that this pattern of misrepresentation occurred because of "the certainty so characteristic of evolutionary ranks since the late 1940s, the utter assurance not only that natural selection operates in nature, but that we know precisely how it works." This certainty produced a degree of dogmatism that Eldredge says resulted in relegation to the "lunatic fringe" for paleontologists who reported that "they saw something out of kilter between contemporary evolutionary theory, on the one hand, and patterns of change in the fossil record on the other."[2] Under the circumstances, prudent paleontologists understandably swallowed their doubts and supported the ruling ideology. To abandon the paradigm would be to abandon the scientific community; to ignore the paradigm and just gather the facts would be to earn the demeaning label of "stamp collector."

As many philosophers of science have observed, the research community does not abandon a paradigm in the absence of a suitable replacement. This means that negative criticism of Darwinism, however devastating it may appear to be, is essentially irrelevant to the professional researchers. The critic may point out, for example, that the evidence for the creative power of natural selection is somewhere between weak and non-existent. That is perfectly true, but to Darwinists the more important point is this: If natural selection did not do the creating, what did? "God" is obviously unacceptable, because such a being is unknown to science. "We don't know" is equally unacceptable, because to admit ignorance would be to leave science adrift without a guiding principle. To put the problem in the most practical terms, it is impossible to write or evaluate a grant proposal without a generally accepted theoretical framework.

The paradigm rule explains why Gould's acknowledgement that neo-Darwinism is "effectively dead" had no significant effect on the Darwinist faithful, or even on Gould himself. Gould made that statement in a paper predicting the emergence of a new general theory of evolution, one based on the macromutational speculations of Berkeley geneticist Richard Goldschmidt.[3] When the new theory did not arrive as anticipated, the alternatives were either to stick with Ernst Mayr's version of neo-Darwinism or to concede that biologists do not know, after all, of a naturalistic mechanism that can produce biological complexity. That was no choice at all. Gould had to beat a hasty retreat back to classical Darwinism to avoid giving aid and comfort to the enemies of scientific naturalism, including those disgusting creationists.

Having to defend a dead theory tooth and nail can hardly be a satisfying activity, and it is no wonder that Gould lashes out with fury at people such as myself who call attention to his predicament.[4] I do not mean to ridicule Gould, however, because I have a genuinely high regard for the man as one of the few Darwinists who has recognized the major problems with the theory and reported them honestly. His tragedy is that he cannot admit the clear implications of his own thought without effectively resigning from science.

The continuing survival of Darwinist orthodoxy illustrates Thomas Kuhn's famous point that the accumulation of anomalies never in itself falsifies a paradigm, because "to reject one paradigm without substituting another is to reject science itself."[5] This practice may be appropriate as a way of carrying on the professional enterprise called science, but it can be grossly misleading when it is imposed upon persons who are asking questions other than the ones scientific naturalists want to ask. Suppose, for example, that I want to know whether God really had something to do with creating living organisms. A typical Darwinian response is that there is no reason to invoke supernatural action because natural selection was capable of performing the job. To evaluate that response, I need to know whether natural selection really has the fantastic creative power attributed to it. It is not a sufficient answer to say that scientists have nothing better to offer. The fact that scientists prefer not to say "we don't know" tells me nothing about what they really *do* know.

I am not suggesting that scientists have to change their rules about retaining and discarding paradigms. I merely want them to be candid about the contradictory evidence and admit, if it be the case, that they are hanging on to Darwinism only because they prefer a shaky theory to having no theory at all. They insist, however, upon presenting Darwinian evolution to the public as a fact that every rational person is expected to accept. If there are reasonable grounds to doubt the theory, such dogmatism is ridiculous, regardless of whether the doubters have a better theory to propose.

To believers in creation, the Darwinists seem thoroughly intolerant and dogmatic when they insist that their own philosophy must have a monopoly in the schools and the media. The Darwinists do not see themselves that way, of course. On the contrary, they often feel aggrieved when creationists (in either the broad or narrow sense) ask to have their own arguments heard publicly and considered fairly. To insist that schoolchildren be taught that Darwinian evolution is a fact is in their minds merely to protect the integrity of science education; to present the other side of the case would be to allow fanatics to force their opinions on others. Even college professors have been forbidden to express their doubts about Darwinian evolution in the classroom, and it seems to be widely believed that the Constitution not only permits but actually requires such restrictions on academic freedom. To explain this bizarre situation, we must define our fourth term: *religion.*

Suppose that a skeptic finds the evidence for biological creation by natural selection obviously lacking and argues that, in the circumstances, we ought to consider seriously that the development of life may have required some input from a pre-existing, purposeful creator. To scientific naturalists this suggestion is "creationist" and, therefore, unacceptable in principle, because it invokes an entity unknown to science. What is worse, it suggests the possibility that this creator may have communicated in some way with humans. In that case there could be real prophets—persons with a genuine knowledge of God who are neither frauds nor dreamers. Such persons could conceivably be dangerous rivals for the scientists as cultural authorities.

Naturalistic philosophy has worked out a strategy to prevent this problem from arising: it labels naturalism as science and theism as religion. The former is then classified as *knowledge,* and the latter as mere *belief.* The distinction is of critical importance, because only knowledge can be objectively valid for everyone; belief is valid only for the believer and should never be passed off as knowledge. The student who thinks that 2 and 2 make 5, or that water is not made up of hydrogen and oxygen, or that the theory of evolution is not true, is not expressing a minority viewpoint. He or she is ignorant, and the job of education is to cure that ignorance and replace it with knowledge. Students in the public schools are thus to be taught at an early age that "evolution is a fact," and as time goes by they will gradually learn that evolution means naturalism.

In short, the proposition that God was in any way involved in our creation is effectively outlawed and implicitly negated. This is because naturalistic evolution is by definition in the category of scientific knowledge. What contradicts knowledge is implicitly false or imaginary. That is why it is possible for scientific naturalists to claim in good faith both that their science says nothing about God and that it has said everything that can be said about God. In naturalistic philosophy both propositions are at bottom the same. All that needs to be said about God is that there is nothing to be said of God, because on that subject we can have no knowledge.

Our fifth and final term is *truth.* Truth as such is not a particularly important concept in naturalistic philosophy. The reason for this is that "truth" suggests an unchanging absolute, whereas scientific knowledge is a dynamic concept. Like life, knowledge evolves and grows into superior forms. What was knowledge in the past is not knowledge today, and the knowledge of the future will surely be far superior to what we have now. Only naturalism itself and the unique validity of science as the path to knowledge are absolutes. There can be no criterion for truth outside of scientific knowledge, no mind of God to which we have access.

This understanding persists even when scientific naturalists employ religious-sounding language. For example, the physicist Stephen Hawking ended his famous book *A Brief History of Time* with the prediction that man might one day "know the mind of God." This phrasing caused some friends of mine to form the mistaken impression that he had some attraction to theistic religion. In context Hawking was not referring to a supernatural eternal being, but to the possibility that scientific knowledge will eventually become complete and all-encompassing because it will have explained the movements of material particles in all circumstances.

The monopoly of science in the realm of knowledge explains why evolutionary biologists do not find it meaningful to address the question of whether the Darwinian theory is *true*. They will gladly concede that the theory is incomplete and that further research into the mechanisms of evolution is needed. At any given point in time, however, the reigning theory of naturalistic evolution represents the state of scientific knowledge about how we came into existence. Scientific knowledge is by definition the closest approximation of absolute truth available to us. To ask whether this knowledge is true is therefore to miss the point and to betray a misunderstanding of "how science works."

So far I have described the metaphysical categories which scientific naturalists have used to exclude the topic of God from rational discussion, and ensure that Darwinism's fully naturalistic creation story is effectively true by definition. There is no need to explain why atheists find this system of thought control congenial. It is a little more difficult to understand, at least at first, why Darwinism continues to receive such strong support in the Christian academic world. Many leading Christian professors of science and philosophy, even at institutions generally regarded as theologically conservative, regard with little enthusiasm any attempt to investigate the credibility of the Darwinist evolution story. Given that Darwinism is inherently naturalistic and, therefore, antagonistic to the idea that God had anything to do with the history of life, and given that it plays the central role in ensuring agnostic domination of the intellectual culture, one might have supposed that Christian intellectuals (along with religious Jews) would be eager to find its weak spots.

Instead, the prevailing view among Christian professors has been that Darwinism—or "evolution," as they tend to call it—is both unbeatable and capable of being interpreted in a manner consistent with Christian belief. And in fact Darwinism is unbeatable as long as one accepts the thought categories of scientific naturalism that I have been describing. The problem is that those same thought categories make Christian theism, or any other theism, absolutely untenable. If science has exclusive authority to tell us how life was created, and if science is committed to naturalism, and if science never discards a paradigm until it is presented with an acceptable naturalistic alternative, then Darwinism's position is impregnable within science. The same reasoning that makes Darwinism inevitable, however, also bans God from taking any action within the history of the Cosmos, which means that it makes theism illusory. Theistic naturalism is self-contradictory.

Some hope to avoid the contradiction by asserting that naturalism rules only within the realm of science and that theism can flourish in a separate realm called "religion." The problem with this arrangement, as we have already seen, is that, in a naturalistic culture, scientific conclusions are considered to be knowledge or even fact. What is outside of fact is fantasy, or at best subjective belief. Theists who accommodate scientific naturalism therefore may never affirm that their God is *real* in the same sense that evolution is real. This rule is essential to the entire mind-set that produced Darwinism in the first place. If God exists, He could certainly work through mutation and selection if that is what He wanted to do, but He could also create by some means totally outside the ken of our science. Once we put God into the picture, however, there is no good reason to attribute the creation of biological complexity to random mutation and natural selection. Direct evidence that these mechanisms have substantial creative power is not to be found in nature, the laboratory, or the fossil record. An essential step in the reasoning that establishes Darwinian selection as creator of the wonders of biology, therefore, is that nothing else was available. Theism is by definition the doctrine that something else was available.

Perhaps the contradiction is hard to see when it is stated at an abstract level, so I will give a more concrete example. Persons who advocate the compromise position called "theistic evolution" are in my experience always vague about what they mean by "evolution." They have good reason to be vague. As we have seen, Darwinian evolution is by definition unguided and purposeless, and such evolution cannot in any meaningful sense be theistic. For evolution to be genuinely theistic it must be guided by God, whether this means that God programmed the process in advance or stepped in from time to time to give it a push in the right direction. To Darwinists evolution guided by God is a soft form of creationism, which is to say it is not evolution at all. To repeat, this understanding goes to the very heart of Darwinist thinking. Allow a pre-existing supernatural intelligence to guide evolution, and this omnipotent being can do a whole lot more than that.

Of course, theists can think of evolution as God-guided

whether naturalistic Darwinists like it or not. The trouble with having a private definition for theists, however, is that the scientific naturalists have the power to decide what that term "evolution" means in public discourse, including the science classes in the public schools. If theistic evolutionists broadcast the message that evolution as *they* understand it is harmless to theistic religion, they are misleading their constituents unless they add a clear warning that the version of evolution advocated by the entire body of mainstream science is something else altogether. That warning is never clearly delivered, however, because the main point of theistic evolution is to preserve peace with the mainstream scientific community. The theistic evolutionists therefore unwittingly serve the purposes of the scientific naturalists by helping to persuade the religious community to lower its guard against the incursion of naturalism.

We are now in a position to answer the question with which this essay began. What is Darwinism? Darwinism is a theory of empirical science only at the level of microevolution, where it provides a framework for explaining such things as the diversity that arises when small populations become reproductively isolated from the main body of the species. As a general theory of biological creation, Darwinism is not empirical at all. Rather, it is a necessary implication of a philosophical doctrine called scientific naturalism, which is based on the a priori assumption that God was always absent from the realm of nature. As such, evolution, in the Darwinian sense, is inherently antithetical to theism, although evolution in some entirely different and non-naturalistic sense could conceivably have been God's chosen method of creation.

In 1874, the great Presbyterian theologian Charles Hodge asked the question I have asked: What is Darwinism? After a careful and thoroughly fair-minded evaluation of the doctrine, his answer was unequivocal: "It is Atheism." Another way to state the proposition is to say that Darwinism is the answer to a specific question that grows out of philosophical naturalism. To return to the game of "Jeopardy" with which we started, let us say that Darwinism is the answer. What, then, is the question? The question is: "How must creation have occurred if we assume that God had nothing to do with it?" Theistic evolutionists accomplish very little by trying to Christianize the answer to a question that comes straight from the agenda of scientific naturalism. What we need to do instead is to challenge the assumption that the only questions worth asking are the ones that assume that naturalism is true.

Notes

1. Niles Eldredge, *Time Frames* (Heinemann, 1986), 144.
2. Ibid., 93.
3. Stephen Jay Gould, "Is a New and General Theory of Evolution Emerging?" *Paleobiology,* 6 (1980), 119–130, reprinted in Maynard Smith, ed., *Evolution Now: A Century After Darwin* (W. H. Freeman, 1982).
4. See Stephen Jay Gould, "Impeaching a Self-Appointed Judge," *Scientific American,* (July 1992), 118–122. *Scientific American* refused to publish my response to this attack, but the response did appear in the March 1993 issue of *Perspectives on Science and Christian Faith,* the journal of the American Scientific Affiliation.
5. Thomas S. Kuhn, *The Structure of Scientific Revolutions* 2d ed., (Chicago: University of Chicago Press, 1970), 79.

A Biologist's Approach to Human Nature

Richard D. Alexander

Richard D. Alexander is the Theodore H. Hubbell Distinguished University Professor of Evolutionary Biology and director of the Museum of Zoology at the University of Michigan. With a Ph.D. in entomology from Ohio State University, he is the author of numerous articles and books, including *Darwinism and Human Affairs* (1979), *Natural Selection and Social Behavior: Recent Research and New Theory* (1981), and *The Biology of Moral Systems* (1987). More recently he has written on the evolution of the human psyche, mechanisms of kin recognition, and the reproductive significance of humor. He has also described almost 400 new species of insects and co-authored a monograph, *The Crickets of Australia* (1983).

Even though I am an entomologist by training, I have a deep interest in human nature that existed throughout my formal training as a biologist and accounts for my having written extensively on human behavior during the past 20 years. In retrospect I believe that much of my interest in biology and human nature derives from my childhood on a farm in central Illinois. Life on a farm, operated by horses and producing primarily livestock, helped give me an interest in things biological. The woods that almost surrounded my farm, and the river that ran near it, were full of animal and plant life that provided most of my recreation. Not least important, during my childhood the Methodist church was also an important stimulus; it was not only the location of essentially all social activities in my community, but as well the only place where anyone discussed the ultimate nature of human beings. Neither in school nor in my home was this topic taken seriously. Many years later, when I asked my mother why, she said she thought that we were too busy to discuss such things. I suspect, however, that with more thought she might have agreed that, even though both of my parents were former school teachers, we didn't know enough about the basis for human nature to discuss it. And I also suspect that my household was not different from most others in this regard.

I also remember being frustrated with church, however, beginning at the age of about 12 years, because it seemed to me that one could not easily raise his hand and ask questions or challenge most things being said. I recall considering the fact that, while in the schoolroom I was usually encouraged to question what was said, ironically, basic problems in understanding human nature were not discussed there.

In the announcement of this lecture, someone referred to a line in Robert Frost's poem, *Mending a Wall,* "Good fences make good neighbors." I have used this poem for many years in my course on evolution and human behavior to make a point about analysis that distinguishes science from the humanities. The point comes from my high school English class, in the closest reference to basic human nature that I can recall being made during my elementary and high school days. Frost and his neighbor had an ancient stone wall along the property line between then, with pine trees on one side and an orchard on the other. Each year Frost's neighbor insisted that he and Frost walk the two sides of the wall, replacing the stones that had fallen off during the year. Frost asked his neighbor teasingly why they needed to do this any longer, since there had been no cattle or other animals on either side for a long time and pine cones could not cross the fence and eat apples or vice versa. The neighbor always answered simply, "Good fences make good neighbors." My high school English teacher interpreted this poem as indicating that farmers, somewhat conservative people who do not like to change their ways, thus are likely to cling to an old idea even when it is no longer applicable. I raised my hand to offer a different interpretation. I suggested that when two neighbors walk the property line between them, repairing the fence, they are likely to renew their acquaintanceship and talk about everything that is important to them. Walking along together on either side and discussing whatever problems might come to their minds was an opportunity to get to know each other again and to re-establish a friendship and common understanding. That was my interpretation of the poem—my metaphor for its message. It is also my metaphor for the relationship between science and the humanities and religion. I think the humanities—and in many respects religion as well—are characterized by the fact that there is no way to decide upon one "correct" meaning of, say, a poem or story or work of art. Even if Frost were here today we couldn't necessarily rely on what he told us is the correct interpretation of his poem. Anyone might change his mind as time goes along, and if someone ever suggested an interpretation that Frost liked a lot better than whatever one he might have placed on it when he wrote it, he might just change to the new meaning and we would never know it. This kind of analysis—trying to decide upon the personal or most significant meaning to you or me of a human intellectual or emotional work—is of course in no way trivial. Anyone can derive great inspiration from such efforts and thereby literally change one or many lives. Everyone, I suspect, shares the feeling that a poem, or any artistic or literary or religious theme, can be a wonderful thing. Part of the beauty is that anyone can make his own interpretation, which may provide a solution for whatever question or problem or decision seems most important or interesting to him or her at the time.

But neither religious nor "humanistic" kinds of interpretations describe well how I have spent my career as a biologist exploring human nature. The scientific approach, which I hope is the one I have engaged, might be said to be a seeking of things undeniable—what we sometimes try to label as "facts"—even, in the end, things undeniable about the background or function of human endeavors such as art, music, drama, literature, humor, and other activities labelled as humanities—even of religion. An undeniable thing, such as that the earth is not flat but rather somewhat spherical, is a piece of knowledge that simply cannot any longer be denied; essentially, anyone who tries to deny it is likely to be ridiculed or thought to be something of a crackpot because of the evidence supporting it, which is also contrary to all suggested alternative ideas. This state of affairs can prevail even though we all realize that virtually any fact can be overturned if new evidence becomes available that does a better job of contradicting it than the current evidence does supporting it. Even though I remain fascinated by all forms of literary, religious, and other forms of human endeavor, as far as my formal career of attempting to understand human nature is concerned, scientific analysis supplanted whatever else had impressed or interested me. The point of my presentation today is to argue that scientific analysis of human nature can continue on all fronts—including evolutionary themes—without necessarily becoming adversarial to religious approaches or any aspect of the humanities. I do not believe that there is any necessary incompatibility between scientific and other kinds of analyses of humans or any other natural phenomenon, even though I believe that avoiding such adversarial relations requires thoughtfulness and concessions on both sides. I am referring to the relationship between science—here evolutionary biology—and religion and the humanities because I believe it is the theme of this symposium, and because I have long been interested in understanding the similarities and differences between science and the humanities and religion as ways of thinking about human nature and the products of human nature.

If, for example, we were to take the attitude that every seemingly unsolvable problem in human nature happened because of special creation by a supernatural being, and that's all there is to it, then we might be caused to give up on further analysis and understanding, especially whenever we encountered anything really puzzling or difficult. We might believe that we could not or should not continue. Yet scientists are most likely to answer crucial questions by focusing deliberately on the seemingly insoluble as the best possible challenge and the likely most important or general problem.

Despite whatever we may know or think now about ourselves, no one can doubt that the world is full of human misery. People often do not know why they do the things they do, or why others behave as they do. Governments know they don't know enough about how to govern people. No one understands well enough how people interact collectively. Countless unfortunate things are happening continually to humans all over the world which could surely be changed for the better by additional knowledge about humans that might be gained from scientific study. I believe that the way we approach such solutions is by continuing unrestricted analysis of ourselves and our history on every front.

Here I want to take a single example and illustrate briefly an analytical approach from a biological viewpoint. I hope I can show that such an approach can lead to findings and conclusions that not only are extremely important, but that were not intuitively clear beforehand.

I choose the human mortality curve (Figure 1) as my example of a human trait to analyze. When people look at a mortality curve they may often think it is something one cannot do much about, but I will suggest that there is much we can alter about it, and that how to think about it and change it in desirable ways becomes much more apparent when it is analyzed in detail in terms of our extended history of evolution by natural selection.

At first it may not seem likely that the mortality curve is the same for all humans everywhere. But, at least in a general way, it is. Admittedly, there will be little bumps that change from one situation to another, as when a war causes young men to die at a higher rate. Prior to medical technology the curve rose at a higher rate than it does today. Child mortality obviously varies in different circumstances. But, generally speaking, the mortality curve is a trait of humans as certainly as are five fingers, two eyes, menopause, concealed ovulation, a large complex brain, or a certain developmental pattern. It's a part of the life pattern of humans according to which we all must live. The curve in Figure 1 is a plot of age-specific mortality across the human lifetime. The horizontal axis shows changes in age, the vertical axis deaths per 1000 per year. Males and females are plotted differently

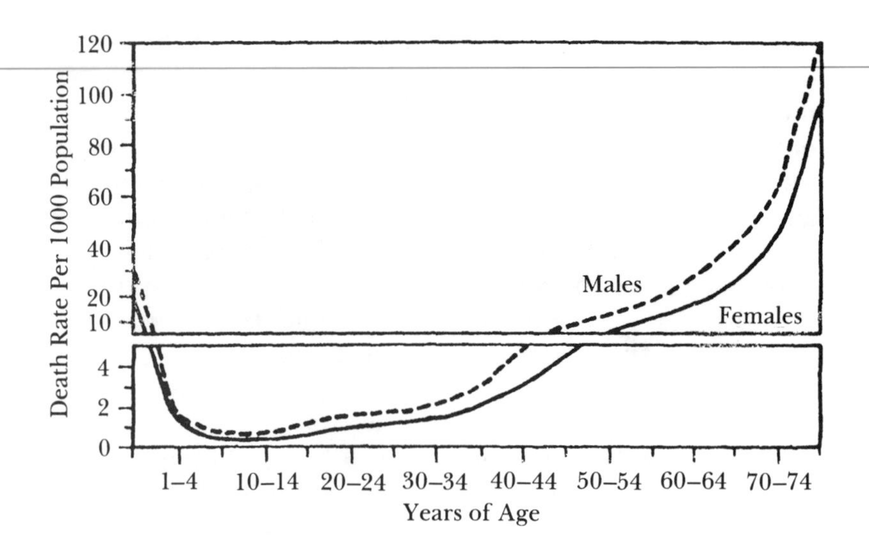

Figure 1. Lifetime morality curves for human males (solid line) and females (dashed line) in modern America in 1950 (from Alexander, 1987). The general shape of the curve remains the same across the world, and the differences between the sexes also remain about the same. The implication is that human lifetimes follow predictable programs, evolved as a result of natural selection (data from U. S. Department of Health, Education, and Welfare, National Office of Vital Statistics, Special Report 37, 1953).

because their mortality rates are different in the same way all over the world.

How can one approach an analysis of this curve? First, we can imagine it as divided into sections that can be examined somewhat separately. One section could involve the increase in mortality during early and middle adult lifetimes. This increase is generally described as owing to senescence, defined as a gradual increase in susceptibility to environmental insults such as diseases and accidents. Why does this increase in susceptibility take place? One might think we simply wear out. This hypothesis, however, makes little sense when we realize that unlike nonliving things, living organisms are not composed of static materials but are constantly changing the molecules that compose them; how could we "wear out" if this is the case? Moreover, each of us begins as a single cell and eventually develop into an organism containing billions of cells, yet, as the mortality curve shows, later in life we cannot even maintain this body; this change in ability to maintain ourselves is what we must explain. Finally, in different species, the individual organisms wear out at greatly different ages—most species in a few hours, weeks, or months, others such as elephants, parrots, turtles, and humans in a hundred years or more, and redwood and bristlecone pine trees only after a few thousand years. Why should such enormous differences among species occur if organisms simply wear out? Some people have noted that only a finite number of cell doublings occur in culture tissues and thought that this limit is what decides lifetimes. But, again, why is the number of cell doublings different in different organisms? Still others have noted that toxic materials accumulate in our bodies and suppose that this is the reason for deterioration. But we still must answer why should they accumulate in a few hours in some organisms and across several thousand years in others. The method I am using here to eliminate certain hypotheses that have been erected to explain senescence is called the comparative method. By examining the array of different kinds of organisms and comparing them to humans, we can falsify many hypotheses invoked as general explanations for something that happens in a single species.

Biologists such as Peter Medawar and George Williams took an approach to this problem of advancing senescence that was quite different from those of their predecessors. They noted that mortality inevitably occurs as a result of accidents, predation, and disease. They also realized that this accumulating mortality gradually reduces the reproductive significance of events happening later and later in life because many organisms are dying, leaving their genetic materials no chance to reproduce themselves, and the residual reproductive possibilities for the organism are being reduced. In other words, any genetic element which contributes the same positive effect toward the maintenance of the organism in which it finds itself throughout the life of the organism cannot create as large a benefit later as it does earlier. The later effects of the genetic unit cannot affect its own spread as much, via benefits to the reproduction of the organism, because most individuals will have died, diluting its later effects, and those still alive at advanced ages will have less of their reproduction remaining. The consequence is that, if conflict ever occurs between early and late effects, the early effect will tend to win. There are two relevant circumstances: first, genes may have multiple effects, some earlier than others. Because development is a unitary phenomenon it is probable that all genes have multiple effects. As one biologist put it, because of the unity of the individual organism, all genes affect the action of all other genes. Genes spread by contributing to the reproduction of the whole organism. If different effects of the same gene are adversarial (some beneficial, some deleterious), early effects tend to be worth more than later effects: indeed, a gene may be saved (may reproduce itself) because of its beneficial early effects even if there are also inevitably accompanying late deleterious effects. Or if a gene only gives a beneficial effect for a short period during the lifetime and is neutral at other times, such time-specific effects will be more beneficial if they occur early. Whenever the beneficial effect is not occurring, the result is in effect deleterious. In a third case, if a gene has precisely the same effect throughout life, but the individual's lifetime changes so that the effect changes from being beneficial to being deleterious, exactly the same consequences will result (for example, if I had a gene that gave me an inclination to play touch football during the noon hour it would long ago have ceased to have any beneficial effects and become increasingly deleterious!).

The overall result of the process I have described as resulting from these three "kinds" of genetic units is that over long periods of natural selection there will be an accumulation of beneficial effects early in life and an accumulation of incidentally accompanying deleterious effects (or lack of beneficial effects) later in life. This is the basis for the "pleiotropic" theory of senescence, published 36 years ago (Williams, 1957); it was named for the phenomenon of pleiotropy, or multiple effects of genes. That senescence remains of great importance is indicated not only by peoples' concern with the finiteness of individual existence, but also by the fact that long series of papers and books have been published on senescence, many within the past few years. One reason for continued attention is the implication, seen repeatedly in newspapers and other popular publications, that there is a medical possibility of increasing the human lifetime dramatically, perhaps even doubling or tripling it. The pleiotropic theory, however, does not support this prediction. Nor does the effect of 100 years of medical technology (Fries, 1980), which appears mainly to have reduced the likelihood of premature deaths, but not increased the longest lives, or what demographers call the maximum average life length. These are not trivial facts, considering the amount of money used in gerontological research under the presumption that massive increases can be effected in the human lifetime.

But does the pleiotropic theory continue to be supportable with closer scrutiny? Let us see. One of its predictions obviously is that over long periods of natural selection a generally higher mortality will lead to higher rates of senescence, the reason being that the higher the mortality rate the greater the reduction of the reproductive significance of gene effects that occur late in life. Therefore, species with higher rates of mortality should have shorter average maximum lifetimes, and they do. Even within species the prediction holds. Men die accidentally and as a result of within-species competition more often than women: they have a higher mortality rate. As predicted from the pleiotropic theory, men also have a higher rate of senescence, and this is the fundamental reason why there are much larger numbers of widows than widowers everywhere in the world and more women than men in homes for elderly people. It is a further prediction that this gender gap will not disappear just because women undertake the same kinds of risky lifetimes that men have led across human history. Because of the residual genetic difference that must have appeared between the two sexes with respect to senescence rates, the gap will only narrow. Another prediction is that the more a population deviates from monogamy, over a sufficiently long period, the greater will be the difference in senescence rates between the two sexes because polygyny tends to cause the two sexes to lead different kinds of lives, in which, under increasingly extreme polygyny, males tend to take higher risks than do females, thus to die at a higher rate from accidents and within-species competition and combat.

One more dramatic example tests the pleiotropic theory by comparative study of mortality rates. In most of the so-called social (or eusocial) insects there tends to be a single reproducing queen living with tens, hundreds, thousands, or millions of her own offspring; in the Hymenoptera (wasps, bees, and ants) the colony—no matter what its size—is a one-parent nuclear family. The workers and the queen have the same kinds of genes: their differences are determined only by the kind of food they receive during development—an aspect of the environment. Nevertheless, the workers have short lives because their particular phenotype has throughout history undertaken the tasks in the colony that more often lead to mortality—searches for food and defense of the queen and the nest. The queen, in contrast, remains inside the nest and is protected there by the workers. In honeybees, for example, the difference in life length ranges from a few weeks of life for a worker to a few years for a queen. Because the queen's phenotype (body, soma) has, across history, tended to outlive the worker kind of phenotype as a result of being kept safe from accidents and predation, that kind of phenotype has also evolved to undergo a relatively slow rate of senescence. Regardless of how well one treats a queen or a worker, the queen lives many times as long as a worker. Thus, the eusocial insects very strongly support the pleiotropic theory of senescence, and in a rather remarkable way.

In still another test of the pleiotropic theory, we can ask why some organisms die suddenly without much evidence of senescence, quite unlke our own gradual increase in mortality across the adult lifetime. The answer again supports the pleiotropic theory. The organisms that die suddenly without evidence of gradual senescence are those, like salmon and soybeans, that reproduce only once in their lifetimes. Ecologists call them "semelparous" (one-time breeders) and ourselves "iteroparous" (iterative or many-time breeders). For a semelparous organism the last reproductive act is the same as the first one, hence is always identifiable. Once an organism has reproduced for the last time, natural selection can no longer protect it from any source of mortality, meaning that if it dies, for whatever reason, because no reproductive possibilities remain there can be no further selection, hence no tendency to remove the source of death. On the other hand, if no act of reproduction is reliably the last one, as in iteroparous organisms like ourselves, then some selection, however weak, will remain against mortality. Long-term selection thus causes semelarous organisms to tend to die suddenly just following reproduction, and iteroparous organisms to become gradually more susceptible to mortality, thus to senesce gradually. Again, the pleiotropic theory is strongly supported by comparative analysis of different kinds of organisms, and so we are increasingly led to believe that it forms the basis for understanding our own mortality curve and what can be done about it.

Why is medical technology unlikely to increase human lifetimes dramatically? What does the pleiotropic theory of senescence predict will happen at the end of life? The chances of reproducing again at this stage of life are almost nothing. Throughout history selection very late in life life would be expected to operate as follows: One or another source of mortality will tend to be most important, and when this is the case selection automatically will work more intensely against the most important source until its effects are reduced so that another source of mortality exceeds it in its reproductive effects. Again, selection will work most intensely to reduce the effects of the new source of mortality, but only until still another source exceeds it. This process will continue, its long-term overall effects being to leave an increasingly great number of sources of mortality lurking just 'below the surface" to affect the aging organism. To reduce the effects of any one—or even several or many—of these multiple sources of death cannot have a dramatic effect on life lengths. Medical scientists have recently begun to realize the trivial effects on population structure of cures for individual problems that occur very late in life, even before they began to understand the pleiotropic theory of senescence. With this theory they know the reason.

If the pleiotropic theory of senescence is the general explanation for mortality curves, medical technology can primarily remove premature causes of death, thereby making the curve more angular (Fries, 1980), but is unlikely to increase substantially the average maximum lifetime. This I believe is an astonishing and non-intuitive result with enormous signficance for the support of research.

There actually is a way to extend the average maximum human lifetime that is consistent with the pleiotropic theory of senescence, but not many people are likely to engage in it. It is simply to have one's reproductive organs removed—to be castrated. We know this not only from domestic animals but from the castrati—humans castrated within recorded history, either accidentally, or on purpose to serve in harems or because of the effects on their singing voices. Just abstaining from sex and other reproductive activities won't delay senescence (though it might reduce the likelihood of certain kinds of accidental and competitive sources of mortality in the individual's lifetime) because our unaltered bodies are still programmed by evolution to senesce at particular rates. Selection has thus caused us to begin the process of senescence not at the first age of actual reproduction but at the usual first age of reproduction, whether or not we actually reproduce then. But, as several investigators have suggested from work on rats and other organisms, staying too lean to reproduce is expected to retard senescence because physiologically it is a little like castration; it inhibits activity of the reproductive organs, and in some regards changes the phenotype temporarily in a direction similar to that of castration. Of course, not everyone can imagine enjoying such a condition even more than, say, castration, and it is also true that emaciation can lead to death from other causes such as susceptibility to diseases.

A little reflection shows that the pleiotropic theory of senescence explains not only the gradually increasing rate of mortality among adults as they age, and the very high rate near the end of life, but as well the extremely high vigor and strength of young adults. Beneficial effects of genes are concentrated among juveniles and young adults; these are the times of greatest ability to resist most sources of mortality and illnesses that lead to mortality. Genes that give their greatest benefits to juveniles and young adults will be more likely to reproduce themselves because they are influencing the greatest number of individuals with the greatest amount of their reproduction still remaining. Such genes are more likely to remain in a population.

Apparently, higher rates of mortality among juveniles than among young adults result either primarily or solely from higher vulnerability. Very young juveniles, for example, tend to be vulnerable just because they are so small, and sometimes because they lack protective structures or behaviors. Lacking suitable parental protection, such juveniles are more susceptible to predation. Compared to experienced adults, juveniles also undergo more novel tests by the environment, and sometimes more severe tests; as a result of being exposed for the first time to this or that disease, those lacking immunity or the ability to develop it tend to die out.

Why doesn't senescence begin in juveniles, or before the usual first age of reproduction? The reason is that, even though deaths are occurring, because none of the individuals in a population are reproducing, and because they are nearing the age of reproduction and as well growing and developing, their likelihoods of reproducing are going up, not down as in adults past the usual first age of reproduction. This set of circumstances causes mortality to be precisely offset by increases in reproductive values of the remaining individuals. A good way to think this through is to consider the offspring of a single parent, given that the parent must provide the protection and calories necessary to bring the offspring to reproductive success. If half of the offspring typically die on the way to adulthood and reproduction, then any individual past the period of mortality will be worth twice as much as one before it. Any individual is worth the most, reproductively, at just the usual first age of reproduction, as can easily be seen by considering at what age one should purchase breeding stock of, say, cattle or other farm animals, if the price is the same regardless of age. The best age would be at the time of first reproduction because none would be lost to mortality before reproducing and no feed or other expenses would be required to cause them to reproduce. Now it can be seen that the reproductive value of an entire population of growing, developing juveniles will be the number of individuals multiplied by the reproductive likelihood of each. If there are half as many individuals, they will be worth twice as much, in terms of the proportionate representation of their genes in the next generation. Unlike juveniles, the reproductive probabilities of adults are diminishing continually, and that is why they senesce and juveniles do not.

Now I am going to discuss briefly one more human trait that has to do with the lifetime and the pattern of mortality across the human lifetime. The trait is menopause, and it is an extremely important trait that affects everyone of both sexes, women directly, but children and men indirectly. Menopause refers to that time in a woman's life, usually between 45 and 50 years of age, when she ceases to prepare ova, and the remainder of her body, for the act of further baby production. In layman's terms she becomes postreproductive. But we will have to examine that term "postreproductive" very carefully. Perhaps the first idea to explain menopause was that women have simply senesced so far by middle age that they cannot continue to produce offspring successfully, so they stop. But this idea leaves many unanswered questions. Why should menopause be virtually restricted to human females, and why should it be such a definite event in a woman's life if it is merely a part of senescence? Why should women have senesced so far as to cease reproduction halfway through the average maximum lifetime of humans, which is somewhere around 85 years? For a long time it was also thought that human ova become so likely to be mutated deleteriously when the mother is middle-aged that the population is damaged by the addition of damaged babies. But that hypothesis will not explain why individual mothers cease reproducing, for those that continued, despite the occasional problem, would surely outreproduce those who abstained. A third hypothesis derived from the realization that humans have added about 50 years to their average maximum lifetimes during the long period of their evolutionary history (we surmise this by comparing the lifetimes of the primates most similar to us, and by evidence from the archaeological record of humans). This added period of life is essentially all postmenopausal for women, so some people argued that selection actually lengthened men's lives and only incidentally dragged women's lifetimes along with it, the correlate being that men continue to make sperm (hence, to be at least potentially directly reproductive) all their lives. The falsifier for this proposition appears to be that women typically outlive men. But the question remained how natural selection could add almost 50 years to the human female's lifetime if it was all postreproductive.

If we attempt to use comparative method to understand menopause, as with several human attributes (such as concealment of ovulation, our uniquely large and complex brains, or our unique sociality), we find nothing among nonhuman species that strictly compares with human menopause. Perhaps some whales, elephants, and maybe a few other species such as horses, have something near the ends of their lives that could be a rudimentary menopause. But nothing like menopause in humans seems to exist in any other species. What else is distinctive about humans that might be relevant? Humans are one of the most extensively and intensively parental organisms. Unlike practically all other species they tend their offspring until they, the parents, themselves die. Indeed, through wills and bequests we humans arrange to provide for our offspring even long after our deaths. The hypothesis was generated, again by George Williams in his 1957 paper on the pleiotropic theory of senescence, that menopause evolved because a time came in a woman's life when it became more reproductive for her to tend the descendants she had already produced than to produce additional ones. This hypothesis has been expanded to include the possibility that women actually undergo changes at the time of menopause that are considerably more profound and involves turning them into much more politically inclined individuals than before, so that in fact they are overseeing the fates of not only their own offspring and grandchildren, but at least sometimes the entire clan of relatives that are reproductively important to them (Alexander, 1990). This hypothesis may be able to explain why elephants and horses and whales give some evidence of rudimentary menopause. They, too, are highly parental, and they live in female-dominated groups of close relatives. As William D. Hamilton showed in 1964, a gene can contribute to its own spread and persistence not only by causing its bearer to produce and assist offspring but also by causing it to assist non-descendant relatives such as nephews, nieces, and cousins. This is true because, just like descendant relatives, non-descendant relatives carry the genes of an individual in proportions that are correlated with social circumstances that can be used to set up particular patterns of social interaction. In other words, genes can increase their spread and persistence through causing their bearers to aid known non-descendant relatives as surely as they can by causing parental or grandparental care. And the more relatives one can help at once, the more likely any genetic unit contributing to such help can spread itself and become consolidated in the species as a whole.

I have discussed only one example of human attributes that can be analyzed by biologists, and some of the questions and possibilities that derive from it. There are many such examples. Moreover, in the space available here, I have had to deliver a greatly condensed version of a very important subject. More detailed discussions can be found in Williams, (1957) and Alexander (1987), and in recent issues of *Science* and *Nature* (e.g., see Letters, *Science,* June 11, 1993).

Senescence is not an easy example for my purposes here because it is a non-intuitive phenomenon, and it is not a direct result of selection, but rather something that happens *in spite of* selection. As my arguments indicate, selection works against senescence and susceptibility to mortality, but cannot entirely prevent it. I chose this difficult topic because it is of great importance in the everyday lives and thoughts of individual humans and to medical practice and the distribution of research money; it is likely always to remain closely connected to issues of very great importance to humans. I felt that it illustrates well the nature of the scientific approach to basic human attributes or human nature.

Returning to the introduction, I would like to draw a fairly simple conclusion. Analyses of human nature, whether evolutionary in their approach or not, need not conflict with anyone's ideas about the nature of the universe, including the human aspects of it, and there seem to be no good reasons for foregoing such analyses. This conclusion presupposes that people will generate and cling to views of religion and other nonscientific topics in fashions and forms that admit to the usefulness of scientific analyses of even the most hallowed subjects; this is what I meant earlier by "concessions on both sides." I think it is a poor practice to adopt views that deny the validity of analytical approaches to anything in the universe, living or non-living. It is equally poor practice, however, to dismiss or disparage the ideas of people who for whatever reasons choose not to engage in this kind of analysis. There is ample reason in our world for scientific studies that seek to identify the undeniable on every hand, and also for searches for personal meaning via religion and the humanities that need not involve science or any general versions of undeniability at all. Good fences really do make good neighbors.

References

Alexander, R. D. 1987. *The Biology of Moral Systems.* Hawthorne, New York: Aldine de Gruyter.

Alexander, R. D. 1990. How did humans evolve? Reflections on the uniquely unique species. *University of Michigan Museum of Zoology Special Publication* 1: 1–38.

Fries, J. F. 1980. Aging, natural death, and the compression of mortality. *New England Journal of Medicine.* 303:130–135.

Hamilton, W. D. 1964. The genetical evolution of social behavior I,II. *Journal of Theoretical Biology* 7:1–52.

Williams, G. C. 1957. Pleiotropy, natural selection, and the evolution of senescence. *Evolution* 11:398–411.

Where in the World Is God?

Owen Gingerich

Owen Gingerich is a senior astronomer at the Smithsonian Astrophysical Observatory and Professor of Astronomy and of the History of Science at Harvard University, where he also chairs the department of science. Besides over 300 technical articles and reviews, Dr. Gingerich has written popular articles on astronomy in several encyclopedias and journals. In 1989 he published *Album of Science: The Physical Sciences in the 20th Century* and in 1992–93 two anthologies of his essays, *The Great Copernicus Chase and Other Adventures in Astronomical History* and *Eye of Heaven: Ptolemy, Copernicus and Kepler* in the *Masters of Modern Physics* series from the American Institute of Physics. He is also the co-editor of *A Source Book in Astronomy and Astrophysics.*

The title of this essay is not to be read, "Where in the world is God?" as if God is lost or missing, but rather, "Where, in the world, is God?" I wish to inquire, as a natural scientist, about the interaction of God in the physical world, and as background to this inquiry it is necessary to prepare a framework about the nature of scientific knowledge.

Let me begin, however, by turning the clock back almost precisely 500 years, to November 7, 1492. Just before noon a brilliant fireball exploded over Switzerland, and near the Alsatian village of Ensisheim a stony meteorite plunged three feet into the ground. Three weeks later the Emperor Maximilian rode into town and, puzzled by the stone, consulted his advisors. They decided exactly what it was: a miracle, a wonder of God, a signal of favor to the Emperor.

In the five centuries since 1492, people have commonly

This essay is based in part on the Gross Memorial Lecture delivered at Valparaiso University in 1992.

come to accept meteorites, comets, the northern lights, and other such former mysteries as natural, normal phenomena and not as miracles or signs from God. There are, nevertheless, many very intelligent people who somehow wish they were still in a world where brilliant fireballs were generally seen as miraculous events. Before I have finished I shall return to this claim, but several other points require attention first.

I have in hand an apple. I let it go, and it drops to the floor. Why? I could say that it is God's will that the apple falls. I am not being facetious, for I firmly believe that God is both Creator and Sustainer of the Universe, and part of this sustaining power is the maintenance of the laws of the natural world. In fact, the very origin of the expression "laws of nature," from the time of Newton and Boyle, arose through the concept of divine law, and it is probably not accidental that modern science arose in such a philosophical/theological environment. But much as we might assert that the apple falls because of divine will, such a statement does not pass muster as a scientific explanation. What science requires is a broader explanatory scheme, one that links falling apples and the fall of the moon, and that enables us to calculate the trajectories of rockets or the spin of a skater.

After Newton published his *Principia,* critics complained that he had not really "explained" gravity, and that for the moon, or the apple, to be pulled toward the earth by invisible means was just plain occult and superstitious. Newton was sufficiently troubled by this to add a "General Scholium" to the second edition of his book, in which he admitted that he could not explain the essence of gravity. "I feign no hypotheses," he said, but he added that space was the "sensorium of God" and that somehow God's sustaining action throughout space could let the moon or the apple know immediately that the earth was attracting it. Thus we can see that there are multiple levels of explanation for any phenomenon, but over the years one vast, panoramic scientific picture has been put together that has been singularly successful in explaining phenomena in the natural world. I shall argue that scientists, as scientists, need to play by the rules of the game that have been developed for doing science, and I shall argue that the bottom line is not scientific proof but scientific coherence.

In order to place all of this into a fuller context, I would like to describe a few aspects of a project that I have been working on for the past few years. A dozen years ago the most widely publicized and most widely viewed science program aired on public television. It was Carl Sagan's "Cosmos," a thirteen-part series that celebrated the vast richness of the universe and extolled the crisp, rational approach of natural science. As an advisor to the series, I suggested filming locales and scripting details for the historical sequences on Kepler and on Huygens.

Nevertheless, there were parts that I found hard to swallow. At the outset Sagan stood before the camera and intoned, "The cosmos is all that is, or ever was, or ever will be." For many viewers, this was a flat out declaration of atheism. "Really?" asked one of his somewhat startled producers. "We just put that in because it sounded poetic."

In any event, the materialistic and anti-religious bias of the "Cosmos" series is flagrant enough that my students regularly notice it when I show the Kepler episode to my class at Harvard. Would it be possible to present science in a different light, as an intellectual activity that grew out of a Judeo-Christian philosophical tradition, in a series that sensitively portrays the epistemological boundaries of science, and that declares the glory of God? Some of my friends in the American Scientific Affiliation, a flourishing group of scientists who take both science and the Bible seriously, thought there ought to be an opportunity to organize some science television with a subtly different spin from the fare that has been hitherto offered.

We began brainstorming the possibilities with what seems in retrospect astonishing naivete. We supposed, for example, that if we could find financial backers and produce a first-rate series, then PBS would cheerfully buy our programs, and our backers would get their money back. No way! If the tapes were really good, PBS would agree to show them free, but would be a lot happier if we added another million for publicity to guarantee that the stations would all show them together in prime time.

I am pleased to say that we raised enough money to get some top professional help to block out treatments for six episodes. I proposed to call the series "Six Riddles of the Universe," but Geoff Haines-Stiles, who had been associate producer of "Cosmos" and "Creation of the Universe" and who helped us script our programs said, "Why not be up front with what you're doing? Why not call your series 'Space, Time and God?'" and that is the title that has stuck. The individual episodes have titles such as "Can Facts Lie?," "Was Copernicus Right?," "Does the Universe Have an Edge?" and "Are Atoms Forever?" In the course of this essay, I would like to use the proposed but as yet unfunded series as a background for raising the question of how and where God fits into a physical universe. But first I want to give you some flavor of the mix of images and ideas that might transform some of the abstract concepts into what we think could be visually compelling television.

The thrust of the second episode "Was Copernicus Right?" is to show how science attempts to build a coherent vision of the universe, something that makes sense in the way it hangs together, and that such a structure of explanation often goes beyond immediate observations and so-called "scientific proofs." The scene begins at the Pantheon in Paris, where on January 8, 1851, Jean Bernard Leon Foucault swung his now-famous pendulum to demonstrate the rotation of the earth. As I am about to enter the building, a motorcycle courier rushes up with an urgent message: a challenge to find a "scientific proof positive" that the earth moves—in fact, it offers a $1,000 prize. I go into the Pantheon and set the pendulum swinging in a re-creation of this *experimentum crucis.* It is a very long pendulum, suspended from the ceiling high overhead; its rhythm is slow and stately, and it will keep swinging for a long time. In the course of this critical demonstration the plane of the pendulum's swing will appear to rotate as the earth itself turns.

The scene shifts to Torun in Poland, to the house where

Nicholas Copernicus was born in 1473. With a wonderful model, called a "shadow orrery," it is possible to show the heliocentric arrangement of the planets and to watch their motions: swift Mercury on the inside, Venus, the earth, Mars, Jupiter, and, finally, the outermost planet known to Copernicus, Saturn, barely creeping along. By switching on a bulb on the earth in order to view the sight lines from the moving earth, we can see how a simple sun-centered arrangement produces rather complicated apparent motions.

In Copernicus' day, the whole business of throwing the earth into motion seemed rather ridiculous. What Copernicus saw in mind's eye flew in the face of all common sense experience, which teaches us that the earth is firmly fixed. If it were spinning and speeding about the sun, would not the birds whirl off this dizzy planet? Would not a rock, thrown upwards, land in another county? It was neither observation nor exasperation with an overly complex received system that set Copernicus on his path, but simply the aesthetics of a beautiful arrangement that so neatly explained the major apparent complexities of motion, and, as a compelling bonus, provided tight linkages that automatically placed the fastest planet, Mercury, nearest the sun and the slowest, Saturn, at the most distant reaches of the planetary system. It was an arrangement "pleasing to the mind," as he put it.

The scene shifts again, to the Vatican gardens where Galileo told Pope Urban VIII that he could not admire enough those who had accepted the Copernican system *despite* the evidence of their senses. Yet Galileo argued that he had finally found a physical proof of the Copernican system—namely, the tides. But Urban reminded him that even if the tides could be explained by the motion of the earth, God in his infinite wisdom could have created the tides in many other ways. The Pope was more right than he knew: Galileo was wrong, and the tides are today explained by the gravitational effects of the moon and sun, something Galileo dismissed as "occult."

Yet the Pope lost the argument. Even though Galileo had no satisfactory proof—no "scientific proof positive"—he had many splendid examples of phenomena that were explained more logically or more clearly by a heliocentric system—so many, in fact, that the whole picture began to hang together and make a lot of sense. Its sheer explanatory coherence was convincing. It was, to use a slightly pejorative term, rhetoric rather than proof, but it won the day.

Once again the scene shifts, to Woolsthorpe, the Newton homestead with its legendary apple tree. Curiously enough, even Newton had no "scientific proof positive" that the earth moved, but his entire system of the world, as it was called, made no sense without a massive, comparatively immobile, sun near the gravitational center of the system. Newtonian mechanics was so thorough and consistent that it was believable; it had every mark of truth, whether or not it was proved in some dramatic specific way. Eventually Foucault's famous experiment would provide direct evidence for the rotation of the earth, but it would have little impact simply because people were already convinced.

So now it is back to the Pantheon. The pendulum has been swinging for 40 minutes, and the plane of the swing has rotated. Clearly the earth's motion has been demonstrated. A scientific proof positive! Or is it? As I leave the Pantheon, I suddenly remember the challenge in my pocket. Can I collect the thousand dollars? I do not have space here to spell out the denouement of the episode, but in a nutshell, Einstein's theory of relativity tells us that there is no absolute reference frame, that space itself has no meaning apart from the measurable masses within it. You can choose any coordinate system you like, including one fixed in the earth, though the calculations are decidedly messy if you insist on considering the earth as the fixed reference frame. Messy, but enough to keep me from collecting the prize money.

The point I have tried to make is that science paints a marvelous explanatory picture of the universe, the chief and central quality of which is the coherence of the scheme rather than individual proofs. This notion becomes of critical importance in understanding theories of cosmology and, even more especially, of biological evolution. Thus, with episode two as essential background, let me skip ahead to episode five, to a place where Space and Time intersect with God, that is, to a question that has been central to this volume: How God's agency impinges on the origins of life on earth. I want to use my historically informed view of the nature of science to look at a major scientific theory, biological evolution by variation and natural selection.

In episode five I would propose to address some of the evolutionary issues, always remembering that science is trying to build a coherent explanatory structure of the universe. Of course, theology has also tried to build coherent, explanatory structures of the universe. One explanatory tack might be to say that what we observe is simply Divine Providence. That is how the seventeenth-century astronomer Johannes Kepler explained why Tycho Brahe left Denmark in a huff, because that move was essential for the two astronomers to get together. One might also say that it is God's will for apples to fall when dropped. Much as we might believe that gravitation continues to act through God's continual sustenance of the universe, this does not pass as a satisfactory *scientific* explanation. Scientific explanations owe their success to an automated, mechanistic way of understanding how things happen. The scientific theory of gravity enables a scientist to calculate how an apple will fall or how to plot a trajectory of a spacecraft from the earth to Jupiter.

Depicting the universe as a mechanistic, automatic system turns out to be one of the highly successful rules for doing science. But it is essential to keep in mind that the universe might not be like that in reality. Treating the universe as an automatic, mechanistic system might be nothing more than a rule of the game. It might not be an intrinsic property of the universe at all. It is this understanding of the rules of the game that is essential for understanding the nature of biological evolution. We need to keep in mind the rules as we inquire in episode five, "Are We Alone?"

The sequence begins, perhaps a little artificially, with me busily photographing a stained glass window that reproduces Masaccio's "Expulsion of Adam and Eve from the Garden of Eden." While I am at work, a young missionary couple approaches, engages me in a discussion about the Biblical story of creation and hands me a book entitled *Life—How Did it Get Here? By Evolution or by Creation?* I tactfully explain to them that I think the book asks the wrong question. The choice should not be "creation or evolution?" but "design or chance?" Evolution is a particular mechanism; it could be the way God chose to create the universe. *Both* creation and evolution could be correct.

But my alternative query, "design or chance?" also has it problems. Recently *Great Ideas Today,* the Britannica's yearbook for their *Great Books of the Western World* series, published an earlier lecture of mine subtitled "Reflections on Natural Theology" in which I cite these alternative questions, "creation or evolution?" versus "design or chance?" In a printed response to my essay, philosopher Mortimer Adler argues that an element of chance is necessary for a theistic position. If the universe were designed with no choices and hence no chance, it would simply *be,* running along a totally determined and godless course. This, he declared, is a great theistic heresy. I quickly realized that the nuances of my intended position would be better served by framing the question as "purpose or accident?" "Design" suggests a master blueprint, perhaps even a rigidly pre-determined plan. If there are no choices, Adler believes, there is no room for God. "Purpose," in contrast, opens an element of choice; it is even possible that by introducing choice and chance into creation, God surrendered some of his omniscience, with the result that even God might be surprised by some of the results.

In all of this I am, of course, articulating the theistic view of the universe. I passionately believe in a universe with *purpose,* though I cannot prove it. A scientist who approaches the world from a diametrically opposite orientation is the Oxford biologist Richard Dawkins. In his book *The Blind Watchmaker* he has deliberately set out to frame the argument of *accident* in such a compelling fashion that atheists can feel intellectually fulfilled. Otherwise, he says, the apparent evidences of design in the world are almost overwhelming. He greatly admires William Paley's *Natural Theology, or Evidences of the Existence of the Deity Collected from the Appearances of Nature* and says that when it comes to complexity and beauty of design, "Paley hardly even began to state the case." Yet he argues that in his conclusions Paley was wrong, "gloriously and utterly wrong." Dawkins has attempted to capture the theory of biological evolution for his avowedly atheistic interpretation of the world. Intelligent life has come to be, he maintains, by a zigzag, opportunistic, accidental path. That we are here as sentient beings with consciences is an astonishing but meaningless freak pattern of events. Notice, however, that this is Dawkins' religion, his "atheology" one might say. His opinion rests on the presuppositions he brings to the data of the natural world, but his is a conclusion not inherent in the data.

What, then, are the data for a theory of biological evolution? Obviously, a TV episode would try to demonstrate some samples, and here is where television images can be a great deal more efficient than a stand-up lecture. First, we have close structural and morphological relationships of living creatures, whether it is the five-digit bone structure that runs from the fins of the ancient coelacanth (a fish sometimes called a living fossil) right through to apes and humans, or whether it is the amazing similarities of genetic DNA coding. It is also the temporal relationships seen in the strata of the geologic column, from the hoary Cambrian seabeds up past the great extinctions, into the Miocene, Pliocene and Quaternary. Finally, it is the geographic distribution of species, the differing ways in which similar ecological niches are filled in diverse, separated zones.

To make a *scientific* theory to account for these data requires an automatic, mechanistic approach, or in the phrase of another contributor to this volume, Professor Dick Alexander, an analytical approach. To say that the species exist because God created them is no more satisfactory as a scientific theory than it would be to say that apples fall because God wills it so. The scientific theory must then look for continuous and natural, that is, chemical or physical, ways of forming new species from existing ones. Now we know that no two individuals of a species, once we get above single-celled clones, are exactly the same. One possible strategy is therefore to suppose that the variations can accumulate, and by natural selection these variations can eventually build differences so great as to define a new species. This is the central thesis of the biological theory of evolution, and it is the only working scientific theory we have. We must not delude ourselves into thinking that the details are even close to being understood, for example, how a wing or an eye can evolve into existence. The fossil record provides hints, but in detail it is an embarrassment because of the paucity of intermediate types and because of the evidence that so many species stay essentially unchanged for hundreds of millions of years. But to say that the theory of evolution is a failure, or ought to be dumped because it has not as yet come up with certain specific details is to miss the point about the nature of scientific explanations.

Let us return for a moment to the Copernican theory. If the earth is moving in an annual orbit around the sun, the nearer stars should show a perceptible annual wobble in their positions, something called the annual parallax. Copernicus knew that this was a prediction of his theory, but explained that it was not observed because the stars were so very far away—"So vast, without any question, is the divine handiwork of the Almighty Creator," he declared. For nearly three hundred years astronomers tried in vain to detect annual parallax. Not until the late 1830s was this tiny effect finally established with convincing measurements. The point is that the Copernican theory was adopted not because of a suspended anticipation that parallax would be found, but because of the coherent, integrated view it provided in the meantime, long before the full details of the proofs had been achieved.

By the same token, the theory of evolution provides a way of organizing the observational data of biology. As a scientific theory, it necessarily assumes that the processes occurred through some mechanistic, internal rules, that is, without outside divine intervention. It is not that science is atheistic or anti-God, or that it supports Dawkins' "blind watchmaker" thesis. Rather, these are the rules of the game, the way science builds its explanatory models. Science has no answer about the question "purpose or accident?" But on the other hand, it cannot preclude divine intervention in the origin of life on earth.

The amount of genetic information contained in the DNA in every cell of our bodies is so awesome that many distinguished scientists, such as Francis Crick and Fred Hoyle, have expressed their disbelief that it could have arisen by chance in the time available, that is, within the five billion years of the earth's existence. To the outrage of some evolutionists who have adopted the "blind watchmaker" thesis as their philosophical stance, Hoyle has compared the probability of this happening to the likelihood of a 747 aircraft being assembled by a whirlwind in a junkyard. This, they feel, is a brutal attack on their atheology; and so it is if you assume that mechanistic science and the world it describes are one and the same, for the evidence suggests that a super-intelligence—the term Hoyle uses—"[has] monkeyed with physics, as well as with chemistry and biology, and that there are no blind forces worth speaking about in nature."

So, what I want finally to discuss is divine intervention, a topic with close connections to the sixth and last television episode. But first I should note the bottom line of episode five, "Are We Alone?" If evolution is a blind, capricious, meaningless process, it is debatable whether intelligent life would ever arise again. Distinguished evolutionists such as the late G. G. Simpson and my Harvard colleague Ernst Mayr have argued vehemently against the existence of intelligent life elsewhere. (A frank look at humankind suggests that high intelligence may not be correlated with long-term survival of the species.) On the other hand, many astronomers and physicists, including Carl Sagan and Frank Drake, have equally vehemently defended a galaxy teeming with intelligent, alien civilizations. I would have to say that scientifically, it is a toss-up.

But what about theologically? Do the great monotheistic religions have anything to say about it? Traditionally, Christianity has depicted humankind as the top of the pyramid. It is true that the human brain is the most complex entity known in the entire universe. The humble blade of grass, so complex in its DNA, is no less impressive than the journey-work of the stars, to paraphrase Walt Whitman. Compared to the human brain, stars are utterly trivial. So there are empirical reasons to suppose that the universe was designed and created for us. Yet, from a theological perspective, we have no basis to circumscribe God's creativity. European Christendom was unprepared for the new forms of life, not to mention the seemingly alien peoples, that Columbus encountered five hundred years ago, and we are still coming to terms with that encounter of another world. Today it might just be sound theology to think of the larger universe as teeming with other, almost unimaginable, life forms. As men and women steeped in a Judeo-Christian tradition, we dare not limit God's creativity.

Now having set the stage with these preliminaries, I want to address the question of where, in the world, God is, or more particularly, the question of divine intervention in the physical universe. We can envision God as creating and recreating the universe from moment to moment. Such a view of God as sustainer of the universe is one to which Newton would subscribe, and one to which I would subscribe. Each moment is an independent creation, yet we observe an apparent connectivity. There would be no meaning to conscience if we could not anticipate future consequences of our choices based on past experience. No one really knows why scientific theories can predict things, or why the causal connectivity exists, but—pace David Hume—it seems to be there. To postulate this moment to moment action of God is, however, more useful as a theological perspective than as a scientific notion. The late Donald McKaye, a neurophysiologist and a thoughtful examiner of the relations of science and religion, compared this activity of God's to the carrier wave of television—it makes it all possible, but it is not the program. And what science is interested in is the program.

So let's look at the program and examine three scenarios for God's involvement or intervention. Just to be specific, I shall take as an example the *paradoxides* trilobite. For many years I showed to my classes a fossil of this unusually large three-lobed creature from the Middle Cambrian sea bottom, remarking that it was called *paradoxides* because it seemed to have no obvious ancestor in the Cambrian strata. Not long ago I had a teaching fellow from the geology department, and after the lecture he came up and whispered to me that the real paradox, when the creature was named, was that the fossils occurred only on the eastern coast of Massachusetts and in Morocco. Today, we understand that these two areas, contiguous 500,000,000 years ago, have split and drifted apart. But how did *paradoxides* come to be in these ancient seas? I would like to consider three options or scenarios.

Option 1 is to say that at one moment once upon a time there was no *paradoxides* and the next moment it was there, like the magician's rabbit pulled from an empty hat. Perhaps *paradoxides* came slithering up out of the mud, full grown, female, and pregnant. This is not so much different than the views of our medieval predecessors who thought eels were born out of mud. Let me embellish the scenario slightly. God says, "It has been at least five years since I created a new species. I guess I will make a trilobite today. I made another one sort of like it, not quite so big, some time back, so I will try to do a little better this time." And voila! *Paradoxides* is born, with all the appropriate structural similarities to the other trilobites in the Cambrian sea.

There is a curiously familiar ring to this option. When Isaac Newton realized that the planets would each be attracting the other, he feared for the stability of the planetary system, but he proposed that God would from time to time readjust the system to maintain its order. Newton's continental rival and critic, G. W. Leibnitz, promptly retorted that this was "a very mean notion of the wisdom and power of God." Would such an explanation as Newton's deter astronomers from investigating further? It did not stop the French theoreticians, who in the next century closed the gap by showing that the solar system was stable despite such gravitational perturbations. God was no longer actively needed for this task.

Option 1 is the scenario commonly adopted by the creationists. It agrees perfectly with the observations, that is, with the fossil record. Scientifically, however, it is a dead end, because it provides no explanatory framework whatsoever for all the relationships addressed by the theory of evolution by natural selection, or for the observational data that 99.99 percent of all species that ever lived are now extinct. A complete option 1 scenario would require *paradoxides* eventually to become extinct. We see species dying off every year nowadays as habitats change, but sometimes the demise of species seems much more catastrophic. I refer here to the impact of a giant meteorite at the end of the Cretaceous period, which appears to have given the *coup de gras* to the dinosaurs, an essential step for the development of intelligent life on earth. The mammals could not have proliferated and flourished without the deliverance of these ecological niches from the reptiles. From a creationist viewpoint, that impact must be seen as a "wonder of God," just as the inhabitants of Ensisheim in 1492 viewed *their* smaller meteorite as a stone from heaven.

Now for option 2, which starts with a creature similar to *paradoxides,* but with a mechanism that is considerably more detailed. A few cosmic rays zoom through the DNA of the parent creature's germ cells; mutations occur, and its offspring is different. After one, or perhaps a series of steps, a *paradoxides* is born. My anthropologist colleague Irven DeVore likens the chances for beneficial random mutations to the task of tuning up your MG by standing fifty paces back and blasting it with a shotgun. Possibly one pellet nudges the right valve by the right amount before the engine is simply destroyed. But the mutations of option 2 are different: though triggered by uncertain causes and their intentions masked by the uncertainty principle (a fundamental physical limitation in tracking the ultimate movements of atoms), these are sent by God to achieve a definite goal.

Option 2 is indistinguishable from option 1; it too matches the observations. Scientifically, however, it is much more interesting, because it helps explain the structural and temporal relationships between living forms, and because it presents a much greater incentive to probe and understand these relationships. It also would explain the incredible amount of information contained in DNA, which is difficult to account for by the accumulation of variations from seemingly random events. Since evolution requires variations, here is a meaningful, theistic way to make them.

At least one other possibility remains: the option that Howard Van Till has called the "functional integrity" view of creation. In option 3, God's plan and design of the universe prepares for living beings to arise without further immediate intervention according to preordained rules of order. God could create potential forms at the outset, leading to what Van Till has described as "possibility space." The initial creation would then be "pregnant with potentialities conceived in the mind of the Creator." Part of the purposeful planning would involve pathways and catalysts that make it much easier to get from inert molecules to life forms, from prokaryotes to intelligent life. The miracle of life would then be in the planning, not in a series of discontinuities.

Even the atheists must admit that such pathways exist. Otherwise the sheer amount of genetic information contained in the cellular DNA is completely inexplicable by random association of atoms in the time available. The fact that we exist would tell them as much. A theistic scientist, convinced that option 1 provides a satisfactory solution, might refuse to search for such pathways. He might argue that such gaps in our theories are a real feature of the universe and not just a gap in our present knowledge. When pressed for a positive agenda in a recent discussion, Phillip Johnson, an outspoken critic of Darwinian evolution, remarked that he would not waste his own money on scientists looking for such pathways for the chemical formation of life. But since such pathways continue to be discovered, those opting for the first scenario will be increasingly hard pressed to explain why they are present if they are unnecessary.

Let us suppose that *paradoxides* existed in the mind of God as a potential form at the outset of the universe. We can well imagine that, for reasons science can as yet scarcely grasp, such a form might be particularly stable or likely. The theory of evolution claims that the species are formed by a process of natural selection from existing variations, but it seems beyond our ken ever to comprehend why those particular contingent variations arose. As one of my atheist colleagues put it, if the coelacanth had turned left instead of right when he first climbed up on the beach, we might not be here. Within our present scientific understanding there would seem to be no way to design a mechanism to guarantee a specific outcome, since the variations are essentially indeterminate. We would have to consider that God had planned only general purposes, and that in some profound sense might have been "surprised" by the specific possibilities that emerged, including both *paradoxides* and ourselves.

In general, options 1, 2, and 3 lead to the same predictions concerning the observational data. Can we find any evidence in nature that might point more specifically to the form of option 3, in which life in the universe unfolds toward God's ultimate purposes but not necessarily according to specific designs and blueprints? I would suggest that we need to take a hard look at what Darwin calls "imperfect adaptation." Let me cite a modern example, one unknown to him. Most people's red blood cells include a protein named hemoglobin A. In many areas of the tropics, however, a quarter of the population carries hemoglobin S, which differs by one out of the 287 amino acids that form the hemoglobin molecule. Persons with only hemoglobin S suffer from a severe shortage of red blood cells that is called sickle cell anemia. Those with both hemoglobin A and S are notably more resistant to malaria, however. Immigrants to more temperate zones where malaria is not prevalent—persons including much of the black population in America—are significantly more prone to sickle cell anemia, without accruing any advantages from the resistance to malaria. A theory of natural selection can explain the differing distributions of the hemoglobin S and A; it does seem easier to argue that the pairing of properties (advantageous resistance to malaria versus likelihood of severe anemia) results from a blind process leading to imperfect adaptation rather than from deliberate design. I personally know too little of biology to have come to a firm conclusion regarding imperfect adaptation (that is, "blind" selection nevertheless fulfilling God's ultimate purposes), but

I think this kind of scenario would not necessarily be incompatible with my theology.

As we look at these three options from a theistic perspective, to a first approximation they all agree with the observational data. Our individual decisions about which option to choose may well depend on other considerations, such as our psychological or theological orientations, often based largely on what other people whom we respect have told us. But option 1, which might be called the "God the magician" or the "eels from mud" scenario, and option 2, "God the tinkering miracle maker," are both "God of the gaps" theories. They imply that God left his creation imperfect, so that there will always be gaps in the continuity where science cannot enter. The gaps are filled by God's specific action, and are therefore unaccountable by human knowledge. These options are anti-scientific.

For a scientist working within the contemporary rules of science, only option 3 provides a satisfactory answer. Only option 3, with the assumption of full linkages from the initial creation to the slow evolution of the elements, thence to the origin of life from inert matter, and to the rise of intelligent rational creatures, offers us the requisite mechanistic continuity or functional integrity. To this, the theist will add the assumption of purposefully planned pathways whereby God's conceptual potentialities can be worked out. The atheist may argue that such pathways must naturally occur, based on the evidence of our presence. Curiously enough, as far as the observational data is concerned, there is also no distinction between the theistic or atheistic perspectives. I cannot prove the existence of God from elements of biological design any more than Richard Dawkins can prove his atheism on the grounds cited on the dust jacket of his book, "Why the evidence of evolution reveals a universe without design."

As a theist, I would personally find a creation with functional integrity satisfying and inspiring, and as a theistic scientist I would, alongside my atheistic colleagues, pursue the search for the specific pathways that made the development of life possible. I would cheer on agnostic colleagues such as Stephen Jay Gould, who has made it his life work to explore some of these almost inscrutable pathways. The pathways and conceptual potentialities we might find are designs, as much and perhaps even more worthy of an omnipotent Creator than adjustments to creation made in real time, as in options 1 and 2.

When I set out to discuss where, in the world, is God, I mentally noted that in addition to the divine agency or purposeful planning that would be involved in the development of life on earth, there was also the omnipotent intervention at the moment of creation, when the universe began—a universe purposefully designed to bring forth conscious, conscientious, creative creatures. Yet perhaps even that intervention defies a temporal moment. Augustine, at least, appears to have agreed with this.

For some decades we have been happily living with the concept of the Big Bang, a moment roughly 15 billion years ago when in a split second of awesome creativity the universe sprang forth in a blinding flash. While there are still compelling reasons to accept this scenario, it has been challenged and somewhat eroded in the past few years. Part of this challenge has come from Stephen Hawking, who says in his best-selling *A Brief History of Time:*

> The idea that space and time may form a closed surface without boundary also has profound implications for the role of God in the affairs of the universe. With the success of scientific theories in describing events, most people have come to believe that God allows the universe to evolve according to a set of laws and does not intervene to break these laws. However, the laws do not tell us what the universe should have looked like when it started—it would still be up to God to wind up the clockwork and choose how to start it off. So long as the universe had a beginning, we could suppose it had a creator. But if the universe is really completely self-contained, having no boundary or edge, it would have neither beginning nor end: it would simply be. What place, then, for a creator?

From a theistic perspective, the answer to Hawking's question is that God is more than the omnipotence who, in some other space-time dimension, decides when to push the mighty ON switch. Indeed, creation is a far broader concept that just the moment of the Big Bang. God is the Creator in the much larger sense of designer and intender of the universe. The very structures of the universe itself, the rules of its operation, its continued maintenance—these are the more important aspects of creation.

God's creativity, design and purpose may transcend any instant of time that can be specifically identified with a moment of creation. By now some of you may be thinking, "This man claims to be a theist, yet he seems to be arguing against any active divine intervention throughout the history of the universe. He argues just like a deist, that God set it all up at the beginning and then let it run. And what is worse, he's now waffling as to whether the universe had a beginning! Is his a God that matters? Ask him if God intervenes in the universe to create miracles!"

Just to avoid getting sidetracked by this last query, let me support a statement made by Howard Van Till, who has said:

> And what about miracles? Would they be disallowed or downgraded in a Creation marked by a gapless economy? Not at all. In fact, I would say that the status of miracles would be elevated. In special creationist scenarios, numerous "miraculous divine interventions" appear to be obligatory functions—mandatory supplements to the incomplete economy of the created world. Without them there would be no way to bridge the gaps conceived to be characteristic of Creation's developmental history. In a Creation marked by functional integrity, however, miracles would no longer be obligatory; instead, they would be voluntary acts of God freely performed for their special revelatory or redemptive value.

I need to add a gloss to Van Till's remarks and to what I said earlier. When I mentioned option 2, in which God might intervene through that microscopic level where the uncertainty principle reigns, I said it was anti-scientific, but probably I should have said unscientific, in the sense of violating the standard rules of scientific explanation, which call for continuity and mechanism. This does not mean that option 2 is wrong or even impossible; it simply means that it is outside the accepted bounds of science. If we believe in a world in which choice and chance play a role, each in itself a minor miracle to the extent that choice lies outside the bounds of science, then the intersection between the world of physics and biology and the world of theology could well lie in that hazy netherland of the uncertainty principle.

From my own perspective, it simply makes more sense to me to assume that the universe has purpose and meaning, and that our consciousness is not just a macabre joke played on us by a dicey but amazingly complex configuration of atoms. And for the universe to have meaning in human terms, we, the most complex organisms in all known creation, must be part of that purpose and meaning. So here I turn to the Scriptures for help. Without doubt the most crucial sentence of the first chapter of Genesis is verse 27, so essential that the idea is immediately repeated lest we miss it: "God created man in his own image, in his own image created he him, male and female created he them." Succinctly put, the stance of the biblical account is that God is not only Creator and Designer, but there is within us, male and female, a divine creative spark, conscience, and consciousness.

Creativity is the realm of art, music and literature, as well as scientific explanations and understanding. Conscience deals with right and wrong, the tree of good and evil and moral choices. Consciousness allows us to contemplate life and death, space and time, purpose and meaning. To think of these questions is to envision transcendence, something far greater than we are, greater than all our creativity and conscience and consciousness can conjure, a Creator standing beyond and yet within the universe.

Just as I demand coherence as the quintessential criterion in my scientific understanding, I ask for coherence in philosophical and theological understanding, something that hangs together and makes sense. And this brings me at last to the most difficult and challenging of the television episodes, a final episode entitled, "Is the Cosmos All There Is?"

Transcendence seems like too big a word even for PBS, but that's the bottom line, and looking for hints of it in the arts and music, in humankind's quickening conscience, and in the big questions that consciousness opens before us—these must be the fabric of the episode. In the end I am prepared to declare, "The Cosmos is NOT all there is, or ever was, or ever will be." For me, that is the ultimate coherence.

Scientists Who Keep the Faith

Donald B. Heckenlively

Donald B. Heckenlively is Vice President for academic affairs and professor of Biology at Hillsdale College, where he has been a member of the faculty since the early 1970s and where he has also held appointments as Director of Biology, Chairman of the Department of Natural Sciences, and as the Director of Academic Computing. Formerly a teaching fellow at the University of Michigan, he holds a Ph.D. in zoology from the same institution and an M.S. in biology from New Mexico State University. He is the author of numerous articles in such publications as *Nature, Condor, Wilson Bulletin, Collegiate Microcomputer,* and various other science publications.

By training, I am an evolutionary biologist. By conviction, I am a believing and mostly practicing Christian—as with most Christians, the practicing part is the most difficult. I see no contradiction between these positions. My task here is to explain this lack of contradiction, and also, if possible, to help to provide an operational continuity between science and theology. Thus this essay will address three areas. First, I will be discussing some problems with biblical interpretation, especially with regard to Genesis, both from a biblical and from a scientific viewpoint. Second, I will present and discuss evidence for natural selection and its implications, including a brief summary of microevolution, and also an overview of the evidence for macroevolution. Third, I will attempt to draw together these threads into a common statement of faith and science, as viewed from a biological perspective.

Biblical Interpretation

I do not want to belabor this point, but it is important to realize that it is a recent movement within the fundamentalist Christian community that insists on a literal "six days" understanding of Genesis. This view is strongly at odds with science and is one of the few Christian positions that *is* at odds with science. In another essay in this volume, Ronald L. Numbers has shown that such a rigid interpretation of Genesis is a very recent phenomenon, essentially gaining widespread popularity in Christian circles since World War II. I view the growth of this movement to be, in part, an indictment of science education in recent years. The prevalence of such notions could not survive a *real* understanding of what science is saying. My indictment here is two-fold. On the one hand, there has been excessive emphasis in recent times on the secular nature of science, as argued against particularly by Drs. Johnson and Moreland and alluded to by Dr. Gingerich in the public response to Carl Sagan's *Cosmos* television mini-series. On the other hand, there has been very poor dissemination of what science truly has to offer, both in content and as a system for orderly investigation, to the detriment of us all. Biblically, literalism is questionable. What might we do, for example, with Psalm 90: 4?

> For a thousand years in thy sight are but as yesterday when it is past, and as a watch in the night.

This and many other passages in the Bible warn us that it may be presumptuous to equate our measure of time with God's. In other words, we do not really know what is meant by the "days" in Genesis. To borrow from astronomy, it seems a little silly to limit God's actions to the rate at which a relatively small planet spins in space in the vastness of the universe, even if it is our planet. Especially intriguing is Howard Van Till's citation from St. Augustine referring to the idea that the "days" of Genesis should be regarded as topically ordered revelation. Let us use our own imagination to envision some early Israelite seekers of the truth asking God how Creation occurred:

> The Israelites say, "Tell us, God, how you created all this."
> God replies, "I started with a pinpoint of energy with an immeasurably immense mass. In less than a second I expanded this into the Universe. Over eons, some of this expanding mass coalesced into primaeval solar systems with stars and pre-planetoid masses. At the right time on earth, I took a primordial mixture of methane, carbon dioxide, water and various nitrogen compounds and, using energy from volcanic action and lightning, I set in motion reactions that resulted in lipids, peptides and nucleotides as pre-life molecules. Using lipid micelles with intrinsic proteinaceous enzymes I then created proto-cells."
> The Israelites respond, "Huh?"
> So God tries again: "In the beginning I created the Heaven and the Earth. The Earth was without form and void. . . ."

There are several points to be made here: First, those who would invoke a literal six-day interpretation of Genesis are attempting to lock us into an understanding of origins that is many centuries old. Second, perhaps Genesis was not intended to be understood in quite the way the literalists think it should be. As a scientific statement, I cannot get much beyond the peculiar relationships between days one and four in Genesis, much less the interesting events involving animals and humans in the later days of creation. On day one, God created light and darkness. On day four, God finally created the sun and moon. How do we measure "days" before the creation of the sun? Where does the light come from prior to the creation of the sun? I think it is a reasonably well-established tenet of science that light, as we know it, arises from the sun. We have a real puzzle if literalism is pushed too far. I know that it is possible to invoke various *ad hoc* explanations about God's ability to do all things, with special fogs between days one and four, etc., but that is not very satisfying, given the consistency of God-given chemical and physical laws as we know them in other contexts.

I have concluded that Genesis literalism can exist by one of four means, at least as I have seen it among various friends and colleagues over the years:

(1) *Compartmentalization:* An individual may simply refuse to think about the contradictions between what science tells us about the universe and what a literal interpretation of Genesis implies. This is not uncommon among scientists who are fundamentalist Christians.

(2) *Distrust of Science:* An individual may simply refuse to believe evidence because he holds contrary views. It should not be lost on us that such an individual is disputing not just biological evidence, but also saying that virtually all of astronomy, geology, physics, anthropology, and chemistry, as well as various other disciplines, are to be mistrusted or disregarded if biblical literalism is to be upheld in the face of scientific contradiction. The late William T. Keeton, one of the truly great authors of biology texts, wrote some years ago, "Science can say neither that there is a God or that there is not.... Yet, any aspect of the physical universe can be studied by science, and anyone making the existence of God stand or fall on some supposed fact about the universe risks having science destroy his God." His comments, in context, seem intended to be both challenging and sympathetic. But herein lies a dilemma for many: the "God of the gaps" position mentioned by several other contributors to this volume.

(3) *Selective Use of Evidence:* An individual may approach scientific evidence selectively, using whatever fits various preconceptions and ignoring or dismissing evidence that does not fit those preconceptions. Unfortunately, this characterizes much of the "scientific creationism" school of thought. In fairness, I should also acknowledge that anyone, including evolutionary scientists, can use evidence selectively.

(4) *Ignorance of Science:* An individual may not know that Genesis is fundamentally different from what science tells us about the history and development of the universe and particularly about our little corner of it. I have a friend who is an artist and a biblical literalist; quite honestly, I do not think that various contradictions have ever occurred to him because he knows almost no science.

So, what does Genesis really say to us? At bottom, it tells us that we are beholden to a Creator who made it all. But we tend to get into trouble if we insist on using Genesis as a scientific text. In fact, it is many centuries old and most likely was passed along as an oral tradition long before scribes recorded it.

As a theist, I regard the laws of chemistry and physics to be God-given properties of the universe. I also believe that living organisms developed—*evolved,* if I may use the word—within patterns established by God-given biological laws of nature. It is perhaps also worth mentioning here that if one asks a scientist about the laws of physics and chemistry (or other scientific principles, including evolution), they are simply *given properties* of the universe. That is, science, as such, can only describe what *is*. Speculation on *why* it should be that way is largely outside the realm of science, falling much more into the realm of theology.

As a scientist who is a Christian, I regard Genesis as received wisdom from God. That is, for a story of how the universe and life began, it reads well for wisdom given from on high, from God, to a very early human culture many centuries ago. At this level, I regard Genesis as eternally *true*. The central aim of the first book of the Bible is not to offer a scientific explanation but to say who created life, and whom we should continually thank for having done so. As a scientific text, Genesis may be regarded as on a par with the wisdom of Aristotle or the Roman, Pliny the Elder, but I would not want to be locked into any of them in preference to more recent explanations.

In his book, *Darwin on Trial,* Phillip Johnson characterized supernatural considerations as "unacceptable" to scientists and he carries on at some length in his essay in this volume about the liability of this position. In the context of his book, he was responding to a statement from the National Academy of Science that a basic characteristic of science is a "reliance upon naturalistic explanations." From Johnson's response, it is clear that he did not understand what the Academy was saying. It is a basic tenet of modern natural science that it is driven by empirical observations—that is, by repeatable, objective measurements of the natural world. Supernatural considerations in this context are not so much "unacceptable" as "unworkable." There is no way to measure the supernatural. Carl Hempel, the noted philosopher of science at the University of Pittsburgh, formerly at Princeton, characterizes such considerations as "pseudo-hypotheses," that is, having the appearance of an hypothesis but devoid of any means for measurement.

Some of us are old enough to remember the mid-1960s, when Russian cosmonauts returned from orbiting the Earth to announce that their trip had disproven the existence of God because they saw no angels in space. We all smiled to ourselves at such ignorance, but how different is that from insisting that scientists include a supernatural dimension in their deliberations? Naturalistic empiricism is both a strength and a weakness of science. On the one hand, it provides a system for verifiable conclusions about the material universe. On the other hand, it limits the range of topics that can be addressed by science with validity.

J. P. Moreland is less strident on this point, but he falls into the same fallacy. At one point in his essay, he challenges the notion that there is some single issue that distinguishes science from non-science. As a practicing scientist, my first question always is, "Can I measure it? Can I at least measure some of its derivative properties? If so, it is science." To the extent that appropriate hypotheses to be tested by empirical evidence can be derived from *anything,* Moreland's "theistic science" is not totally unworkable, but his suggestions might hold less promise than he seems to hope. It is true that some scientists are insisting that naturalistic methods preclude the existence of God, even to the point of denying that the concept of God can in any way be compatible with a naturalistic understanding of the universe. John Muller, psychologist and president of Bellevue College in Nebraska, has an apt saying for this: Such individuals are "confusing their methods for their metaphysics." That is, they have moved beyond a basic limit of science, that it cannot deal with supernatural phenomena, to conclude that the supernatural does not or cannot exist. This is a fundamental error. Unfortunately, it is not uncommon within science and mathematics today.

The Theory of Natural Selection

On the theory of natural selection, let us begin somewhat intuitively: If I have five kids and you have three, who leaves the most genes to the next generation? [Answer: me] If I have five kids and you have three, but three of my kids die from cystic fibrosis—which is an inherited disorder—who leaves the most genes to the next generation? [Answer: you] That is the essence of the theory of natural selection, except that what is happening in most cases is much more subtle. For example, if I have a set of genes that reduces my ability to leave offspring by three percent and you have a set of genes that reduces your ability to leave offspring by only two percent, who will have the most genes in the next generation? [Answer: you]

Any biological factor can have the net effect of reducing such ability to leave offspring. It could be a genetically inherited defect like cystic fibrosis, but the biological factor need not be something representing a gross defect. It might be something as subtle as a genetically-based physiological ability or inability to cope with high or low temperatures. It might even be some aspect of one's ability to socialize and interact with others, to the extent that such things are genetically-based.

There is a human condition called "sickle cell anemia" that provides a classic model of how natural selection operates. Sickle cell anemia is an inherited condition, in which the hemoglobin molecule that carries oxygen in the blood stream is a variant form, resulting in red blood corpuscles that take on a half-moon, or "sickle" shape. It is due to a recessive gene, so that an individual would have to inherit the condition from two parents who were both carriers of the condition to contract sickle cell anemia. Affected individuals have a number of difficulties associated with delivery of oxygen to the cells of the body and poor circulation of red blood corpuscles. Mortality is high in affected individuals, often at a young, i.e., pre-reproductive age. The geographic origin of the gene is Africa. In some areas of Africa, the frequency of carriers of the sickle cell gene is quite high, representing a majority in a population. In Americans of African descent, the proportion of carriers of this gene is relatively low—about nine percent of the American black population.

Why is there such a profound difference between African and American blacks? It turns out that carriers of the sickle cell condition—that is, individuals who carry one gene for regular hemoglobin and a companion gene for sickle-cell hemoglobin—have a greater resistance to malaria, which is a parasite in the blood stream. In areas where malaria is prevalent, carriers of the sickle-cell gene have a higher survival rate than those individuals who lack the sickle-cell gene. The areas of Africa in which we find the most carriers of sickle cell anemia are also the areas with the highest incidence of malaria. In the United States, where malaria has been virtually wiped out, being a carrier of sickle-cell hemoglobin confers no advantage and is, indeed, a disadvantage. The key point here is that a given gene is advantageous or disadvantageous only in the context of the environment in which an individual with that gene lives. That is, the environment is the principal "selecting" agent in natural selection. (It is also worth noting that a similar gene is known for individuals of Italian descent. It has been well documented historically that one of the impediments to the development of Rome as a city was the prevalence of malaria in southern Italy.)

Some critics of evolution have alleged that we lack evidence of one species changing into another species, or even of one species changing into two species. Actually, the evidence is overwhelming for microevolution. There is not enough space here to consider this exhaustively, but let me lay out the theoretical framework. Suppose that the world were shifting into an ice age, with each year successively colder than the last. The polar ice caps would be getting progressively larger. On our end of the globe, Canada would become progressively covered with thick ice and then a part of the northern United States would also become covered with ice. Suppose that I have genes that help my kids survive cold conditions, while you have genes that leave your kids less well-equipped. Who leaves the most genes in the next generation? [Answer: me]

That seems to be precisely what has gone on during the last million years or so. It has been well documented by geologists that the earth has gone through a series of so-called "ice ages" or "glaciations" in the last million years. These have been characterized by the polar ice caps growing progressively to cover a part of what we think of as the "temperate" areas of the earth, lasting for about 200,000 years, then receding for 100,000 years or so. The last glaciation ended about 12,000 years ago. The ice over Michigan during the last glaciation is estimated to have been about 5,000 feet thick.

Now let me introduce an important variable in this mix: Not all sub-populations of a species live in exactly the same environment. In the event of an impending glacial period, we would see organisms moving out of the way as best they could. The habitats sought out by some sub-populations tended to be different from those sought by others. Evidence provided by migration routes of birds today, for example, indicate that some animals sought refuge in Central and South America, while others shifted into the Caribbean, to the extent that such mobility was possible. For plants, it was a slightly different problem, since they could not just uproot and move, but a similar net shift of plant populations toward Central America also occurred, as shown by residual (or so-called relict populations of plants in the mountains of Arizona and Mexico that are near-relatives of plants growing much further north today.

In these relatively recent glaciations, we have well-documented events that had the net effect of dispersing sub-populations of organisms in diverse directions, into subtly and not so subtly different environmental settings, where they then resided for about 200,000 years, *in isolation from each other*. That is not much time in evolutionary terms, but 200,000 years is ample time for different sub-populations to accumulate a variety of genetic differences, due to differing selective pressures from different environments. In many ways it has been useful for biologists that this was a relatively brief span, because it has given us a wide spectrum of outcomes to study.

About 12,000 years ago, the most recent glaciation ended, that is, the ice receded back to the polar caps, and organisms came back into temperate North America. What might one expect to see (i.e., "predict"), as sub-populations came back together after a separation of several hundred thousand years, assuming my picture of microevolutionary changes is correct? There are several possible outcomes that we could anticipate, and these may not exhaust the list of alternatives:

(1) No significant genetic changes occur in the two or more sub-populations, so they merge back together as if no separation had occurred.

(2) The sub-populations accumulate sufficient genetic changes that they are recognizably different (to us), but still freely interbreed and are thus still one species.

(3) The sub-populations accumulate sufficient genetic changes so that they no longer interbreed, even though humans cannot see differences between them morphologically.

(4) The sub-populations accumulate sufficient genetic changes so that they interbreed only a little bit, but it seems fairly apparent in this case that populations are not going to interbreed sufficiently to bring the sub-populations back into a single, genetically cohesive group again.

(5) The sub-populations accumulate sufficient genetic changes so that they are morphologically different and no longer interbreed with other populations. Under these circumstances, we could say that complete speciation, or the splitting of one species into two or more new species, occurs.

In fact, *all* of the above alternatives are well-known and are well studied. I happen to be especially familiar with the evidence in birds, the group that I have studied in most of my research, but similar patterns have been documented from virtually all other groups of organisms as well. This model is a general one: That is, if some environmental factor subdivides a population in some way so that *genetic continuity* between sub-populations is broken (with sub-populations in different habitats), genetic differences will start to develop between these sub-populations, because each sub-population will be subjected to different selective pressures from the environment. One interesting example is the Northern Oriole, once thought to be two distinct species known as Baltimore and Bullock's Orioles, but now known to hybridize in the southern great plains of the United States. Bullock's Oriole has adapted to an arid, desert habitat, while the Baltimore Oriole has adapted to much more moist habitats. In fact, it may have been premature to consider them as one species again, because their physiological differences may prevent the genes of one sub-population from spreading significantly into the other.

As a general case, if separation of sub-populations continues long enough, sufficient genetic differences will accumulate that the former members of one population will become effectively isolated genetically from each other and no longer interbreed even when the opportunity presents itself by physical proximity. To use an example that may bemuse some of us, DNA hybridization studies have shown that humans and chimpanzees have slightly over 98 percent of their genes in common, yet I know of no one who would seriously regard a sexual alliance with a chimp as anything but perverse. Jared Diamond at UCLA has recently written a book on human social evolution entitled *The Third Chimpanzee* in recognition of the slight genetic differences between us and chimpanzees. What we have here is a picture that is far neat and clean procreation of "each creature *after its own kind.*" Instead we have a biological and genetic mess on our hands, which is precisely what should be expected if natural selection is, in fact, operating.

There are some—perhaps many—who would say, "All right, you have a case that 'microevolution' exists, but what about 'macroevolution,' that is, the development of one major group of organisms from some other group of organisms? One bird species splitting into two or three bird species does not really answer the question of how, for example, fish supposedly developed into amphibians or amphibians into reptiles, or reptiles into birds and mammals. I have attempted to show that evolution is occurring all around us, if we have but eyes to see. There is no known mechanism that would prevent this process of splitting up old species into new species from continuing on to the development of novel groups of organisms as well. Furthermore, as I shall elaborate shortly, there is good reason not to expect such a mechanism, on theological as much as on scientific grounds.

Regarding macroevolution—What kinds of evidence might be sufficient to show that macroevolution, that is the formation of major new groups, occurs by the same mechanisms that are well documented for microevolution? (1) Microevolution in itself constitutes evidence for macroevolution. (2) Fossil intermediates between major groups can be predicted. (3) Living intermediates falling between major groups can also be predicted. (4) Greater or lesser similarities in the genetic structure of various major groups, based on protein sequencing, DNA hybridization and similar studies would also be predicted by macroevolution. Such studies continue, including recent breakthroughs in which it has been possible to salvage intact DNA from fossil plants and animals, as well as new theoretical approaches that attempt to relate the geographical distribution of organisms to the development of genetic diversity. (5) There is also philosophical support for macroevolution, through the concept of interlocking support from compatible theories.

(1) *Microevolution:* Commonly accepted throughout science is the concept of "uniformitarianism," that is, that whatever we might observe today in the operation of scientific principles can also serve as a guide for the same scientific principles in the past or in the future. It is now well docu-

mented within biology that a population, given suitable genetic isolation from related populations, will develop genetic differences from these other populations due to differences in environmental selection. This process can lead to sufficient genetic differences that sub-populations of a previously united group will eventually become subdivided genetically, the process commonly referred to as "speciation." There is no known "barrier" that would prevent this process from developing new populations that were sufficiently different from ancestors that we would regard them as being representative of some new "*kind*" of organism.

(2) *Fossils:* Anti-evolutionists have charged that a central weakness of evolutionary theory is that the idea of one group of organisms developing from another group of organisms is not supported by the fossil record. In a word, this argument is bunk. The question we should be asking ourselves is not why the fossil record is so spotty, but why is it so good? It takes many special conditions for an animal or plant to be fossilized. Fossilization requires especially the right *pH* and the absence of oxygen, along with a host of other special conditions. Yet in spite of such difficulties, we do, in fact, have a variety of fossils that show intermediate forms between fish and amphibians, amphibians and reptiles, and between reptiles and birds and mammals, as well as many intermediate forms for invertebrate evolution and also plant evolution. What more could be asked? A full and complete fossil record will probably never be found because many parts of it are not there to be found.

A telling counter-argument is to ask the question, "Is there a better explanation for the fossil record than macroevolution?" So far, I haven't heard one. My remarks should not be construed to imply that no further fossils of significance can be expected to be found. Obviously, I expect to hear about many new and exciting fossil finds in the future. All I am really suggesting is that various gaps in the fossil record are not to be viewed with alarm or as a weakness in macroevolutionary theory.

(3) *Living Intermediates* It is reasonable to postulate that some intermediate forms not clearly falling into a major group might still exist in specialized habitats. Such organisms are, in fact, known. One remarkable example is the Coelacanth fishes, which were initially known from fossils and thought to be an early and extinct transitional form between cartilagenous fishes and bony fishes. A number of specimens have now been caught out of the deep waters in the Indian Ocean—genuinely living fossils. Likewise, no one knows quite what to do with Paripatus, a "legged worm" that is mid-way between the major group to which earthworms belong and the Arthropods, a major group that includes insects. There are various other examples I could cite, but my point is that a prediction of living intermediate forms has been well borne out.

(4) *Genetic Similarities:* Studies date back over thirty years in which similarities in protein structure, and by implication underlying genetic structure, tell us about greater or less relatedness between groups of organisms. More recent studies have used new techniques of DNA hybridization to study genetic similarities. I have already mentioned the data showing that humans and chimps have about 98 percent of their genes in common. Similar relationships are being explored regularly between a variety of organisms. Once again I ask, "Is there a better explanation for such similarities than macroevolution?" Again, so far, I have not seen it.

(5) *Philosophical Support:* A concept that arises in the philosophy of science is that an hypothesis gains theoretical support to the extent that it successfully interrelates with other pre-existing theories. As currently understood, macroevolution provides no contradictions and neatly dove-tails with currently understood theories, including genetics, population genetics, physiology, ecology, geology, astronomy, physics, chemistry, and paleontology. Alternative explanations to macroevolution, especially those invoking various kinds of special creation, tend to be contrary to many of these theories.

Faith and Science from a Biological Perspective

It is sometimes tempting to regard God as a "watchmaker" who started it all and then stepped back to watch life "tick on its own." Sometimes characterized as a "Deist" view, this fails to regard each new life as a miracle. As a biologist, I have studied "life" for over 30 years. At this stage of my career, I can distinguish "living" from "dead" with reasonable certainty, but a simple list of what constitutes "living" from "nonliving" is insufficient to distinguish even a fresh cow-pie from a living organism. All I can really say is that I know living when I see it.

Let me advance a novel idea: that God intervenes in the formation of each new living organism with a spark of life. Allegedly this concept of "vitalism" was laid to rest in the late nineteenth century. In large part, it was the work of Louis Pasteur and his contemporaries—showing that all known life comes from pre-existing life—that did away with such ideas as spontaneous generation and attendant notions of vitalism. During the twentieth century logical positivism, as well as a generally reductionist assumption abroad in science during the twentieth century that holds that we will one day be able to understand all essentials of living processes by the use of chemical and physical explanations, have done their mischief in turn.

Call my proposal "neo-vitalism" if you like, but I have no better explanation as a student of living processes. I expect that we will continue to discover important new insights into the ways in which living organisms function, down to and including the molecular and sub-molecular levels. These insights will even continue to provide important progress for biomedical research. But I will be very surprised if we discover anything that will give us explanations beyond a cow-pie level of understanding "life," in the end. Mary Shelley said as much in *Frankenstein.* Even if we learn to manipulate life, I am doubtful that we will truly understand it fully, unless a spiritual dimension is also acknowledged. This may sound like a "God of the gaps" position, but it is not what I am suggesting. The spiritual dimension to life remains regardless of our mechanistic understanding.

What are we really seeing in the natural world? The environment has varied tremendously, in significant ways, from one generation to the next and from one eon to the next. Geologists tell us that this tired old globe we call home has varied from age to age, with enormous changes in climate, shifts in plate tectonics, volcanic eruptions and similar environmental factors. Natural selection provides a mechanism by which populations of organisms adapt genetically to such changes with the net effect of maximizing survival of organisms in the face of such changes. In his essay in this volume, Howard Van Till alludes to God's will in such random factors as genetic mutation and variability, but provides no examples. We have here at least one situation in which a rich and varied gene pool for each species would be advantageous, given the many changes in the environment over the long haul.

One problem that we humans have is that we too often tend to project our own conditions onto the past and the future. Some of the past conditions on earth were very inhospitable to the set of organisms (including us) currently inhabiting the planet. As the earth's conditions have shifted, natural selection, as currently understood, has allowed populations of organisms to adapt within several generations. Evolution is therefore, in my view, a mechanism provided by God, who has provided a means by which populations of organisms can continually adjust in an ever-changing environment. What could be more benevolent as a mechanism provided by a loving God?

Between Jerusalem and the Laboratory: A Theologian Looks at Science

Michael Bauman

Michael Bauman is Associate Professor of Theology and Culture and Director of Christian Studies at Hillsdale College. He is also Lecturer and Tutor in Renaissance Literature and Theology at the Centre for Medieval Studies and Renaissance Studies, Oxford, where he serves as an associate dean of the Centre's summer school program. Formerly an editorial assistant at *Newsweek,* a pastor, a chairman of the general education program at Northeastern Bible College, and an associate professor of religion at Fordham University, Dr. Bauman is the author of *Pilgrim Theology: Taking the Path of Theological Discovery* (1992), *Roundtable: Conversations with European Theologians* (1990), *A Scripture Index to John Milton's De Doctrina Christiana* (1989), *Milton's Arianism* (1987), and co-editor of *Are You Politically Correct? Debating America's Cultural Standards* (1993), *The Best of the Manion Forum* (1991), and Hillsdale College's *Christian Vision* series.

> "It is absolutely safe to say that, if you meet somebody who claims not to believe in evolution, that person is ignorant, stupid or insane."
>
> Richard Dawkins, Oxford zoologist,
> in *The Blind Watchmaker*

We live in but one world; science and theology are united in that they both seek to understand it and to explain it. They do so according to their own respective method (or methods) of knowing. In that sense, both science and theology are a hermeneutic, or a way of interpreting, the world around us. Because we have but one world to interpret, and not a scientific universe along side a theological universe,

Portions of this essay appeared in *Faculty Dialogue.* Reprinted by permission.

only one full and correct answer exists for any well-formed question relating to it. A well-formed question is one that seeks, and helps makes possible, an answer that is both full (that is, comprehensive) and true (that is, accurate). The importance of such well-formed questions is hard to overstate. As Aristotle observed long ago, he who would succeed must ask the right preliminary questions. The answer to a well-conceived question, whatever that answer might be, is correct because it comports fully with reality. Answers that do not are at least partly inadequate, if not flatly wrong. An ill-formed question, by contrast, is one that makes comprehensive and accurate answers not only more difficult to find than they need to be, but might actually make them impossible. If the divine is a factor in the physical world, and both history and theology seem to me to say it is, then questions that seek and identify only materialistic conclusions, questions of the sort now asked by modern science, cannot be the well-formed and fully serviceable questions toward which Aristotle's dictum would direct us.

The instances where scientists and theologians agree in their description of our one reality are many and varied. For those agreements I am grateful. But in this essay they are not my main concern. Rather, I intend to focus attention on those places (they too are numerous) where the scientists and theologians diverge. I do so in order to offer some suggestions on adjudicating between the respective truth claims of science and theology and in order to reduce the scope of their future disagreement, as well as its attendant animosity. In the process, I intend to direct my criticisms primarily toward the scientists. I do so precisely because I am not a scientist. That is, if scientists are to be undeceived about their own shortcomings or blindspots it will probably be because someone who did not share those blindspots was able to point them out. Such is my intention: I want to suggest to the scientists that, at least to some outsiders, they occasionally appear narrowly informed, unteachable and as dogmatic as any ecclesiastical or political inquisitor could ever hope to be. I leave it to others to identify for the theologians just what the theologians cannot see and where they fail. Because I do not wish to hold the reader in suspense, much less to be vague or disingenuous, I tell you now that I think much of the adjustment and retrenchment in the sometimes heated dialogue between scientists and theologians needs to be done by the scientists, and that much of the error and unteachability in this dialogue seems to circle around the laboratory and not the seminary. The burden of this essay, therefore, is to explain why I think as I do. I offer but five observations, observations that are, at the same time, both caveats and pleas.

First, the history of both science and theology as intellectual disciplines tends to make me significantly more skeptical about the allegedly secure answers offered by the scientists than those offered by the theologians. That is, science seems a far more fickle pursuit than theology, especially when viewed over time. While Christian orthodoxy seems to have remained impressively stable over two millennia and while the constant refinement of Christian tenets in the crucible of hard reality seems not to have required any fundamental reorientation in orthodoxy,[1] the record of science is far different. The constant testing of fundamental scientific beliefs has yielded a long series of significant reorientations, some so far reaching as to topple many, sometimes most, of the supporting pillars of any and every previous (and ardently held) scientific worldview. The post-Einsteinian worldview is beginning to succeed the Einsteinian, which succeeded the Newtonian, which succeeded the Copernican, which succeeded the Ptolemaic, which succeeded I know not what. What shall succeed the post-Einsteinian (and what shall succeed *that*) we can only guess. If the history of science is a guide to its future, we can be confident something shall and that, whatever it is, it shall depart quite noticeably from its antecedents both near and far. As Austin Farrer wryly observed, "cosmological theories have a short life nowadays."[2]

But not so the Apostles' Creed, which, though it has grown over time, has never required anything resembling a fundamental overhaul, much less several. Liberal theologians of every age (with the not inconsiderable aid of non-Christian thinkers of all sorts) have tried to argue against it and have tried to put orthodoxy under siege. But their dissenting and often idiosyncratic schools of thought themselves have proved transitory and have passed into deserved obscurity. But not the creed. In other words, theological orthodoxy, unlike its numerous scientific counterparts, has undergone centuries of analysis and assault and survived largely and widely intact. Christian orthodoxy has successfully sustained meticulous scrutiny by both its friends and its enemies and yet has shown itself, and continues to show itself, sufficient to many of the most brilliant minds in history, even over a period of centuries, a claim no scientific explanation of reality can yet make. The scientists in every age, I imagine, suppose they can escape, indeed suppose they have escaped, the fate of their predecessors. They fancy they shall avoid being greatly transcended, though none has yet managed the trick. The face of scientific orthodoxy seems to have a nose of wax.

The transitoriness of scientific speculation and the uniformity and staying power of theological orthodoxy often get hidden behind both the wide diversity of theological beliefs prevalent at any one moment in time, on the one hand, and the absence of many public indications of division within the scientific community, on the other. Widespread theological disagreement seems obvious to the man on the street, who sees the Presbyterian church, the Baptist church and the Roman Catholic church all standing tall and serene on their respective street corners, their spires rising toward the heavens. What the man on the street does not see is the underlying unity of the Presbyterians, the Baptists, and the Catholics (to name but a few). He does not readily recognize their common belief in—and devotion to—the same God, the same Christ, the same creed, the same salvation. Nor does the man on the street see the various schools of thought in science, which do not erect edifices of difference on tree-shaded side streets in every city and village in the Western world. And he does not see hundreds of buildings (or view hundreds of television programs, for that matter), dedicated to Newtonian or Ptolemaic theories, standing next to the edifices of post-Einsteinianism. Unlike their ecclesiastical counterparts, those Newtonian and Ptolemaic buildings were rarely ever built, are not now being built, and shall not be built in the future because the scientific worldviews they represent have been so fully overthrown that they are consigned almost entirely to the dustbin of history. This is not to say that no valuable or enduring elements from within those systems have survived the collapse of the system from which they emerged; it does mean that those systems themselves have been greatly and widely transcended.

Here is my point: While a cross section of views at any one moment yields more agreement among the scientists of that age than among the theologians, a cross section taken over time yields the opposite result, and that result, I argue, is more significant because it reveals both the fundamental staying power of the theological interpretation of the world and the (to date) transitory nature of scientific speculation. Science does not speak with one voice, especially over time. That fact notwithstanding, science still seems to me far less willing to take any cues[3] from theology about in which direction to proceed than theology is to take cues from science, which might help explain the transitoriness of the one and the stability of the other. So also might the fact that, unlike nature, God wills to be understood and actively reveals Himself to us.

We apparently are not near the end of scientific intellection, though we are closer now than when Aristotle or Galileo walked among us. We do not know where the next grand turning in the road of scientific learning will lead us, or when it will come, any more than did Ptolemy, Newton or Einstein. We ought, as a result, to be far more hesitant than we have been to identify scientific theories as final. If you contend that scientists do not treat scientific theories as final, I simply point to the theory of evolution, which gets treated almost universally not as theory but as established and unassailable fact requiring, at most, not proof, only further nuance. The epigraph by Richard Dawkins, which heads this essay, is a telling case in point, and can be multiplied *many thousands of times,* both in print and in the classroom. But the missing link, after all, is still missing. It seems to me that we ought to be far more wary of Darwin and his hide-bound modern disciples than we now are, because even though those followers of Darwin now admit that Darwin was not entirely right, they too often refuse to admit that Darwin's theological critics are not entirely wrong. To make the point from a different branch of science, one of the positive effects of quantum theory on the dialogue between theology and science seems to be the increasing awareness we gain from it that virtually no physical or geometrical picture of scientific phenomena is wholly accurate, even though such notions or paradigms were (and still are) widely and enthusiastically set forth, whether as paradigms or as heuristic devices. We need to be more measured in the confidence we place in the scientist and in our estimate of what exactly the scientist has actually accomplished.

Second, because scientists are human, and because human beings tend to resist the overthrow of their most cherished beliefs, scientific theories, once accepted, are often exceedingly difficult to supersede. The shameful treatment of Pierre Duhem at the hands of his institutional superiors is a well known case in point. All too often, the new, even when it carries great weight of evidence, gets routinely derided as outlandish. That scientists are intellectually conservative, of course, is good. Their conservatism helps protect them from the multiple embarrassments of intellectual trendiness, of identifying fad as fact. But that scientists are unduly entrenched, when they are, is lamentable. That entrenchment reveals that scientists sometimes are, like the rest of us, resolutely unteachable. The Dawkins epigraph is but one example of the entrenchment, perhaps even intellectual bigotry, about which I speak. Scientists who think in that fashion seem to me to be what one dictionary defined as "proof-proof": the state of mind of one upon whom contrary evidence and argument have no persuasive effect, regardless of their strength. I am not alone in this observation, of course. Many writers, Kuhn and Laudan among them, have shown how dogmatism—yes, dogmatism—characterizes the periods of what we might call *normal* science. Whether we want to admit it or not, there is a remarkably comprehensive scientific orthodoxy to which scientists must subscribe if they want to get a job, get a promotion, get a research grant, get tenured, or get published. If they resist, they get forgotten.

Given how changeable previous scientific worldviews have been, one wonders how chimerical they would have proven without this dogmatism. I am not here debating the relative merits or weaknesses of dogmatism; I simply say that scientists are by no means free from it and should not be treated as if they were or permitted to speak and act as if dogmatism were a characteristic only, or even primarily, of theologians, which is preposterous.

Third, scientists often fail to admit, sometimes even to recognize, that so many of the issues and findings of science are neither purely scientific nor genuinely empirical. Because all empirical endeavors build upon, and proceed according to, various presuppositions, and because those presuppositions and procedures are inescapably philosophical, no scientist and no scientific procedure is truly philosophy-free. Empiricism and empiricalism are, after all, philosophy-laden worldviews and techniques, and perhaps not the best. If ideas have consequences, and if (as some philosophers strongly argue) empiricism and empiricalism are highly suspect, and perhaps even greatly flawed, intellectual systems, then scientists are likely to be misled if they apply these philosophical systems uncritically to their work. To put a point on it, if, as some scientists insist, real science is truly empirical and reduces only to empirical methods and the conclusions reached by using them, then there is no real science—first, because such philosophical theories are not the result of the methods they advance; and second, because theory-independent observation, analysis, and conclusions are simply not possible. That is partly why, in the middle ages, science was known as "natural philosophy." Because none of us is presupposition-free, and because (despite much contrary insistence) scientific theories often deal with the unobservable, the laboratory is no philosophy- or theology-free zone. Scientific methods and conclusions cannot be purely empirical because the unavoidable philosophical and theological underpinnings upon which those scientific methods rely are not the result of those allegedly empirical methods.

Put another way, the claim to objectivity and empiricality falls down on both sides—on the side of the scientist and on the side of science. When eating their curry, many people like to build for it a nest of rice. To employ a more American image, people like to mold a bowl in their mashed potatoes in order to hold their gravy. Science, it seems to me, has its nest, its bowl. Science always has its philosophical and theological underpinnings; physics always has its metaphysics—always.[4] To declare science a philosophy-free zone is to have a philosophy; to declare science a procedurally agnostic or atheistic endeavor is to have a theology; to claim that science is, and ought to be, value-free is to make a value statement. The question, you see, is never whether or not the scientist in a laboratory has a philosophy, a theology or an ethic when doing scientific work; the question is whether the philosophy, the theology and the ethic the scientist has are any good and are worth having. This problem they cannot escape.

Even in the pursuit of something as fundamental as self-definition, science alone is utterly insufficient. To the question, "What is the proper definition of science?" one can give only a philosophical answer because the question itself presupposes and requires a vantage point from outside science. Because we cannot tell who are the scientists and who are not until we know what science itself is, one cannot answer this question, as scientists too often do, by resorting to the tautology that science is that which is done by the scientist. The question "What is science?" is a question about science, not a question of science. Scientists want, indeed claim, to be empirical. But please note: "empirical" is a philosophical category. Without the aid of the humanities, science cannot even identify itself, much less justify, or even invent, its procedures.

To make the point in a different direction, science is not theology-free, and that is so precisely because science intentionally operates according to a procedural agnosticism, if not atheism. That is, science operates as if God cannot be known or else as if He were altogether irrelevant, if not entirely absent. By its means and its conclusions, science implicitly, perhaps even explicitly, denies that Christ is Lord of the laboratory, an inescapably theological denial. What I, as a theologian, want to tell my scientific colleagues is that, as Lord of the universe and all that it is within it, Christ is not something *in addition* to science, He is someone *in relation* to it. To operate as if He were utterly irrelevant to the laboratory is to answer, probably without careful analysis and theological acumen, the question raised long ago in the gospels: "What think ye of Christ?" Because Christ is foundational to the universe, He is foundational to science. As Thomas Torrance once explained to me,

> the countries of the Far East and of the Southern Hemisphere want our science and technology, but they have no doctrine of creation. They do not realize that science and technology rest upon, indeed arise from, Christian foundations. This is true both historically and epistemologically. We must show them that it is the Creator God himself who stands behind everything, and that he provides the rational ground upon which the various sciences rest, as well as the world those sciences unlock and help to tame. Theology and technology come as a pair. We must be quite firm about both this and their function in serving and respecting the integrity of nature.[5]

Like it or not, the systematic and procedural denial, not to say the intended destruction, of metaphysics and of theology is the death of scientific truth, if for no other reason than that it posits a dual or dichotomized universe, which we noted at the outset was untrue. Answers to questions predicated upon that same bifurcated basis, while they are perhaps true as far as they go, do not go all the way, and are not the whole truth. Perhaps an illustration will serve. No physicist today can reckon with miracles and interventions from outside the cosmic order, with interventions that break that order open. No theory they devise, no answer they propose, permits such ideas or recognizes such data, even though such data and ideas might possibly be absolutely and comprehensively true. But that inability reveals the limitations, indeed the blindness, of modern physics. Modern physics does not reveal the limitations of God and his actions, much less God's non-existence or irrelevance, assumptions implicit in scientific method as now understood and practiced. God, if we need to be reminded, works in perfect freedom, and not according to any physicist's theory of determinedness, or to any of its current variations or future descendants.

Let me put it more graphically: Any intellectual endeavor in which theology is segregated from the other disciplines and relegated to an intellectual ghetto is an instance of Jim Crow come again to the college campus because it explicitly asserts that the best intellectual paradigm is not well informed academic integration but some form of "separate but equal," which, as we learned in the old South, meant separate but unequal, not because of actual inferiority, but because of bigotry. By acting as if God Himself were irrelevant to the universe He has made and to our understanding of how it operates, scientists, in effect, practice "disciplinism," a widespread form of intellectual prejudice, even tribalism, whereby the research and discoveries of scholars are systematically disregarded simply because those scholars are members of another discipline. The Queen of the Sciences has been banished to the back of the bus by her own bigoted descendants. The fool has said in his heart that there is no God, and the scientist permits himself to operate as if the fool were right.

Science is not an autonomous set of empirical disciplines. Nothing about science properly, or actually, prevents philosophical or theological concepts from entering into it. Science, like all intellectual disciplines, ought not to conduct its business in what it falsely imagines is an air tight compartment, isolated from all other strivings of the human mind after knowledge. Because too many scientists have cut themselves off from those other strivings, they condemn themselves to discovering all on their own many things already widely known by others. For example, even though such ideas appeared new and revolutionary to some of the unphilosophical practitioners of science, many of Mach's notions were already standard fare in the writings of a number of earlier philosophers. So also was Darwin's theory of evolution. The price some scientists pay for their intellectual isolationism is having repeatedly to re-invent the intellectual wheel.

But there's more to theology in science than procedural agnosticism and atheism. Our alleged ape ancestors are treated with immense respect, even toadying homage, as the secular Adam and Eve. No attacks upon their status, much less their existence, are tolerated. Read Dawkins' epigraph again. Not to do obeisance to ancient animals ranks as scientific sacrilege, as heresy. Religion, albeit pagan, has come to the laboratory.

Furthermore, many of the scientists who insist on divorcing religion from science seem especially eager to use their science as a basis for making or altering theological pronouncements. And even when they are not eager to do so, they do so nevertheless. The literature of science (and not merely of Darwinism) is full of anti-theistic language and conclusions: The universe was not designed; the universe has no purpose; human beings result from random and mindless natural processes, or so we are repeatedly told.

To the adoration of God and of virtue, in other words, we have added the adoration of science, or at least what goes by that name. But you cannot deify the scientific method without at the same time devaluing or debasing both theology (the human understanding and application of revelation) and philosophy (the human understanding and application of reason). In the eyes of an uninformed public, many scientists, without meaning to do so, undermine our only sources of morality and freedom: God, tradition and reason. They do so by propagating the notion that only those things that are testable under controlled laboratory conditions qualify as hard knowledge; all else is merely opinion. But even a moment's reflection reveals that if every question of morality, of politics, of philosophy, and of theology, is a matter of mere untestable opinion, they can be settled only by force, not by reason. In that way (and in others) scientists sometime lead us into tyranny. Fascism and pseudo-liberalism are the not-too-distant offspring of modern man's widespread belief that science alone is trustworthy and that whatever lies beyond its pale is little more and little else than irrational prejudice, unsubstantiatable conjecture, and transitory emotion incapable of reasoned support. This vision of life, in all likelihood, modern man learned in the science classroom. Too often scientists teach and write as if the only real options available to us are science or mysticism, empiricism or bias, fact or feeling.

Simply because no test tube yields a "should" or an "ought," "should" and "ought" are not thereby banished or made suspect; science is. Moral questions—questions about right and wrong or good and bad—cannot be answered (or even raised) by the scientific methods now prevalent in either the natural or the social sciences. That does not mean, however, that they cannot be answered, have not been answered, or have no answers. It means only that with regard to the diagnostic and fundamental questions of life, science is impotent, though dangerous. The one who has not learned to ask, much less to answer, the fundamental questions of life, is indeed no man at all, but still a child, still benighted. To answer such questions, even to raise them, science is powerless. Technical schools and scientific laboratories are important and laudable things; but to advertise them as colleges or universities, or to say that those who have passed through them are thereby truly educated men and women, is a lie.

To put the point differently, God is the Lord of the entire world of knowledge, including science and technology. Science and technology that are atheistic in both conception and conduct, that are consciously cut loose from all formal considerations about God and morality, are not your dream come true; they are your worst nightmare. To utilize science and technology wisely or else to become their victims, that is the choice before us. But the wisdom that saves us from our science and technology is no commodity derived from either of them or from both. To paraphrase something C. S. Lewis said in another context, science ceases to be a demon only when it ceases to be a god. It can never cease until it figures out a way to let God be God, even in the laboratory.

Finally, with regard to science and theology, if German theologian Wolfhart Pannenberg is correct that "God is a field of force without limits of extension or power, pervading all reality, and giving rise again and again to new creatures,"[6] then both God and his actions are, in principle, detectable by science. Perhaps they already have been detected but, because of the scientific worldview now prevalent among scientists, have not been duly recognized. Strictly naturalistic presuppositions render any such detection impossible. After all, you see only what you are able to see, and the unreconstructed secularism of modern science makes us unable to see or recognize much of what might truly exist. If God is there and can be recognized, but our truncated epistemology cannot make such recognition possible, we need to get one that can.

Fourth, we ought to be more skeptical than we are both of scientific taxonomy and of the translation of the world outside our heads into numbers. That is, scientists do not actually deal with the world as they find it, they manipulate that world into words of their own choosing, into categories of their own making, into experiments of their own devising, and into numbers. Forcing a creature into one or more categories based upon our intellectual manipulations and deductions regarding, for example, its body pattern and parts, or upon our understanding of its physical makeup and prehistoric biological descent, is at least partly arbitrary, partly subjective. Such categories, though helpful and serviceable, are man made. They unintentionally, and sometimes unwittingly, collapse the distinction between what we discover and what we invent. While the beings that populate such categories most emphatically do, families, orders, classes and phyla, as such, *do not exist outside the taxonomist's mind.* Such categories are a taxonomist's useful fiction. That is, while they are mental constructs based upon careful observation, they are mental constructs nevertheless. Of course, I am not saying anything so silly as that there exist no genuine and recognizable differences between a dog and a man, or that "dog" and "man" are useless delusions devoid of all external reference.

But let us not too quickly or uncritically exchange "useful" for either "true" or "real," things that in many cases and ways are quite different.

Yet, not only are we required to accept the taxonomist's scheme of classification as both real and true, we are required to believe that the occupants of these various man-made categories are linked by a long series of now dead intermediate creatures (also duly classified and arranged), most of whom are not found to exist anywhere in the fossil record, a radically incomplete record we interpret according to the taxonomical grid provided for us. (The circularity of this procedure seems to go unnoticed and unremarked.) Furthermore, we are also required to believe that all the apparently discontinuous and taxonomically divisible groups now alive are the descendants of a common ancestor, another phantom of which (or of whom) we have no hard evidence. Please note that "ancestor" and "descendant" are part of a taxonomical scheme, and are no less so than "phantom," or "which," or "whom," words from which my scientist readers would naturally have recoiled. Their own language, the scientists must remember, is the source of recoil as well, though after years of using it the scientists themselves no longer feel its pinch. It rarely seems to occur to many scientists that the rapid evolutionary branchings posited in some theories are but a euphemism for mystical scientific leaps, though they are called by other names. Of such leaps, and the taxonomical sleight-of-hand that hides them, I am more than a little skeptical.

Further, not only is taxonomical classification theory laden, it is context dependent. That which we classify as the observed in one case fails to be so classified in another, even though that which is involved in both cases might be basically the same. That is, what is foreground and what is background vary according to the judgment of the observer, an observer who is never context-free or presuppositionless. Thus, scientists are driven back, whether they acknowledge it or not, upon the problem "What is context and what is content?," the answer to which seems to vary from situation to situation depending upon the experimenter and the experiment, regardless of the similarity of the aggregation of things involved. Even the experiments themselves are not pristinely empirical and objective, for experiments are highly stylized sets of phenomena, sets from which as many variables as possible have been artificially eliminated by the will and work of the experimenter, however well or however poorly. Of course, I am not saying that the data yielded by such experimentation are therefore untrue, only that they are not pristine. In other words, some scientists need frequently to be reminded of the significantly non-literal and pragmatic nature both of their experiments and of their theories, as well as of the language in which those experiments and theories are conceived, articulated, and defended.

Like taxonomy, quantification might itself be a movement away from the world around us, not into it. The translation of things into numbers is, after all, a translation. Frequently, neither the words nor the numbers in scientific theories are complete and exact representations of the constitution and behavior of the universe, much less are they the things themselves that they are intended to describe in words or embody in numbers and formulae. Newton had his numbers; Einstein had his; post-Einsteinians have theirs. Newton's and Einstein's formulae worked and were the basis for considerable correct prediction regarding natural phenomena. Nevertheless, on many important points, Newton and Einstein were also quite wrong, something from which their seemingly correct numbers did not and could not save them. I am not reluctant to think that the same fate awaits their number-crunching scientific descendants.

The classification of physical phenomena as data, the arrangement of data into groups, the translation of that data into numbers, the manipulation of those numbers via computation, and the transformation of the results of computation into more data and hypotheses are all guided by philosophical deliberations that are prior to and apart from science's allegedly empirical nature and militate against it, all of which ought to cause us to hold science's supposed assured results with less assurance. Judging from the philosophical and theological naivete of most of the scientists with whom I have ever spoken, those intellectual deliberations might not have been deliberations at all, but merely the unexamined and unacknowledged *a priori* assumptions of a mind untrained in a number of difficult but acutely relevant fields throughout the humanities.

The related assertion that science is measurement is, of course, a philosophical assertion, an assertion that might be flatly unprovable, perhaps even wrong. We cannot prove this assertion by invoking the principle of prediction and thereby assert that a scientific hypothesis is true if it can be shown accurately and successfully to predict the action of physical phenomena. The principle of prediction, while clearly important and serviceable, is at least as closely related to pragmatism as to truth. That is, to be able to predict more accurately than all other theories means only that one's theory is pragmatically preferable, not that it is true. We must remember that false, or partly false, theories have demonstrated impressive powers of prediction in the past. The ancient Babylonian astronomers, for example, were by no means shabby forecasters, even though they were working from many premises and principles that were quite off the mark. In other words, while prediction might (or might not) be a necessary attribute of a true theory, it must not be considered a sufficient attribute. Prediction is not proof, no matter how impressive it seems. Too many scientists, nevertheless, still think, write, argue, and teach as if accurate prediction demonstrated truth. How many times this has been done, is now being done, and shall continue to be done, only God knows. But it seems not at all likely to stop. Or, to make the case in a different direction, if prediction were really the reliable indicator of truth that some think it is, then physics itself, which has an abysmal record of prediction with regard to individual entities, would be radically undermined. Put yet another way, clear thinking philosophers and theologians understand that, on its own, pragmatic superiority is an utterly insufficient basis for knowing right and wrong. If pragmatic preference is an exploded mode of knowing in ethics, I am inclined to regard it as such in science. Pragmatism's epistemological failures are not magically eradicated simply because we now concern ourselves with a laboratory.

Fifth, to turn from the presuppositions and methods of science to its attendant morality, one begins to suspect that, because science itself yields no code of ethics, science pays too little attention to the virtues or evils of research, especially research involving the human body. In this regard, although I could marshal illustrations ranging from fetuses to cadavers, for the sake of brevity I limit myself to the latter only. After his resurrection, Christ's body still bore the marks and wounds inflicted upon it during his crucifixion. Those marks, in fact, helped persuade Thomas that this indeed was the same Jesus he had known for years. In that same scarred body, Scripture says, the Son of God lives and reigns forever. That fate, resurrection of the body, awaits us all. If Christ is an indication of what that resurrected life and body are like, and again Scripture says He is, then the things done in and to the body might well have everlasting significance, something we ought to consider very carefully before we carve up any more human bodies in anatomy or biology class. The human body is not meat, is not a "specimen," is not equipment. The human body is sacred and enduring. It ought to be treated in a way that honors its sacredness and treated in no other way. To call this body, which a few days or weeks ago was alive and now is dead, a cadaver, is vainly to impersonalize it. That such attempts are unsatisfactory even in a secularized environment like a science classroom is evident in the way so many teachers and students feel compelled to give those bodies names: Sally, Bob, Zack, Ralph, etc. A body does not become mere matter simply because it is dead. To think so is to do bad theology, not good science. To justify a public carving of human bodies on the grounds that such research aids other human bodies is simply to assert that ends justify means, is simply to offer as justification for one's efforts the same justification offered unconvincingly by Nazi scientists for theirs, is simply to resort to pragmatism, which is to do bad philosophy, not good science. In light of Christ's incarnation, resurrection and ascension, the Church has long understood the sacredness of the human body. Because of those overwhelming historical realities, the Church has taken great care in the way in treats dead bodies. It buries them in the churchyard, in the womb of the Church, where they await the resurrection of the last day. That is why the Church historically has refused to bury the bodies of suicides in consecrated ground, burying them instead at crossroads, *head down,* in careful reminder that some of the things done to human bodies, even done by those whose bodies they are, are colossally vile. The Church knows what is sacred and what is sacrilege, and it does its best not to confuse or mix the two as if there were no difference. But not so modern science, which has no category of the sacred, though that self-condemning omission does not mean that the the sacred does not exist or that science does not shamelessly violate it. No fact was ever altered simply by pretending it wasn't one. Can such violations be overcome by the grace of God? Of course. Ought they therefore to be continued? Even to answer that question one would need to stop being a modern scientist.

What scientists have done to the unborn, who are undeniably alive, treating them as if they were cash crops suitable for cultivation, harvest or destruction, is an even more horrific consideration.

Those, at any rate, are my observations and caveats. That is how the laboratory looks from the seminary, or at least to this member of it. Having watched many of them in action, I think the scientists would be better served (and would serve better) if they were more humble and more eclectic in pursuit of their quite worthy enterprise. I should hope that when they do their work the scientists would listen at least as much to those outside the laboratory as they would like those outside the laboratory to listen to them when pursuing their own non-scientific tasks. This, after all, is the golden rule of scholarship.

Finally, though it is clearly beyond both my intention and my competence to dictate to the scientists exactly how their jobs ought to be conducted and in what specific direction they ought to proceed, let me offer but one outsider's opinion, an opinion motivated by sincere goodwill for my laboratory colleagues. I believe that what we need now is not something akin to an aimless collection of more data, but research (of every sort) directed by principles, illumined by ideas. Those guiding principles and those illuminating ideas must, by their very nature, come to science from outside science. Science, to be kept serviceable and humane, must be kept humble and teachable. It must acknowledge its extra-disciplinary debts, debts it always has.

To the question "Is science enough?" the answer is emphatically "No."

Notes

1. Creeds are not imposed by simple ecclesiastical fiat. Instead, like scientific findings in other branches of knowledge, creeds typically undergo what might roughly be described as a five stage development: observation, reflection, articulation, testing, and confirmation or rejection. In the first stage, Christian thinkers examine carefully the text of Scripture (that is, the content of revelation) and the course of their own and others' experience of living in agreement with Scripture, at least as they understand it. Second, they reflect deeply and carefully upon what they have observed, in order to grasp its true significance. Because they must not be content with an inarticulate devotion and understanding, to this perceived significance and to their conclusions concerning it, they naturally try to give thoughtful and precise expression. Their newly formulated ideas are then submitted to testing in the twin crucibles of life and thought to see if those ideas can withstand the rough and tumble of genuine human experience and the rigors of systematic intellectual scrutiny. If they cannot, they are rejected, or else modified and tried again. In this informal but effective way, the Church has invested decades, even centuries, in capturing in precise creedal form the tremendous truths revealed in the historical events connected with Jesus of Nazareth and the words of Scripture used to describe and explain them. Of course, this is not to say that creeds have nothing to do with the pronouncements of bishops and councils; they often do. But creeds typically find their roots elsewhere, in revelation and in the life and thought of the church. This is especially true of the Apostles' Creed, which though at some points is still controverted, has been

tested by long experience and careful, repeated reflection upon that experience in the light of Scripture and reason. Furthermore, because the Apostles' Creed has grown out of centuries of biblical exegesis, human experience and reflection, it continues to be both relevant and reliable. It continues to ring true because, like all good theology, it is deeply rooted in divine revelation, on the one hand, and human reason and reality, on the other.

2. Austin Farrer, *A Science of God?* (Geoffrey Bles, 1966), 32.

3. What might be the precise nature and content of such cues I cannot now say. How philosophy and theology ought ideally to be introduced into the sciences is a question the answering of which might require a radically new way of doing science. This paradigm shift might be as far reaching and profound as that made by Copernicus or Newton or Einstein. That I myself, as a theologian of culture, am unable to make it is neither an embarrassment to me nor a refutation of my claim that it might be needed. I offer only an analogy, drawn from criminology. When a detective attempts to solve a crime, he not only searches for clues, he invents hypotheses. In this search and invention, the detective has this great advantage: He knows he is deciphering not some random occurrence, but tracking the work of a mind. Knowing this, the detective suitably modifies the character of his hypotheses and alters both the nature and focus of his search for clues, as well as his definition of what might or might not be relevant data. Human criminals, for example, unlike mindless and lifeless matter, have discernible motives and concoct false alibis in order to cover their tracks. In short, they leave clues of a very distinctive sort. The scientist, by the same token, if he were to entertain the God factor in his laboratory and decide to trace the workings of Infinite Mind rather than of mindless matter, might need to alter what he considers the boundaries of acceptable hypothesis, what he admits as relevant data, how he forms and executes his experiments, how he draws and articulates his conclusions, and what he imagines constitutes a convincing refutation.

4. I am not saying that all physicists must or do have the same metaphysic, only that while they are doing their work they cannot avoid having one and applying it.

5. Michael Bauman, *Roundtable: Conversations with European Theologians* (Baker Book House, 1990), 115.
6. Ibid., 52.

God and Evolution: An Exchange*

I
Howard J. Van Till

Although the rhetoric Phillip E. Johnson employs in his article "Creator or Blind Watchmaker?" (*First Things*, January 1993) differs in some details from that of the "scientific creationists" of North American Christian fundamentalism, the effect of his pronouncements is the same. That is, it perpetuates the association of Christian belief with the rejection of contemporary scientific theorizing, thereby ensuring that the gulf between the academy and the sanctuary will only grow wider. Moreover, ironically, the concept of creation implicit in his argumentation is one that has moved far afield from the Christian theological heritage.

The title of the lecture series from which Johnson's article was adapted was: "Theistic Naturalism and the Blind Watchmaker." That title was considerably more accurate, because the thrust of his contribution is not to offer the reader a choice between belief in the Judeo-Christian Creator or in Richard Dawkins' "blind watchmaker." Rather, his agenda is polemical in character, focused on affixing the label of *theistic naturalism* (a term used ten times) to the positions espoused by some of his Christian critics and arguing that such positions are substantively indistinguishable from the detestable "blind watchmaker hypothesis" of evolutionary naturalism, which, by the heavy-handed effort of the "scientific establish-

*Originally appeared in *First Things*, 34 (June/July 1993): 32–41. Reprinted by permission.

ment," is fast "becoming the officially established religion of America."

To borrow a phrase from his earlier article in *First Things* ("Evolution as Dogma: The Establishment of Naturalism," October 1990), there is in Johnson's writing "just enough truth to mislead persuasively." If, for instance, one were to peruse a representative sample of the popular and semi-popular literature written by the strident preachers of antitheistic naturalism (some textbook literature also qualifies), one could, as did Johnson, find an abundance of reckless assertions that modern science, especially evolutionary biology, has soundly discredited all forms of theism. Finding such offensive rhetoric is not at all difficult, and, in full agreement with Johnson, I find such statements wholly unwarranted and grossly out of place in the public education system.

* * *

But Johnson's attack does not stop at an exposé of the triumphalist scientism espoused by a number of highly visible and self-appointed spokesmen for natural science. No, he proceeds zealously in a more ambitious campaign to establish the position that not only is the exploitation of scientific theories for the purposes of antitheism to be rejected, but the scientific theories being thus exploited are to be rejected as well. One of Johnson's central claims is that "doctrinaire naturalism is not just some superfluous philosophical addition to Darwinism that can be discarded without affecting the real 'science' of the matter," but is the very source of the evolutionary paradigm. Johnson's entire program proceeds from his belief that scientific theories regarding macroevolutionary continuity are the products, not of legitimate inference from empirical data, but of naturalistic assumptions that have been imposed on science by Darwin and his followers.

In his book *Darwin on Trial* Johnson says, "Biological evolution is just one major part of a grand naturalistic project, which seeks to explain the origin of everything from the Big Bang to the present without allowing any role to a Creator.... The absence from the cosmos of any Creator is therefore the essential starting point for Darwinism." Hence, "Naturalism is not something about which Darwinists can afford to be tentative, because their science is based upon it." In Johnson's view, then, the only reason for giving credence to theories that incorporate the idea of genealogical continuity among all lifeforms is their value in promoting the antitheistic worldview of naturalism.

But here's the rub: If biological evolution is, as far as Johnson can see, inextricable from the presuppositions of naturalism, and if evolutionary naturalism is radically opposed to the existence of a supernatural Creator, then how is it possible for a person to be what Johnson calls a "theistic naturalist"? How could one possibly by an authentic Christian theist—one whose worldview is built on belief in the Creator God—and at the same time a proponent of naturalism? Isn't "theistic naturalism" an oxymoron of the highest order?

It would seem so, and this appears to be precisely the kind of conclusion that Johnson would have readers reach. As he defines it, *theistic naturalism* is a transparently incoherent stance that no rational or intelligent Christian could possibly take. Hence, to be a proponent of such (Johnson offers Diogenes Allen, Ernan McMullin, and myself as prime examples), it would appear that one must give up either rationality, or intelligence, or authentic Christian faith.

* * *

It is important to notice how this polemic is crafted. How does Johnson—who, in his own words, approaches the creation-evolution dispute "not as a scientist but as a professor of law, which means among other things that I know something about the way that words are used in arguments"—craft his case against those of us who do see the distinction between scientific theorizing and naturalistic propaganda, who do find considerable scientific merit in the concept of common ancestry among all of God's creatures, and who do so, not in defiance of our Christian heritage or of intellectual integrity, but as an expression thereof? Simply put, by using (or abusing) words and selected connotations in order to lead a reader to discover for himself the intended conclusion.

As an illustration of an especially mischievous use of word associations, consider the word *naturalistic* and the closely related words *naturalism* and *naturalist.* One of the fundamental flaws in Johnson's essay (and the rest of his writing on this issue) is that there are two significantly different meanings of the word *naturalistic* that he uses without a hint of differentiation.

One meaning, I shall call it *naturalistic (narrow),* is very limited in scope and simply refers to the idea that the physical behavior of some particular material system can be described in terms of the "natural" capacities of its interacting components and the interaction of the system with its physical environment. Hence there is a *naturalistic (narrow)* theory of planetary motion, or of star formation, or of earthquakes, or of cell behavior, or of photosynthesis, or of the development of a zygote into a mature organism.

So understood, *naturalistic (narrow)* speaks only to the idea of the functional integrity of a material system as it acts and interacts in the course of time. No stance regarding the ontological origin of its existence is either specified or implied. Nor is the ultimate source of its capacities for behaving as it does, its purpose in the larger context of all reality, or its relation to divine action or intention. Defined in this way, *naturalistic (narrow)* has no elements or connotations that would in any way be objectionable in principle to Christian belief.

The other definition, I shall call it *naturalistic (broad),* is far more expansive in scope. It not only includes all of the elements of *naturalistic (narrow),* but also superimposes the strong metaphysical stipulations that neither the existence nor the behavioral capacities of material systems derive from any divine source (thereby making a Creator unnecessary) and that the behavior of material systems can in no way whatsoever serve in the attainment of any divine purpose. So defined, *naturalistic (broad)* is essentially identical to *materialistic* and is absolutely irreconcilable with Christian theism.

Nowhere does Johnson give evidence of recognizing or honoring the distinction between these two vastly differing meanings of *naturalistic.* Most often the broad and essentially antitheistic meaning is implied (as in his definitions of Darwinism), so that no Christian in his or her right mind could "accommodate" or "compromise with" such a position. However, in the context of applying the pejorative label *theistic naturalism* to the views of Van Till, Allen and McMullin, the meaning flip-flops between *narrow* and *broad* without any recognition of their profound difference. This strategy ensures that the label *theistic naturalism* will function to convey strongly negative connotations and cast grave doubt on both the intellectual and spiritual integrity of those persons tagged with this epithet.

This sort of semantic sleight of hand may work well to win a legal case in a courtroom, but it does not at all serve to clarify the discussion at hand. Toward the end of his article Johnson calls upon the scientific community to replace "vague words like 'evolution' with a precise set of terms that can be used consistently to illuminate the points of difficulty." Reflecting on the merits of this advice, Johnson goes on to say that "Nobody on any side of the issue should object to clarifying the issues that way—nobody, that is, who really wants to find out the truth." By the measure of his own advice to the scientific community, the law professor's continuing exploitation of verbal ambiguity represents, I believe, the visible tip of an iceberg of misconstrual. Whether intended or not, the propagation of confusion continues.

* * *

A second aspect of Johnson's stance that deserves critical evaluation is his definition or expectation of just what divine creative action is and how it would manifest itself. Although Johnson does not offer us a careful development of this important matter, there is nonetheless a conceptualization of divine creation implicit in his writing. As I see it, Johnson conceives of God's creative activity not only as that singular and uniquely divine act of bringing the universe into being from nothing at the beginning of time, but also as a succession of extraordinary acts in the course of time whereby God forces matter and material systems (such as DNA molecules and living organisms) to do things beyond their resident capacities and therefore different from what they would ordinarily do. One could call this a "theokinetic" concept of creation.

Implicit in Johnson's discussion is the expectation that "real" creative action is of the "miraculous intervention" sort that would "make a difference," specifically a difference that could be unequivocally confirmed by means of empirical science. But is this performance of theokinetic acts the historic Christian picture of what God's creative activity is and how it is manifested? Before we can take up this question, however, we need first to focus on Johnson's own picture and how it relates to the rhetoric of evolutionary naturalism.

I understand Johnson to be saying that if molecules and organisms have in fact accomplished the changes envisioned in the macroevolutionary paradigm simply by employing their own resident capacities (that is, without special "divine assistance"), then molecules and organisms would have accomplished all of the work of creation traditionally ascribed to extraordinary acts of a "supernatural Creator." Furthermore—and this is the part that Johnson's theistic naturalists presumably fail to comprehend—the proponents of evolutionary naturalism would then (by Johnson's measure, that is) be justified in concluding that evolution has made the Creator unnecessary.

If this is Johnson's reasoning, then it would appear to me that he has trapped himself in a misshapen apologetic engagement with antitheistic naturalism. By the apologetic rules imposed by naturalism (ironically similar to those of young-earth creationism), theistic talk regarding creation can mean only *special* creation through acts of "supernatural intervention." Consequently, the proponents of antitheistic naturalism have occasion to delight whenever they can identify a material mechanism (as a Christian theist I would prefer to call it creaturely action) that accomplishes something that special creationists have reserved for supernatural intervention.

However, since our scientific knowledge of creaturely action is (and always will be) incomplete, the special creationist can always hold out the possibility that there are other missing elements in the developmental economy of the physical universe. Although Johnson wishes to distance himself from the position of young-earth creationists, he tends to employ the same rhetorical strategy of treating the absence of evidence (say, for some process or activity thought to be an important contribution to evolutionary change) as if it were evidence for the absence of full genealogical continuity. By this means a place for "real" creation by a supernatural Creator is secured, giving rise to "a nature that points directly and unmistakably [by scientific measure, presumably] toward the necessity of a creator."

In discussions of this sort Johnson adamantly denies that he is espousing a "God of the gaps" strategy, but I must admit that I cannot distinguish his argumentation on this point from that of the young-earth creationists, which is built on the assumption that there must exist gaps in the developmental economy of the created world—gaps that can be bridged only by acts of supernatural intervention into the course of otherwise natural phenomena. Gaps in our scientific understanding are not important in themselves, but they gain profound significance by being recognized as indicators of gaps in the economy of the created world. Hence, Johnson is tolerant of a great deal of "microevolution" within the limits of some category of classification, provided that such phenomena (or any other natural processes) not be presumed capable of warranting a macroevolutionary theory concerning how these distinct categories of creatures "came to exist in the first place."

* * *

Caught in the jaws of this fruitless apologetic debate, in which the existence or nonexistence of an "active" Creator is to be decided on the basis of whether there are or are not gaps in the genealogical history of lifeforms, Johnson speaks as if the only conceivable reason for favoring an unbroken genealogical continuity is that it appears to give the proponents of antitheistic naturalism an apologetic advantage. Against the background of the dynamics of this apologetic struggle, we can see why Johnson wishes to place under a dark cloud of doubt and suspicion those Christians who are caught in the act of favoring the concept of a created world endowed with a gapless economy that could conceivably provide the basis for the full genealogical continuity envisioned in the macroevolutionary paradigm. They must be identified publicly as persons of questionable intelligence and dubious faith who seek a "compromise" of irreconcilable perspectives, who have "embraced naturalism with enthusiasm" and strive to "baptize" it for incorporation into the body of contemporary Christian belief. Beware, dear friends, of those *theistic naturalists,* whose twisted reasoning "establishes a remarkable convergence of Christian theism and scientific naturalism." So goes the accusatory rhetoric.

But we must get back to the issue of what kind of activity divine creation is and how we would recognize it. Johnson and other skeptics of macroevolutionary continuity appear to be looking expectantly for "evidence" (I presume this to mean the kind of evidence to which natural science has privileged access) that confirms that God's creative activity has "made a difference." To the question, "What difference would it make if there were no Creator?" traditional Judeo-Christian theism has replied, "If no Creator, then no created world." In other words, the very existence of the world of which we are a part is sufficient evidence for the action of the Creator. No further proof, not even modern scientific argumentation, is necessary. Contrary to all of the rhetorical bluster of materialism in its many forms, neither the existence of the world nor the character of its functional economy is self-explanatory.

It appears, however, that this traditional answer is not sufficiently convincing to the law professor. Hence we must seek evidence for divine creative action of the sort that would convince any honest and intelligent twentieth-century person that we had proved our case beyond the shadow of doubt in the court of scientific rationality. In Johnson's words, "If God stayed in that realm beyond the reach of scientific investigation, and allowed an apparently blind materialistic evolutionary process to do all the work of creation, then it would have to be said that God furnished us with a world of excuses for unbelief and idolatry."

This remarkable statement follows Johnson's appeal to Romans 1, from which he presumably derives his claim that we should expect to find, by unbiased scientific analysis of the empirical data relevant to the formative history of distinctly differing life forms, evidence for the kind of "supernatural assistance" that had "made a difference." One cannot help but wonder concerning the sorry plight of all those poor folks who, "ever since the creation of the world" and before the advent of modern biological science, were deprived of this essential evidence.

In personal correspondence, I once asked Johnson to help me understand how this evidential test would work by telling me just how one would establish a "no divine action baseline" to which actual processes and events could be compared. Armed with a knowledge of this baseline we could perform the crucial test and settle the apologetic question of the ages once and for all. Johnson chose not to answer my question. Perhaps he would be willing now to do so and tell us just what biological history would have been like if left to natural phenomena without "supernatural assistance."

* * *

Now it is time to return to the historical question regarding the way that God's creative action and its visible manifestation have been pictured by Christian stalwarts of the past. Because of my personal interest in this matter I have been studying the relevant works of Basil and Augustine from the Late Patristic period, especially their reflections on the creation narratives of Genesis.

In the words of one Patristic scholar, "Saint Basil's work on the *Hexaemeron* is one of the most important Patristic works on the doctrine of creation." Delivered as a series of nine homilies, this work has the style of material spoken to inspire praise of the Creator, not the style of a treatise written to be subjected to philosophical or theological scrutiny. Nonetheless, to examine Basil's homilies for their general concept of the nature of the created world and the character of God's creative activity is an instructive exercise.

Summarized as succinctly as possible, Basil's picture of creation is one in which God, by the unconstrained impulse of his effective will, instantaneously called the substance of the entire Creation into being at the beginning and gave to the several created substances the harmoniously integrated powers to actualize, in the course of time, the wonderful array of specific forms that the Creator had in mind from the outset. Both matter and the forms it was later to attain were the product of God's primary act of creation. Reflecting, for example, on the earth being initially without the adornment of grass, cornfields, or forests, Basil notes that, "Of all this nothing was yet produced; the earth was in travail with it in virtue of the power that she had received from the Creator."

In Basil's judgment, harmony, balance and provision for all future needs are characteristics of the created world that deserve our profound appreciation. Both fire and water, for example, are necessary for the economy of terrestrial life as we know it. But these two elements (as understood in Basil's day) must be provided in correct proportions so that neither one will consume the other. Observing the comfortable balance that appeared to prevail between these two contending substances, Basil says that we owe "thanks to the foresight of the supreme Artificer, Who, from the beginning, foresaw what was to come, and at the first provided all for the future needs of the world." From this it follows, of course, that the Creator need make no special adjustments at some later date to compensate for inadequate provision at the beginning. "He who, according to the word of Job, knows the number of the drops of rain, knew how long His work would last, and for how much consumption of fire he ought to allow. This is the reason for the abundance of water at the creation."

Because each element is called upon to contribute its natural activity to the functional economy of the created world, Basil considered it essential to make clear that even these natures are the product of God's creative word and are not the manifestation of any powers independent of God. "Think, in reality, that a word of God makes the nature, and that this order is for the creature a direction for its future course."

The divine command recorded in Genesis 1:11, "Let the earth bring forth grass . . . ," is for Basil God's empowering of the earth for all time with the capacities to assembly and sustain all manner of plant life. This command from God "gave fertility and the power to produce fruit for all ages to come." In several ways Basil expresses his conviction that although the Creator's word is spoken in an instant, the Creation's obedient response is extended in time. "God did not command the earth immediately to give forth seed and fruit, but to produce germs, to grow green, and to arrive at maturity in the seed; so that this first command teaches nature what she has to do in the course of the ages." And in language that seems almost to anticipate modern scientific concepts Basil goes on to say that, "Like tops, which after the first impulse, continue their evolutions, turning themselves when once fixed in their centre; thus nature, receiving the impulse of this first command, follows without interruption the course of the ages, until the consummation of all things." Furthermore, "He who gave the order at the same time gifted it with the grace and power to bring forth." This is consistent with an earlier comment on the Holy Spirit's activity in creation, "The Spirit . . . prepared the nature of water to produce living beings."

In his reflections on the words, "Let the earth bring forth the living creature," Basil speaks eloquently of the Creation actively carrying out the effective will of the Creator. "Behold the word of God pervading creation, beginning even then the efficacy which is seen displayed today, and will be displayed to the end of the world! As a ball, which one pushes, if it meet a declivity, descends, carried by its form and the nature of the ground and does not stop until it has reached a level surface; so nature, once put in motion by the Divine command, traverses creation with an equal step through birth and death, and keeps up the succession of kinds through resemblance, to the last."

Consistent with the world picture of his day, Basil, of course, envisions no historical transformation of these varied kinds; but at the same time he offers no theological objection whatever to the concept of spontaneous generation of living creatures from earthly substance alone. For instance, "We see mud alone produce eels; they do not proceed from an egg, nor in any other manner; it is the earth alone which gives them birth. 'Let the earth produce a living creature.'" It would seem, then, that Basil envisions the first appearance of each kind of living creature occurring in like manner, the earth having been endowed from the beginning with all of the powers necessary to physically realize the whole array of lifeforms created in the mind of God. The elements of the world, created by God from nothing at the beginning, lacked none of the capacities that would be needed in the course of the ages to bring forth what God intended. The economy of the created world was, from the outset, complete—neither cluttered with things that had no useful function nor lacking any capacity integral to its functional economy. In Basil's words, "Our God has created nothing unnecessarily and has omitted nothing that is necessary."

In his work *De Genesi ad litteram (The Literal Meaning of Genesis),* St. Augustine provides an extensive commentary on the first three chapters of Genesis. His goal is to demonstrate a one-to-one correspondence between the text of these chapters and what actually took place in the creative work of God; in fact, this is precisely how he defines the term "literal" in his endeavor. In contrast to modern biblical literalism, however, Augustine shows no disdain for interpreting certain words and phrases in early Genesis in a figurative sense, but even these figurative readings are firmly bounded by the controlling assumption that Genesis 1–3 is "a faithful record of what happened."

In constructing his literal reading, Augustine makes extensive use of the analogy of Scripture; the meanings of words or phrases in Genesis are often decided by comparison with other relevant texts. But Augustine is equally insistent that the literal meaning thereby derived may never stand in contradiction to one's competently derived knowledge about the "earth, the heavens, and the other elements of this world," knowledge that one rightfully "holds to as being certain from reason and experience." In a tone that leaves no doubt concerning his attitude, Augustine soundly reprimand those Christians who defend interpretations of Scripture that any scientifically knowledgeable non-Christian would recognize as nonsense. "Reckless and incompetent expounders of Holy Scripture bring untold trouble and sorrow on their wiser brethren when they are caught in one of their mischievous false opinions and are taken to task by those who are not bound by the authority of our sacred books."

For a number of reasons, Augustine, like Basil, concludes that God created "all things together" in one initial, all-inclusive, and instantaneous creative act. But the initial and simultaneous creation of "all things together," reported to us within the literary framework of a six-day narrative, should not be taken to mean that all created things suddenly materialized in mature form at the beginning. With considerable labor and repetition, Augustine developed a rather sophisticated program of interpretation by which he sought to distinguish what took place at the beginning from what took place in the course of time. In the beginning, according to Augustine, God called into being all created substance and all creaturely forms. At this beginning all created forms existed both in the mind of God and in the formable substances of the created world. But in the formable substances the creaturely forms did not exist actually, but only potentially. Although the creaturely forms were not yet actualized in visible, material beings, these forms were there potentially in the powers and capacities, called by Augustine "causal reasons" or "seed principles," with which the Creator had originally endowed the created substances.

Perhaps we should let Augustine speak for himself on this issue: "But from the beginning of the ages, when day was made, the world is said to have been formed, and in its elements at the same time there were laid away the creatures that would later spring forth with the passage of time, plants and animals, each according to its kind. . . . In all these things, beings already created received at their own proper time their manner of being and acting, which developed into visible forms and natures from the hidden and invisible reasons which are latent in creation as causes. . . . [W]hat He had originally established here in causes He later fulfilled in effects." Finally, "some works belonged to the invisible days in which He created all things simultaneously, and others belong to the days in which He daily fashions whatever evolves in the course of time from what I might call the primordial wrappers."

Now, lest we be tempted to infer that Augustine is thereby proposing a macroevolutionary scenario in which these emerging lifeforms are genealogically related, we must immediately note that he in fact offers no suggestion whatsoever of any historical modification of the created "kinds." Consistent with the world picture of his day, Augustine envisioned each unique "kind" of creature to have been individually conceptualized in the Creator's initial act of creation and independently actualized as the causal reasons functioned to give material form to the conceptual forms created in the beginning. Standing in the tradition of a hierarchically structured cosmos populated with fixed kinds of creatures, Augustine had sufficient reason to envision the independent creation and formation of each kind. And without any knowledge of genetic variability or of the temporal succession of lifeforms over a multibillion-year timespan, Augustine had no basis for questioning either that tradition or the concept of spontaneous generation.

In the context of our present concern, however, I wish to draw attention, not to the particulars of Augustine's portrait of God's creative work, articulated in the conceptual vocabulary of his day, but to one of his underlying presuppositions concerning the character of the created world: the universe was brought into being in a less than fully formed state but endowed with the capacities to transform itself, in conformity with God's will, from unformed matter into a marvelous array of structures and lifeforms. In other words,

Augustine envisioned a Creation that was, from the instant of its inception, characterized by *functional integrity*. Every category of structure and creature and process was conceptualized by the Creator from the beginning but actualized in time as the created material employed its God-given capacities in the manner and at the time intended by the Creator from the outset.

* * *

What is the point of bringing Basil and Augustine into our critique of Johnson's essay? Are Basil and Augustine to be treated as authorities on the chronology or the historical particulars regarding the formation of species? Of course not. Since their day, fifteen centuries ago, we have learned, for instance, that the spontaneous generation concept of that time fails to be viable. And we have learned that the history of lifeforms spans billions of years and is marked by patterned change. The first organisms were unicellular; today a marvelous diversity of both unicellular and multicellular forms exists. We have learned that species come and go, and that most of the lifeforms that once lived are now extinct. and we have learned that on the molecular level the present array of species exhibit relationships that strongly support the idea—drawn earlier from morphological, biogeographical, and paleobiological considerations—that all species share a common ancestry. (This thesis is most strongly affirmed by similarities, not in the small portion of DNA that functions genetically, but in the greater portion, sometimes called "junk" DNA, in which no similarities at all would be expected on a special or independent creationist picture. In fact, they would have to be considered mischievously misleading.)

No, Basil and Augustine have no lessons for us on matters biological. But as I reflect on the sorry state of contemporary discussion regarding the relationship of Christian belief and evolutionary science, I am convinced that the fruitfulness of our discourse would be vastly improved if we could recover from their theological work what I have come to call "the forgotten doctrine of Creation's functional integrity." Basil and Augustine held high views of what God brought into being. The created world invisioned by Basil and Augustine was a world endowed by the Creator with a functionally complete economy—no gaps, no deficiencies, no need for God to overpower matter or to perform theokinetic acts in order to make up for capacities missing in the economy of the created world. (The question of miracles performed by God in a world having such a gapless economy is an entirely different matter and is under no threat from the concept of functional integrity. The issue here is the character of the world within which God acts and with which God interacts.)

But if we grant that molecules and organisms do have the capacities to bring about the genetic and morphological changes envisioned in contemporary biological theorizing, have we then capitulated to naturalism? Are physical/chemical/biological processes like mutation and selection (plus all of the other relevant processes) doing the *creating*? From a theistic perspective, certainly not. These processes need not and cannot create anything.

I believe that we Christians are warranted in seeing every potentially viable lifeform (or every viable variant of DNA) as something thoughtfully conceived in the mind of the Creator. As did Basil and Augustine, I believe that we may rightfully speak of God calling into being at the beginning, from nothing, all material substance and all creaturely forms (whether inanimate structures or animate lifeforms). And, still standing with Basil and Augustine, I believe that we may rightfully presume that the array of structures and lifeforms now present was not yet present at the beginning, but became actualized in the course of time as the created substances, employing the capacities thoughtfully given to them by God at the beginning, functioned in a gapless creational economy to bring about what the Creator called for and intended from the outset.

In the context of this traditional Christian vision of God's creative work (notably different fro Johnson's theokinetic picture), we might now wish to employ the vocabulary of twentieth-century science and speak about the full array of functionally viable forms of DNA (and the creatures thereby represented) as constituting a "possibility space" of potential lifeforms—this possibility space itself, along with all connective pathways, being an integral component of the world brought into being at the beginning. Furthermore, in the language of this theistic paradigm of evolutionary creation we would speak of DNA being enabled by the Creator to employ random genetic variation as a means to *explore* and *discover* (in contrast to *create*) viable pathways and novel lifeforms so that the Creator's intentions for the formative history of the Creation might be actualized in the course of time.

* * *

See, then, what this evolutionary creation paradigm accomplishes: Do material processes have to create? No, the possibility space of viable and historically achievable lifeforms is an integral aspect of the world that God created at the beginning. Material systems need only employ their God-given functional capacities to discover some of the possibilities thoughtfully prepared for them. But, one might ask, how can such "mindless" material processes function to bring about what appears to be the product of "intelligent design"? The point is that they are not really mindless at all. Rather, every one of these processes and every connective pathway in the possibility space of viable creatures is itself a mindfully designed provision from a Creator possessing unfathomable intelligence.

It seems to me that this theistic paradigm provides precisely what the naturalistic (broad) paradigm—the blind watchmaker hypothesis—could not. It provides the answer to the question, How is it possible that such a remarkable array of lifeforms is not only viable but historically realizable within the economy of the world at hand? Could anything less than the infinite creativity and faithful providence of God suffice?

Surely not. Hence my rejection of the blind watchmaker hypothesis of Darwinism, but without the necessity of rejecting the possibility of genealogical continuity along with it.

I have a dream that some day the forgotten doctrine of

Creation's functional integrity will be recovered; that it will once and for all displace all variants of the "God of the gaps" perspective; that the empirically derived confidence in the concept of genealogical continuity will no longer give apologetic advantage to the proponents of antitheistic naturalism; and that the whole enterprise of scientific theory evaluation will no longer be distorted by counterproductive entanglement with the authentically religious debate between theism and atheism. When that happens, the declarations of atheistic purposelessness offered by Jacques Monod, William Provine, or Richard Dawkins and company will have to be defended on their religious merit alone. They will have lost the services of science, once held hostage by strident preachers of materialism, and once held in distrustful suspicion by a misguided portion of the Christian community.

II
Phillip E. Johnson

Perhaps the best way to start is by answering Howard Van Till's question: just what would biological history have been like if left to natural phenomena without God's participation? If God had created a lifeless world, even with oceans rich in amino acids and other organic molecules, and thereafter had left matters alone, life would not have come into existence. If God had done nothing but create a world of bacteria and protozoa, it would still be a world of bacteria and protozoa. Whatever may have been the case in the remote past, the chemicals we see today have no observable tendency or ability to form living cells, and single-celled organisms have no observable tendency or ability to form complex plants and animals. Persons who believe that chemicals unassisted by intelligence can combine to create life, or that bacteria can evolve by natural processes into complex animals, are making an a priori assumption that nature has the resources to do its own creating.

I call such persons metaphysical *naturalists.* Throughout this reply, as in the original paper, I use the term "naturalism" in what Van Till would call the broad sense. Of course, theists recognize that experience has shown that a great many phenomena have natural causes that are accessible to scientific investigation. To a theist there is nothing surprising about this, because the universe is a product of the mind of God and the inquiring mind of man was created in God's image. Whether such extraordinary events as the origin of life, the origin of the plant and animal phyla, or the origin of human consciousness can be satisfactorily explained in terms of unintelligent natural causes should be an open question for theists. A person who assumes a priori that such creation events *must* have scientifically ascertainable material causes is a metaphysical naturalist. If he believes in God he is a theistic naturalist, who limits God's freedom by the dictates of naturalistic philosophy.

The subject of my essay was not "genealogical continuity," or "common ancestry," or even "a gapless economy of creation." I agree with Howard Van Till that concepts like these can easily be incorporated into a genuinely theistic worldview. My theology does not require that God create by what Van Till calls "theokinetic acts," or by any other particular method. If God exists at all, He could create by whatever means He chooses, whether or not the choice pleases me, Van Till or the rulers of evolutionary biology. Determination of the method that God actually employed should be left to unbiased scientific research. On the other hand, thesists should not accept a definition of "science" that excludes the possibility of divine action, nor should they accept Darwinian theory uncritically merely because it is the leading naturalistic explanation for life's diversity and complexity. We ought to scrutinize the evidence independently, and consider the possibility that Darwinists have derived their theory more from naturalistic philosophy than from empirical evidence. Maybe what God chose to do just isn't known to the evolutionary biologists of today.

My target was the Blind Watchmaker thesis, the crucial Darwinian claim about *how* very simple life forms were transformed into the highly complex organisms that inhabit the planet today, including ourselves. The Blind Watchmaker thesis says that natural selection, in combination with random mutation, has the kind of creative power needed to make complex plants and animals out of very much simpler predecessors. If Darwinian selection does not have the required creative power, then "evolution" in some general sense may still be true, but science does not know how creative evolution has occurred.

* * *

The evidence that Darwinian mechanism either could or did make flowers, insects, whales, and human beings from single-celled microorganisms is not impressive. The fossil record is notoriously inconsistent with the Darwinian model of continuous change in tiny increments. Selective breeding, which in any case presupposes the guiding power of human intelligence, produces change only within the limits of the existing gene pool. The peppered moth story, which involves no creation whatsoever, is still the most important example of the creative power of natural selection. If one considers only the empirical evidence, the Blind Watchmaker thesis is a fantastic extrapolation from clearly inadequate evidence.

The fundamental error that theistic evolutionists like Van Till make is to assume that, because the modern neo-Darwinian evolutionary synthesis is classified as "science," it is supported by impartially evaluated empirical evidence. This is not true, and I think Van Till at some level realizes that it is not true. He accuses me of "treating the absence of evidence (say, for some process of activity thought to be an important contribution to evolutionary change) as if it were evidence for the absence of full genealogical continuity." The process or activity in question is the Darwinian process of creation by mutation and selection. The absence of evidence for *that* process is hardly something to be brushed aside as "rhetoric." It means that, contrary to the expansive claims of Darwinists, empirical investigation has not discovered a mechanism by which the fantastically complex structures of plants and animals can be built from vastly simpler organisms like bacteria and protozoa.

Whether "genealogical continuity" in some sense unites all living things is another question. Certain features, like the existence of natural groups and common "junk DNA" sequences, support an inference that there was some sort of process of development from some common source. We may call that process "common ancestry," but it does not necessarily follow that we are referring to the ordinary process of reproduction that we observe in today's world, where ancestors give birth to descendants very much like themselves. Normal reproduction is not known to produce radically new organs or organisms, and if it did so it would have to proceed one tiny step at a time. In fact there is a great deal of evidence that innovative transformations must have involved organisms doing something "different from what they ordinarily do." The hypothetical single-celled organism that produced as descendants all the animal phyla appearing suddenly in the Cambrian era—without leaving a trace of the developmental process in the fossil record—was not doing just what single-celled organisms ordinarily do. The same is true of the hypothetical four-footed mammal ancestor of whales and bats. What actually did cause such a vast transformation remains utterly mysterious, as far as anyone can determine from scientific evidence.

* * *

That is where the philosophy of scientific naturalism comes in, to make a weak case practically invulnerable to criticism. Naturalism teaches that intelligence and purpose did not come into existence until they evolved, and so chemical and biological evolution had to be purposeless, unguided processes. The task of science is to propose plausible mechanisms by which such naturalistic evolution could have occurred. Darwinian selection is the most plausible candidate that anyone has been able to suggest, and so despite the poor fit with the evidence it holds its position as the "best scientific theory." The evidence that is consistent with this theory is cited as confirmation. The evidence that conflicts with it is ignored or dismissed as unimportant.

Metaphysical naturalists understandably don't require much confirming evidence for a thesis that is so congenial to their philosophy. They also see no point in criticisms that point out the inadequacy of the supporting evidence. If this particular version of the Blind Watchmaker thesis is faulty, then something else very much like it must be true anyway. What else could have happened? If one believes in the existence of an omnipotent creator, a lot else could have happened. Nonetheless, many of the most influential voices in Christian academia are as protective of Darwinian "scientific theory" as the metaphysical naturalists. Even though they acknowledge that practically all the leading Darwinists of the twentieth century have employed their theory in popular presentations and textbooks to discredit the idea that God had anything to do with our creation, these Christian intellectuals insist that the theory itself is entirely benign, and even conducive to a theistic interpretation.

Van Till exposes the reason for this protective attitude clearly enough in his opening paragraph, when he accuses me of trying to "perpetuate the association of Christian belief with the rejection of contemporary scientific theorizing, thereby ensuring that the gulf between the academy and the sanctuary will only grow wider." As he sees it, the job of Christian intellectuals is not to challenge the picture of reality provided by a science committed to naturalism, but to accept the picture and show how it can be given a theistic interpretation. Reconciliation is achieved by softening the blunt edges of the Darwinian claim with soothing language. When translated into the vocabulary of theistic evolution, the claims of the Darwinists sound innocent enough. All the scientists are really saying, we are told, is that there is evidence for "genealogical continuity"—like junk DNA sequences—and modest claims like that do not rule out the possibility that evolution is a God-directed process. More than that, "evolution" can be likened to the complex theories of creation stated by revered early Christian authorities like Augustine—provided, of course, that we ignore the naturalistic metaphysical baggage that the word "evolution" carries when it is used in the Darwinist literature. If we let such reassurance lull our critical faculties to sleep we can sleep in peace. Science and religion can lie down together like the lion and the lamb, as long as the lambs do not provoke the lions by challenging their theories.

* * *

I do not doubt that Van Till and others can interpret "evolution" to their Christian audiences in a genuinely theistic manner. What those audiences need to understand, however, is that theistic evolution is not what the reigning scientific and educational authorities have in mind when they propose to teach every school child that "evolution is fact." They mean fully naturalistic evolution, complete with the Blind Watchmaker thesis, because they regard metaphysical naturalism as the indispensable philosophical basis of science. If persons like Van Till were in charge of science education things might be different, but in fact theists have very little influence. It is the view of evolution taken by authorities like Stephen Jay Gould, Richard Dawkins, Carl Sagan, and Douglas Futuyma that actually teaches the public and the students, and that view is rigorously and uncompromisingly naturalistic.

It is Van Till and not I who characterized theistic naturalism as "a transparently incoherent stance that no rational or intelligent Christian could possibly take." I do think that theistic naturalism is ultimately incoherent, but the incoherence is not obvious and it is understandable that many rational and intelligent Christians have overlooked it. First, we have all been taught to think of "science" as a neutral, objective process of fact-finding that is not biased in favor of a comprehensive metaphysical naturalism. In consequence the conclusions of science must be accepted by anyone who wants to be considered rational by the standards of the academic world. When "science says" that natural selection can accomplish wonders of creativity, that is the end of the matter. Religion cannot survive in a naturalistic academic culture if it opposes science, and so religion must accommodate to science on the best terms it can get. Effectively, that means that God must be exiled to that shadowy realm before the Big Bang, and He must promise to do nothing thereafter that might cause trouble between theists and the scientific naturalists.

In short, theistic naturalism is best understood as an intellectual strategy for coping with a desperate situation. It was barely tenable as a philosophical position as long as the leading scientists believed, or pretended to believe, that science is a limited research activity which does not aspire to occupy the entire realm of knowledge. Today many of the world's most famous physicists are proclaiming the imminent prospect of a "theory of everything"—and they do mean *everything.* It may be that these physicists—and the evolutionary biologists who talk just like them—are no longer practicing "science" and have become metaphysicians. What is important is that they mix metaphysics and science together and present the whole package to the public with all the awe-inspiring authority of science. I have read that 400 million persons have seen Carl Sagan's *Cosmos* series, many of them in the public schools, and very few of them were warned that "What you are about to see is metaphysics, not science." The *Time* cover story for December 28, 1992 says it all: the title asks "What Does Science Tell Us About God?" The answer is *plenty,* and more all the time.

Obviously I offended Van Till with that phrase "theistic naturalism." In a way I am sorry for that, for he is a decent and honorable person whom I would like to have for a friend. But it is necessary to send a wake-up call to a Christian academia that has complacently assumed that mild protests against the most explicitly metaphysical claims by scientists are all that is needed to maintain an intellectually respectable place for theistic religion. The situation is far more serious than that. Metaphysical naturalism has taken over mainstream science, not in a superficial sense but in a profound sense. Purportedly factual claims—like the power of mutation and selection to create complex organs—are based upon philosophical reasoning rather than empirical investigation.

The real danger is not from the metaphysical statements that come explicitly labelled as such, but from the implicit metaphysics that generates seemingly objective facts and theories. Van Till writes that we must carefully distinguish "between scientific theorizing and naturalistic propaganda."

I agree, but we also need to recognize that the persons who now rule science do not themselves know how to make that distinction, and do not even want to make it. We will have to teach them that naturalistic philosophy and scientific investigation are not the same thing, and we cannot even begin to do that if our first priority is to avoid conflict with the rulers of science.

Proffering Some Advice

Art Battson

The following is a letter to the editor that appeared recently in the journal of the American Scientific Affiliation, *Perspectives on Science and Christian Faith.* The writer, Art Battson, is director of instructional resources at the University of California-Santa Barbara and is affiliated with ACCESS Research Network in Colorado Springs. His letter makes some provocative recommendations that relate directly to the themes discussed in this volume of *The Christian Vision.*

Christians have a reason to be frustrated when the world's leading scientists insist that the origin of all biological information must be attributed to purely mechanistic, materialistic processes. Most of the frustration stems from the fact that modern science is limited by methodological naturalism. Creation events are by definition non-natural, and are, therefore, not subject to the scientific method. However legitimate *methodological naturalism* may be, when it is folded, spindled, stapled and mutilated into *philosophical naturalism,* it distorts the natural sciences in ways far beyond those attributed to the Medieval Church. The illogical leap from not being able to study creation events scientifically to assuming that God played no role whatsoever in creation has left scientists with little alternative but variations on neo-Darwinian theory, a theory which, if geological succession is correct, forces scientists to literally ignore the pervasive patterns in the natural history of life on earth. Yet no other theory seems to be possible once we consider the subject of origins (from

Letter to the Editor, *Perspectives on Science and Christian Faith,* June 1993, 147–148. Reprinted by permission.

time, space, matter, and energy to biological information) to be legitimately within the realm of the natural sciences.

As Christians we all acknowledge that we are more than the result of natural processes that did not have us in mind. The Cosmos is not all that is, or ever has been, or ever will be. This knowledge gives the scientists working within a Christian framework much greater latitude in studying the natural world than any scientists working within the bounds of philosophical naturalism could possibly have. The unbeliever has but one option: the assumption that the origin of life and the origin of all biological diversity and disparity must be the result of purely mechanistic and materialistic processes. The Grand Evolutionary Story and the Theory of Common Ancestry must be a fact, Fact, FACT! Evolution, as Sagan, Gould, Simpson, or Dawkins define it, is an unfalsifiable truth.

The Christian, on the other hand, should not only be open to the possibility that God may have created sufficient processes and initial conditions to allow the universe to unfold naturally (Van Till's "functional integrity"), but should also be open to the possibility that natural processes alone are insufficient to account for origins. This latter possibility seems to have been a major theme of the ASA's *Teaching Science in a Climate of Controversy* and Johnson's *Darwin on Trial.* Unfortunately, it also seems to be the cause of Gingerich's frustration, "So what does he (Johnson) want us to do about all this? . . . he seems to offer no prescription. If he understood how science functions, perhaps he could have proffered some advice."

The frustrating thing about the "insufficiency of natural processes" approach is that it leaves the scientist with little alternative but to continue on the path of naturalism to find purely mechanistic solutions to today's unsolved problems of origins. It also leaves the theist with little more than a series of gaps which God is allowed to bridge for the time being.

A third alternative exists for the Christian which eliminates the God-of-the-gaps and insufficiency problems, undermines philosophical naturalism, and offers scientists an alternative research program subject to methodological naturalism. The alternative is developing a theory of "macrostasis" to describe the natural processes which prevent major evolutionary change from occurring and which account for the natural phenomenon of higher taxon-level stasis. At the level of chemical evolution the alternative includes the study of natural processes which prevent life from arising spontaneously, the mechanisms which account for Pasteur's Law of Biogenesis.

This alternative involves a shift in focus away from the question of origins to the question of change. Do life forms gradually transform into substantially different body plans through time or do they retain their original "functional integrity" (with apologies to Van Till) throughout their tenure on earth?

Although critiquing current macroevolutionary theories is important, it is even more important to provide scientists with an alternative research program. Developing a theory of "macrostasis" would constitute a paradigm shift in science away from developing theories which explain data which paleontologists don't have, to theories which explain the data they do. As Stephen Jay Gould put it, "Stasis is data." Fossil after repeatable fossil documents stasis. The study of macrostasis would certainly shift science back to a more empirical base.

Another major advantage of focusing on the questions of change and stability rather than on origins is that both macroevolution and macrostasis, unlike creation and evolution, can be studied under the same rules of methodological naturalism. Opening science to the study of macrostasis requires that we do more research, not less. The evolutionist can continue his attempt to explain how major evolutionary change could occur without leaving any transitional forms leading to the higher taxa, while the scientist explains why major transformations in body plans do not occur naturally by either saltation or gradualism. It may ultimately turn out that natural processes do not exist which can overcome the genetic, developmental, and environmental constraints which account for macrostasis. However, there would be no reason to abandon macroevolutionary research if results looked promising.

Redefining neo-Darwinian theory, however, does not look very promising:

> 1) Darwin had to virtually ignore the pervasive patterns of natural history in order to preserve his theory of evolution. The two key features of the fossil record are stasis and sudden appearance, not gradualism. This is true at lower taxonomic levels and becomes even more pronounced at higher taxonomic levels.
>
> 2) Darwinian theory (including punctuated equilibrium) predicts that the accumulating diversity of the lower taxa will ultimately produce the disparity of the higher taxa. Natural history, however, reveals that disparity preceded diversity. From a systematic point of view, Darwinian theory is in reverse order to geological succession.
>
> 3) Speciation acts to restrict evolution to minor changes, changes which do not accumulate to create major disparity. Speciation also prevents major evolutionary change from occurring by saltation. In fact, speciation even reduces microevolutionary potential as gene pools are subdivided.
>
> 4) Natural selection tends to eliminate incipient and transitional stages thus preventing major evolutionary change from occurring on a gradual step-by-step basis.

Despite these shortcomings, it may be premature to take Occam's chainsaw to neo-Darwinian theory. The theory still explains the transitional forms we don't have better than any other theory (although the God of Chance would certainly have an easier time without the constraints of speciation, natural selection and that frustrating geological data). The time is definitely ripe, however, for a theory which explains why the major kinds of plants and animals retain their basic body plan and "functional integrity" throughout their tenure on earth. Stasis is the basis for a new research program which all scientists should welcome.

There is nothing like a good theory, and neo-Darwinism is nothing like a good theory. Knowing that some of the world's leading scientists still defend it should bring great comfort to Christians. If this is the best there is, what threat could it possibly be to "what was from the beginning, what we have heard, what we have seen with our eyes, what we beheld and our hands handled, concerning the Word of Life" (1 John 1)? Just whose faith is empirically based anyway?

Index

213
B347
C.2
#29451359
90351
LINCOLN CHRISTIAN COLLEGE AND SEMINARY